D0893724

The Puritan Smile

The Puritan Smile

A Look Toward
Moral Reflection

Robert Cummings Neville

State University of New York Press

Cover designed by Beth Neville;
photographs by Naomi Neville;
cover model, Leonora Neville

Published by
State University of New York Press, Albany

©1987   State University of New York

Printed in the United States of America

For information, address State University of New York
Press, State University Plaza, Albany, N.Y., 12246

Library of Congress Cataloging-in-Publication Data

Neville, Robert C.
    The Puritan smile.

    Includes index.
    1. Ethics.   I. Title
BJ1012.N48   1987   170   86-30162
ISBN 0-88706-542-2
ISBN 0-88706-543-0 (pbk.)

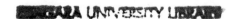

Contents

Dedicated to
Daniel Callahan and Willard Gaylin

Preface

Moral reflection has so many important and valid dimensions that an author is well advised to discover a few kindred ones and pursue them for what they are worth. I confess to being a slow learner in this regard. The need for moral reflection derives from the objective conditions of society, not from the philosophical talents at hand. Either the objective need calls forth the necessary dimensions of reflection or society is ill-served. What more seductive call can turn a philosopher's head than a clear and insistent social need? In our time, that call is often for the clarification of immediate and bluntly defined cases of moral confusion. The clarification depends upon theoretical categories of analysis, and it expresses some particular sense of the function of reflection in addressing morals; these in turn are conditional upon, and sources of, very basic metaphysical ideas. If only that continuity were as simple to work through as it is to state.

This book began as an effort to put in systematic book form certain ideas I had developed in connection with definite practical problems; for instance, the moral limits of psychosurgery on involuntarily detained persons, the political regulation of drugs and other behavior control technologies, the sale of blood for profit, and the sterilization of the mildly mentally retarded. The common themes for what I had to say about these topics, however, were properly located in political and social theory. Indeed, my contributions to political and social theory stem from an axiological approach to morals and from a normative approach to reality. The special quality of these approaches is not anything particularly novel but rather a regrouping of ideas developed in several historical traditions of moral reflection. Unfortunately, those traditions have been historically incompatible and can be made compatible only by being shown to rest within an integrating metaphysical context. Metaphysics is the novel part of moral reflection kindred to my talents. So in this book, finally, there is hardly anything left of the specific practical problems, and the topic is the conflict and reconciliation of fundamental traditions or approaches to moral reflection, especially those of Liberalism, Puritanism, and Confucianism. The thematic way of handling that conflict and reconciliation is by an inventive metaphysics that allows me to keep the parts I want of each, integrating them together, while abandoning what is dangerous or unduly limited in each.

This is not a metaphysics book, although it employs and illustrates metaphysical categories I have developed elsewhere, for instance, in *God the Creator, Soldier, Sage, Saint,* and *Reconstruction of Thinking.* Nor is it a theoretical book on morals and politics; much of that is contained in *The Cosmology of Freedom.* It rather is a book in the genre of criticism, taking as its subject matter the need of culture for moral reflection, and the traditions and categories serving as resources for that reflection. Its plot is that the subject matter is in need of fundamental metaphysical reconsideration, and some of that is undertaken here. Most criticism employing the essay form begins and remains within the language of common thought, which makes most criticism accessible. The criticism here, however, must objectify the moral structures of common thought as its subject matter, and it must present enough of the metaphysical considerations to be intelligible. I apologize, therefore, for the fact that this book, though accessible, sometimes requires the reader to stop and learn how to think the thoughts presented. Thinking metaphysical ideas is not a cultural habit that needs only to be cued in; it is a cultural art that must be learned. The reward is that with the achievement of that art new vistas of appreciation are opened. Beyond the exhilaration of recognizing the depths and breadth of life's deep problems by means of metaphysics, only the critical community of readers attaining some distance can judge whether the ideas presented here are ultimately helpful.

The ideas would have a far poorer case for being helpful if I had published the earlier draft I once thought finished. My colleague Thomas J. J. Altizer told me flat out not to publish that draft, and

the readers for SUNY Press conveyed that message with polite indirection while recommending publication. William Eastman,
Director of SUNY Press, was the perfect editor, saying "It's fine
now, but if you can make it better, please do so." The result of the
specific criticisms from these people and others is that I took both the
audience and arguments more seriously and wrote a harder and
more serious book.

The dedication of this book is to Daniel Callahan and Willard
Gaylin, founders of the Institute of Society, Ethics, and the Life
Sciences, now called The Hastings Center. On the basis of reading
my first and most abstractly metaphysical book, *God the Creator*, they
invited me to join the staff of the Institute to become expert in crisis
issues of behavior control. Although neither of them would admit
much practical importance to metaphysics, they pushed me into the
task of developing a continuity running from metaphysics through
political, legal, social, and cultural theory, to applied moral case
studies, and back again. In my own philosophic practice there are
legally actionable potholes in that continuity. But it has become a
clear task for our culture's philosophy to develop a continuous lore of
moral reflection spanning the extremes of abstract and concrete.
The clarity of that task in our current situation is largely due to the
efforts of Callahan and Gaylin. They transformed "medical ethics"
from concerns about fees and Good Samaritan liability to reflection
on the moral meaning of biological technology; and they brought into the reflective discourse not only the benefactors (perpetrators),
beneficiaries (victims), monitors (whistle blowers), and funding
agencies (exploiters), but also historians, lawyers, social theorists
and analysts, critics of culture, and philosophers with specialties in
ethics, epistemology, religion, and even metaphysics. The result is
the creation of a culture of moral reflection far more practical on the
one hand and civilized on the other than existed prior to their work.
Its potential scale extends far beyond the fields of biology and
medicine. Yet were they to have expanded their research beyond
those fields prematurely, the essence of reflective moral discourse
would have been lost; namely, the acquired lore about the practical
details of the issues that everyone needs in order to participate in the
discussion. Despite the fact that the practical focus of my own interests has drifted to problems in education and religion, despite the
criticisms developed below about the hidden a priori commitments
of a case study approach, and despite my conviction that the most

urgent practical need of current culture is for better metaphysical ideas, the contribution of Callahan, Gaylin, and their colleagues at the Hastings Center has been an historical turning point. For all the complaints lodged below about the sorry state of moral refleciton, the very platform for making those complaints was made possible by the institutionalized discourse they invented beginning in 1969. It is a pleasure to pay tribute to them and to display in this book something of what I have learned about moral reflection from our association.

Ancestors of portions of this book have been used in various contexts and some of them published. Although the material has been greatly rewritten, especially in the final draft of this book, I would like to express my deep thanks to the respective editors and publishers for permission to use or build upon the following items: Three sections of Chapter Two derive from an address to the International Society of Chinese Philosophy in 1985 entitled "The Chinese Scholar-Official as a Model for Ethics," published in its original form in the *Journal of Chinese Philosophy*, 13/2 (June 1986). The contrast between chaos and totalization in Chapter Four derives from the thorough criticism of a presentation I made at a conference on Conflict and Harmony sponsored by the Chinese University of Hong Kong in 1985; the original presentation is in the Conference Proceedings, edited by Shu-hsien Liu and Robert Allinson, that will have appeared from the Chinese University Press before this book is published. Portions of Chapter Nine derive from the historical discussion of Liberalism in "Philosophic Perspectives on Freedom of Inquiry," published in the *Southern California Law Review*, 51/5 (July 1978), an article whose topic was freedom of inquiry to pursue research in genetic engineering; that topic barely appears in this book. An early version of other portions of Chapter Nine appeared as "Various Meanings of Privacy: A Philosophical Analysis," in *Privacy: A Vanishing Value?*, edited by William C. Bier, S.J. (New York: Fordham University Press, 1980), and is reused by permission of the publisher. Chapter Ten is a rewrite of the oldest material in this book, the essential pivot of religion and morals on which my whole argument ultimately turns; the original appeared as "Man's Ends" in *The Review of Metaphysics*, 16/1 (September 1962), and despite what is now revealed as its egregiously sexist language it persuaded my wife, before she was such, that philosophy is practical enough that my calling might be an honest one. An early version of parts of Chapter Eleven appeared under its current title, "A Taste of Death," in *Philosophical Aspects of Thanatology* Volume I, edited by Florence Hetzler (New York: MSS Information Corporation, 1978).

My greatest personal debt for this book is to Thomas J. J. Altizer for telling me not to publish the earlier version, despite the fact that he mainly agreed with it. A close second is my debt to David Hall who said I should surely publish that earlier version, revised only to make it more accessible, despite the fact that he mainly disagreed with it. The comments of both, and of the anonymous readers for SUNY Press, have been integral to the revision. I thank Marilyn Smith for a careful reading of the introductory material and for helpful suggestions about how to avoid the appearance of being a Right-wing Puritan. Reflecting about the many sources of my thoughts about moral reflection, I recognize and publicly acknowledge my cumulative debt to William Sullivan. To David Weissman I express my deep appreciation for his generous capacity to make moral reflection an existentially serious concern, even, or especially, in the most unreflective of situations. Moral reflection is, by definition, of great practical moral importance, but philosophers rarely take it to be as personally serious as he has taught me it is. I thank Jay Schulkin again, as in earlier works, for the conversations that make philosophy in the richest sense the substance of true friendship.

1

Metaphysics and Irony: New Twists on Moral Reflection

The pretensions of human cultures and civilisations are the natural consequence of a profound and ineradicable difficulty in all human spirituality. . . . Man is a creature of time and place, whose perspectives and insights are invariably conditioned by his immediate circumstances. But man is not merely the prisoner of time and place. He touches the fringes of the eternal.

— Reinhold Niebuhr[1]

There are times, such as our own, when the resources that have guided a culture's self-consciousness and moral reflection seem exhausted. The leading ideas seem inapplicable to obvious realities and become the ideological property of special parties. Moral discussion becomes hopelessly confused and degenerates into intellectual politics. The dominant resources for moral reflection in modern European and American culture have been those arising from the development of Liberalism, its emancipation from conservative modes of thought, its supplanting of early competitors such as Puritanism, and its competitive relations with its dialectical offspring, Marxism. It is this complex of Liberal fortunes that has become inadequate in contemporary culture, and this book is one of several recent studies to take a new look.

Specifically, I shall argue that helpful resources for moral reflection may be found in Puritanism and Confucianism, as well as in Liberalism of various sorts. Roughly put, the emphasis on atomic individualism and economic freedom in Liberalism dissociated most of the important things in personal and social life from the public sphere, while handing the major controls of life over to the economic marketplace. By contrast, both Confucianism and Puritanism emphasize the developing identity of human beings through social participation and interaction, which is the proper sphere of moral reflection in their views. Where Liberalism seems abstract, Confucianism and Puritanism are concrete, historical, and committed to morally significant social action. Yet both Confucianism and Puritanism have strong tendencies toward totalitarianism, against which Liberalism has been the only effective proof. As to their own relations, Confucianism is conservatively establishmentarian, whereas Puritanism is radically revolutionary; and Confucianism defines people thoroughly in terms of their relations with others, ultimately as being of "one body with the world," whereas Puritanism is individualistic.

How is it possible to borrow themes from traditions that are so obviously in contradiction with one another? Is it not hopelessly superficial to say that moral reflection should extend throughout the interactions that bind individuals and their institutions together, and say at the same time that individuals should have freedom from at least some of the claims laid upon them by that seamless web of moral connections? History itself has shown the existential antagonism of Liberalism and Puritanism, and little imagination is required to bring Confucianism into the conflict.

The way to reorganize resources so as to combine what is contradictory at one level is to go deeper to the metaphysical level. Liberalism, Puritanism, Confucianism, and every other fundamental cultural outlook has a set of metaphysical suppositions, or a family of such sets as we view them as developing cultures. These assumptions articulate what it is to be a thing, to be valuable, to enter into relations, to cause and be caused, to occupy time and space, and a variety of other basic metaphysical categories. Each culture is relatively coherent, or has tended toward coherence, because it has a more or less clear commitment to a coherent set of metaphysical assumptions. Furthermore, each culture excludes or contradicts the others because its metaphysical assumptions are incompatible with the metaphysics of the others. How, for instance, could Liberalism's commitment to the individual integrity of persons who are only externally related to one another tolerate a social program stemming from Puritanism's metaphysical commitment to the definition of individuals in terms of God's overall plan of salvation?

Progress may be made with regard to integrating apparently contradictory resources by advancing a new metaphysics that picks up those elements in each tradition that would be desirable to bring along while excluding the undesirable elements. This in fact is the pattern in the history of metaphysics. Each metaphysical vision incorporates certain elements of its predecessors, but always with loss of other elements. The trick is to incorporate the good parts and trivialize the bad, and the difficulty is that the most basic judgments about the good and the bad are carried by the categories of the incorporating metaphysics itself. If one were to do metaphysics solely with an eye to capturing the best insights of one's predecessors, the valuational scheme embodied in one's categories would be wildly arbitrary, giving circular judgments about what is worthwhile in the antecedents. Metaphysics should be practised only in close connection with the many domains of experience and knowledge that bear upon it, metaphysical antecedents being but one. With regard to morals, there are a great many sources of judgment concerning what would be valuable to bring along as resources for reflection.

The moral discussions in subsequent chapters will be closely related to metaphysics. They will develop a metaphysical view that I believe allows us in some rather great (though not perfect) degree to integrate the positive contributions of Liberalism, Puritanism, and Confucianism (as well as many other cultural contributors to the dialectic), and to eliminate those elements of each that are undesirable or that inhibit the appreciation of the positive elements of the others. Although metaphysics is not the topic of the following chapters, it is brought in as an important instrument. It is the way to get deeper into the resources that moral reflection might have, and to integrate them so as to make those resources coherent and viable. The basic metaphysical categories will be introduced in the next chapter, repeated, and elaborated upon throughout.

Surely one should have a sense of irony about using metaphysics to reconcile contradictory moral traditions and to eliminate their evils. Such a pretentious undertaking is impossible to complete perfectly, and the imperfections may contain hidden dangers far worse than the evils avoided, if anyone pays attention to the enterprise at all. As I shall discuss at length later in this chapter and in the next, irony is required to attempt a finite grasp of an infinite subject in full consciousness of the incommensurability of the sides. So, any attempt to think systematically and coherently about the field of morally relevant structures is a pretentious wrestling with angels, best undertaken with ironic humor.

This elementary irony required of a metaphysics of morals lies behind the title, *The Puritan Smile*. With due regard for its limitations, certain of the insights of Puritanism need to be lifted ahead of the competing perspectives of Liberalism and other alternatives: namely, its emphases on the social definition of individual identity, on participation and interaction, and on responsibility. This justifies the reference to Puritanism in the title. But in light of its limitations, especially its tendency to totalization, Puritanism ironically needs the counterpressures of the Liberalism that historically supplanted it. Thus, the Puritan needs an ironic smile. An unsmiling, unironic Puritan would be socially dangerous, resisting the reconstruction of metaphysical categories required for even a partial renaissance.

I. The Situation

Serious moral reflection currently suffers three general defects. First, the social context is inhospitable to extended critical consideration of the normative aspects of personal, social, and cultural life. This is, alas, the usual situation. Perhaps only during the late eighteenth century in Europe and America, and a few other times in Chinese history, have the political and cultural leaders of nations actually enjoyed the habits of sustained moral reflection. Most other times the distinguished moral thinkers have considered themselves voices in the wilderness, complaining about inhospitalitiy (or worse) and saved only by their publishers.

The second defect is that moral reflection has been cut off from other fields of philosophy that could provide critical analyses of the structures and categories it presupposes. Moral reflection has been alienated from its connecting philosophical endeavors, especialy philosophical anthropology, political theory, philosophy of culture, and most especially metaphysics.

The first three of these fields largely have been taken over by cognate disciplines in the social sciences. This is an advance when empirical study is sharpened because its agenda are set by proximity to opportunities for research. The very virtue of the social science approach, however, is a vice regarding its philosophic service. Moral reflection needs from the empirical study of personal and social life not just the latest theoretical advance nor data about a suddenly accessible topic but a considered evaluation of the significance of its findings for moral concerns. That "considered evaluation" is a philosophic task, whether undertaken by the scientists or by professional philosophers. This part of the defect is being slowly rectified through the development at universities and independent research organizations of substantial interdisciplinary research programs. These interdisciplinary studies, however, rarely include metaphysics.

The separation of moral reflection from metaphysics is more serious, particularly given the role affirmed for it in this study, and I see little happening to effect its remedy. The most fundamental problem is that until recently metaphysics itself has languished as a respected field of philosophy to which the best minds are attracted. Between the first three decades of this century—when the great metaphysical accomplishments of Bergson, Whitehead, Dewey, Heidegger, Nishida, Bradley, Royce, Scheler, and Wittgenstein were achieved—and our own time, the antimetaphysical influence of analytic philosophy, Marxism, phenomenology, and existentialism all but suppressed the practice of metaphysics. The most telling damage of these influences was not in refuting metaphysical systems but in seducing the brightest students into believing metaphysics has no legitimate attraction. Of course, bright students are needed in many areas of philosophy, but in none more than metaphysics. Unlike many kinds of philosophy, metaphysics in its systematic practice requires erudition as well as original critical imagination and methods for grasping the logical connections between propositions. Blanshard, Buchler, Findlay, Hartshorne, and Weiss (and perhaps a few others) alone were able to fulfill rich careers of metaphysical speculation during that interval. More recently, their younger colleagues and students have revived the appeal of metaphysics, and perhaps we may anticipate a period of sharp growth in the quality and variety of morally useful speculation.[2]

In addition to the comparative lack of helpful metaphysics, the recent approaches to moral reflection have not been particularly attentive to metaphysical suppositions. One thinks of John Rawl's *A Theory of Justice*, Robert Nozick's *Anarchy, State and Utopia*, and Alasdair MacIntyre's *After Virtue*. If their approaches, diverse as they are, still prescind from metaphysical matters, it might well be because of their recognition of the scarcity of good work in the field. Yet the price each pays, MacIntyre less than the others, is that his moral position is vulnerable to the simple rejection of important presupposed metaphysical positions; for instance, certain nominalisms in the first two cases, and Aristotelian substance philosophy in the last. Of course, the connections between metaphysical nominalism and social individualism are complicated and filtered through many layers of qualification; a thinker persuaded by a refutation of nominalism might not abandon private individualism in moral and social philosophy. Nevertheless, the moral philosophy would soon become suspect, for the most general ideas through which it is expressed would be recognized to be unsupportable on their own terms.

Whereas it is heuristically important to enter the study of ethics and metaphysics each at the point of its central problem, avoiding any suggestion of deducing one from the other, the context presupposed for ethics includes metaphysical considerations (and vice versa). Thorough moral reflection requires critical examination of the relevant metaphysical presuppositions, just as it does of the suppositions about structure and causation in human nature and society. As mentioned earlier, this book aims to develop a metaphysics appropriate for moral reflection. Because I have dealt directly and extensively with metaphysics elsewhere, the approach here will be to define the categories and principles in context, through illustration more often than conceptual analysis. The point will be to explicate the continuity of moral reflection with the metaphysical elements of its context.

The third defect suffered by current moral reflection has to do with the quality of the ideas dominating the discussion. With the exception of a few such as Max Scheler and Emmanuel Levinas, most twentieth-century Continental philosophers have eschewed moral reflection and a fortiori have had few good ideas on the subject. Marxism, particularly in the work of the "humanistic" Marxists, or in that of the Frankfurt School, has made decisive critiques of social and intellectual structures. The power in the Marxist approach is its technique of sweeping a situation into a tightly integrated vision so as to criticize it as a totality. The Marxists follow Hegel in their belief that the normative dialectic of history proceeds by negation and that a situation must be totalized in order to be negated. Of course, the power of the Marxist analysis is at the same time a great weakness: Totalization is a lie when applied to the particularities of a situation or to cases. The most important moral consideration about a particular situation might be very different from the most general framing considerations. That one exists in a decadent capitalist system, for instance, might be less important to know than certain other factors in considering whether to mortgage one's house to send a child to college. Furthermore, dialectical totalization might be mistaken as an entire strategy; perhaps things are not organized so well as to constitute a sufficiently connected collection for totalizing principles to obtain.[3] At any rate, most Marxist moral reflection has been social criticism of a most general sort.

British and Anglo-American philosophy, taking the "linguistic turn" seriously, has concentrated on meta-ethics, not on moral reflection.[4] Meta-ethics is descriptive and analytical, but not pre-scriptive as one would hope for at least certain aspects of moral reflection.

In response to the normative aridity of meta-ethics, whatever other value it has, many philosophers in the Anglo-American tradi-tion have turned to applied ethics, by which is meant the develop-ment of moral norms through the consideration of specific cases or types of cases. The move to applied ethics is socially useful and has served to connect philosophy once again with public concerns of social life. Nevertheless, the consideration of cases as the entry into normative moral reflection itself expresses a nominalist bias. That approach makes it extremely difficult to develop a feel for how the values we apprehend in particular circumstances are themselves functions of more general social conditions, tendencies, and institu-tions. More especially, moral nominalism detracts attention from moral criticism of those general conditions, tendencies, and institu-tions by saying that the payoff is in the cases. Whereas Marxist moral reflection is strong on social criticism and often mendacious about particulars, Anglo-American applied ethics is responsive to cases but deceptive in its supposition that the moral character of general conditions, tendencies, and institutions can be reduced to consequences for particulars.

Alasdair MacIntyre has argued that the comparative poverty or limited applicability of contemporary moral ideas is not a result of twentieth-century difficulties alone. On the contrary, the twentieth century is witnessing, according to his astute analysis in *After Virtue*, merely the playing out of the consequences of philosophic strategies ill-formed at the beginning of the modern era.[5] I am in substantial agreement with his analysis of the long-term inevitable decline of modern moral reflection. MacIntyre's response to this decline is to construct a new conception of human virtue, building upon Aristotle's but qualifying it to take into account what has been learned for better or worse since ancient time. I agree that at least that much must be true, although more is involved in moral reflection than is easily statable in a virtue-ethics. The aim of this book is the introduction of a distinctive moral view, one appropriate to the best moral reflection we can hope for today, and one grounded in a metaphysical system that picks out at least a few of reality's natural joints.

The inhospitable social context for moral reflection is a fault of our time, not of philosophy except as it expresses the time. In these most desperately unmoral days, moral reflection can hardly be undertaken with a straight face. Across the world the popular languages of morality have been captured by the ideological Right, for whom critical philosophy is a subversive symptom of immorality. Intimidated by the power and complexity of current economic, military, and technological systems, political leaders have been backed into defensive "management" postures, often devoid of critical reflection on moral worth. Perhaps the most desperate element in the situation is the gravitation of higher education in the West toward modular styles of learning, appropriate for technological and elementary scientific subjects but not for anything reflective. The typical modernization of universities in areas outside the West emulates the most primitive and degenerate Western models in the attempt to build quickly a cadre of technocrats.

The social context in which fully serious moral reflection either fails to occur or is expressed only as ideology is an untenable one. Moral reflection is a response to the urgent needs of societies for wisdom about what should be prized or despised, refrained from or pursued. In the last twenty years, professional philosophers have begun to revolt against existential disdain for moral reflection and against the narrowing of it to meta-ethics. The rise of applied ethics and the enthusiasm so widely felt about MacIntyre's call for new models of moral thinking express this new movement.

In a sense, the arguments in this book are part of this revolt. But in another sense, the rejections of moral reflection scouted above express a deeper criticism of the cultural Modernism of the past century. For Modernism, the worth of something should be self-contained and self-intelligible, justifiable in itself without the vagaries of indefinite appeals to context. At root, Modernism says that worth is aesthetic worth, not moral worth.[6] Or morality, if there is such a thing, has access to demonstrable worth by founding itself on self-justifying first principles; hence the philosophers' concerns with meta-ethics. The arguments against aesthetically encompassed moral reflection are complicated and run throughout this book.

Because of its emphasis on the self-contained and self-intelligible, on beauty in and by form itself, Modernism shows a predilection for nominalistic philosophies. The most prominent current influence of nominalism, albeit usually unintended, is the framing of practical ethics as a matter of individual cases or types of cases. Or, in the analysis of a general problem, such as the ethics of abortion, the nominalist approach is to move the discussion to examples and counterexamples of real or imagined cases.[7] The case-study approach to normative ethics, although rightly cited as the recovery of practical philosophy from the sterile abstractions of Modernist meta-ethics, is in fact a dialectical extension of Modernism itself. Of course, practical decisions often have to be made about cases, particularly when we have not attended antecedently to the context and conditions within which the cases arise. Nevertheless, the relevant aspects of cases, and the important reasons to deal with them one way or another, might not appear from the cases alone but from their context and conditions. The case-study approach to normative ethics too often gives rise to the conclusion one would expect from the ideology of Liberal nominalism, a coincidence that itself calls for moral reflection.

II. The Ironic Relation of Aesthetics and Morals

There is nevertheless a profound truth in the view that value in itself has the character of beauty before it has any character conveying obligation or commanding responsibility. Yet moral reflection takes place from within a human context where the question is not merely what is intrinsically good but what is worth valuing one way or another relative to enjoyment and action. The return to moral reflection, or the search for new modes of it, is part of a general cultural abandonment of European Modernism. Acknowledging the importance of something like aesthetics for appreciating value as such, a nonaesthetic, non-Modernist sense of moral reflection must therefore take up a somewhat ironic mode of argument. Perhaps irony is the way to look at moral reflection from the aesthetic standpoint.[8] Or again, perhaps irony is the way moral reflection looks at itself in contrast to the aesthetic view of morality. Or perhaps irony is the means by which the aesthetic standpoint is incorporated into the moral and reconciled with responsibility. The root of the irony is that moral reflection is based on general intrinsic values of things appreciated aesthetically, and yet in its concern to identify responsibilities must put itself away from the divine universal disinterestedness of the aesthetic. The aesthetic standpoint is infinite and everywhere; the moral is finite and only where you are.

The contrast between the aesthetic and the moral — the contrast itself — is the epitome of irony. Irony is the profound existential attitude that comprehends as if they were united two fundamentally incoherent ontological facts; the infinity of creation and the selective finitude of recognition, knowledge, interpretation, and culture. There is no mystery about the ontological facts. On the one hand, reality is infinitely complex and dense. Any part of it has connections extending in a host of directions and has values relative to all those connections. On the other hand, the human interpretive response to reality is always selective, employing a finite set of signs to lift out certain aspects as important and connected, implicitly ignoring the rest. Furthermore, because we select by means of signs, the connections and unities we see are functions first of the networks of signs employed, and only latterly of any serious testing of the sign-system in reality. So we create cultures that arrange reality into a "world." With different cultures there are different worlds, all pragmatically acceptable at some level because all pick out genuinely important features of reality, but perhaps conflicting or even incommensurate when compared with one another. Sophisticated cultures know that they are selective, that there are alternatives, and that reality is infinite and thereby unrepresentable as a sum. Hence, cultural irony.

Plain as these two ontological facts may be, even entailing one another in a sense, they are incoherent. There is no way one can accept or contain within itself a proper status for the other. The finite human world is a moral world. Whatever its selective order, certain things are valuable in recognizable connections, and these contend for respect while they command moral energies. In the pragmatic

commonalities of known cultures, human suffering is bad unless it
serves a higher good, and the things that prevent or alleviate suffering are positive values; so are things that nourish, that secure the
human ecological niche, that satisfy needs and ambitions, and that
serve the needs of the spirit. All cultures have means to effect trade-
offs among values and to adjudicate at least the frequent conflicts.
However defined, wanton destruction and murder are evil. In the
great civilizations, competing cultural or moral traditions arise, for
instance, the Confucian and Taoist in China; yet they compete over
moral stances, even (as in the Taoist case) when the moral stance is
akin to aestheticism.

     Nature is infinitely dense in its values. Each part has its value,
and it participates in complexes of values according to its infinite array of connections. Each part is a center for which the rest of nature
is environment. There is no priority of value, since the focal point is
arbitrary, or infinite. Only God, in the Western theistic conception,
can be equally close to all potential centers of value. Hence, the
divine perspective is infinite and aesthetic. It makes no sense to say
there is a whole or totality of nature if that were to mean that some
one structure sums up everything. Any one totalizing structure,
however true as far as it goes, stands in contrast to an indefinite
number of other structures each true in its way. Rather, the infinity
of creation is chaos, which David Hall aptly defines as "the sum of all
orders."[9] Aesthetics is oblivious to moral values except as understood
within a game, where the game is defined by the arbitrarily chosen
focal point. Aesthetically, cancer is bad for human beings, but it is
the mode of flourishing for cancer cells; Hitler was a moral monster,
but he was neatly efficient. The aesthetic point of view takes any one
part of reality as a center of value, an order of things relative to itself.
Contending moral claims are, from the aesthetic point of view,
merely differing relative standpoints, none comparably better than
another, except from yet another relative standpoint. The aesthetic
view of cultures is that they are all games, at best dances of the
Gods.

     Human life is essentially and ineluctably cultural, and thereby
finite. As intentional creatures we interpret and use signs. As we
take critical responsibility for having good signs, we systematize
them and represent more or less coherent aspects of real structures.
Self-consciousness itself entails that we organize active and interpretive responses around fundamental categories that define world-

liness. Among these categories are those articulating the relations between the values of things brought into order by our culture, and hence we have a moral universe. That everything is filled with value does not by itself constitute a moral universe; but that the values are ordered one to another, so that Hitler's merry villainy contravenes the goods of those he murdered, constitutes the moral universe. Because of its essential finitude, human life has an inescapable moral dimension.

Irony is the existential attitude recognizing both of these onto-logical facts. The finite side is earnest or evil when it is innocent, and dogmatic when it has fallen through contact with alternate moral universes. The finite side is playful or heedless when innocent, and cynical when its innocence has been crushed by an encounter with moral force. Irony combines the playfulness with moral earnestness in an uneasy contrast. It is tempting to assimilate irony to the aesthetic side, as David Hall tends to do. For, the final truth about both the infinity of reality and the finiteness of human culture is that one's order of value is relative to one's position. But irony of the aesthetic sort is only disguised cynicism. An equally final truth is that any finite thing has, is, and defines its own position, and there-fore has real values relative to that position. Unless we could be posi-tionless, that is, infinite, we cannot occupy the divine aesthetic standpoint. A new guise for the Sin of Pride! Therefore, we are normed by the values of our situation. The moral problem is to have an adequate view of the breadth of our position and to avoid men-dacious selfishness. Our "position" is at least the entire field of poten-tial communicators. Because of our finitude, the commandment to moral earnestness is the truth about us.

An ironist is not funny. True irony can only arise out of moral earnestness that does not take a holiday. Yet at the same time, the ironically earnest effort cannot regard itself as absolute; there is an indefinite number of other moral tasks, limited only by our imagina-tion. Therefore, irony can laugh only at its own earnestness, never at the world. Irony requires both engagement and the distance sym-bolized by humor that puts its own project in infinite perspective. The rhetorical style of irony is to protest some pretension as falsely infinite, often through parody and ridicule, yet secretly to affirm it. The final failure to affirm the infinite importance of some finite pro-ject is to abandon irony for the ultimate pretension of having the divinely infinite point of view. As Milton illustrated in the character of Satan, this results not in sublime infinite aesthetic vision but in miserable cynicism.

Irony is closely related to a religious attitude. Religions have been staunch guardians of moral codes. At the same time, and almost from the earliest literate times, they have understood the relativity of moral codes. The divine lawgivers are above the laws. Spiritual experience extended to mystical depths is alleged to transcend the finiteness of cultures and symbols, though always expressed in that clothing. On the other side, the aesthetic standpoint has been characterized again and again as that fit only for infinite divinity; only God can appreciate all standpoints without taking sides. Both the aesthetic and moral dimensions push beyond themselves to the religious, and precisely because of their juxtaposition as grasped in irony.

Our own culture has endured the death of God. My references to divinity in these matters can only be symbolic. Or ironic. For our own time, therefore, we must ask whether it is finally possible to live in an ironic situation or moral reflection. Only thirty years ago, humanists were debating whether it is possible to have tragedy in a Christian universe. Now the question for many is whether it is possible to be ironically moral in a universe without the old God..

III. Puritanism

These remarks about irony are abstract to an extreme, and will be made concrete during the course of this book. The title, *The Puritan Smile*, alludes to an historical irony. No tradition has been more morally earnest than the Puritan, unless perhaps it has been the Confucian. There is irony intended in both the smile and in the reference to Puritanism. Not that the historic Puritans didn't have their straightforward fun and humor, if a bit more straightforward than jolly. Edmund Leites has recently demonstrated that Puritanism intensified wit and warmth, particularly within the household, only eschewing those extremes of feeling that threaten the social bonds.[10] But smiling is not the popular image of Puritanism. I bring the smile into the title in part to confuse and break that popular image.

It is an irony to call up the ghosts of the old Puritans for contemporary moral reflection, because theirs is a dead tradition. I have no desire to resurrect it; Puritanism died for good reasons and would be a horror if restored. The political resurgence of the simplistic moral Right in contemporary America with its messianic sensibilities finds resonances in a form of Puritan imagery with opposite implications from the conclusions I want to draw. Nevertheless, there was a large and important truth in Puritanism that is better than any social philosophy we have today, and I want to recover that in a form that by necessity must be ironic. So, another cause for the Puritan smile in this book is that the Puritan is to be a working ghost.

My reference to Puritanism is literary and not intended to be a serious historical commitment. In one sense, my intent is antihistorical; to re-mythologize Puritanism as a culture emphasizing personal responsibility, social participation, and political change. The seventeenth century saw the rise of two cultures in England in response to the material and intellectual conditions of modern society: Puritanism and Liberalism. The Liberal tradition resonated with the scientific world, civilizing its major themes, eventually inspiring its own Marxian counterfoil, and creating the culture of technology that has wrought a globe-encompassing society. In our own time, Liberal culture has become a popular whipping boy. Among its faults are that it fights against itself, that it had its greatest fling in Modernism, that it fosters many kinds of economic oppression, and that it gives us the terror of nuclear annihilation. True enough. To its credit, on the other hand, it has conquered most diseases, developed marvelous technologies of food production, and manufactured civilized ideologies of population control, individual freedom, equality before the law, tolerance, and the fear of the intrinsic wickedness of tyranny. The strength of Liberalism, and its weakness too, is that it glorifies the capacities of individual creativity and freedom, and protects them from government and social control. Creaking with both strengths and weaknesses, Liberalism remains a living culture and gives what meaning it has to the technological age. In a large view, Marxism is but a variant of Liberalism that seeks to bring its benefits to the proletarian class.

Puritanism, by contrast, died. It was a culture in which both individual and communal life possess their meaning and worth as expressions of a deeper divine, cosmic, and ontological ground. More important, it was a revolutionary movement that began by turning over the individual soul, and in its conception of that required turning over the entire society. Liberalism won out at the end of the seventeenth century in part as a calming agent applied to the furor of

Puritan social concern. Much of the calm came from the Liberal separation of the pursuit of individual interests from pursuit of desirable social structures. Of course, the Puritans were right: individual and society cannot be separated, and the Liberal pretense that they can masks the social interests of the powerful self-seekers of capitalism. For Puritanism, there is an organic continuity between the individual and the social fabric. In extreme forms, alas, that continuity passes over into an ideal of totalitarianism against which the Liberal myth seems our only protection.

The individualism of English and Anglo-American culture was fed more powerfully by Puritan than Liberal sources. Its preachers developed a rhetoric of "plain" speaking that could address people of any class and background. The Puritan sermon related the drama of the soul's fall into sin, its struggle for salvation, and the vicissitudes of the saved going on to sanctification.[11] Opposite to the medieval morality plays that universalized the drama, the Puritan sermon personalized it to the audience in social as well as psychological terms. The intent and frequent effect of the preaching was an intense response on the part of the hearer to identify himself or herself as one in deep trouble, and to undertake specific steps in remedy. The "identity" of the individual was just that dramatic or historical personage. Puritan identity thus had both a vertical dimension and a horizontal dimension. The former defined the soul and its destiny in relation to God, the ground and goal of existence, the glorification of which is the ultimate meaning of personal life and history. The horizontal dimension defined the specific content of individual life in terms of the particular conditions within which one sinned and struggled for righteousness: home, family, friends, employment, leisure, participation in the army, the tax structure, the system of foreign and domestic trade, and so forth.

Puritanism was a culture of responsibility rather than freedom because of its unique sense of individualism. Liberalism softened the vertical dimension to a belief that a person's life can be meaningful in itself, and it softened the horizontal dimension to imply that one is what one owns. So for Liberalism, freedom is the virtue that glorifies what remains of the vertical dimension and that defines excellence (i.e., protection of property) horizontally. Responsibility is the analogous virtue for Puritanism: One is obligated to a role in God's drama, and this means normative participation in the structures of

one's situation. Edmund Leites has called attention to the decisive
ways in which this part of Puritan culture develops an extraordinarily
powerful conscience and habit of moral constancy.[12]

The historic Puritans in England and America were a diverse
lot. On the right, as it were, stood those who became the Presby-
tyrians and whose intitial concern, as Haller put it, was "taking over
the establishment and running it according to the scheme of the *Book
of Discipline*."[13] From their ranks arose dissenters with stricter criteria
of church membership and an emphasis on great autonomy for local
congregations ("Congregationalists"), and to the left spread out the
Brownists, Barrowists, Separatists, Baptists, Millenarians, Seekers,
Ranters, Quakers, Muggletonians, and so forth. As Haller noted:

> No denunciations were more bitter or more complete than
> those which these bodies upon occasion leveled at one another,
> but we should not permit the differentia of the Puritan sects to
> confuse our understanding of Puritanism . . . The disagree-
> ments that rendered Puritans into presbyterians, independents,
> separatists and baptists were in the long run not so significant as
> the qualities of character, of mind and of imagination, which
> kept them all alike Puritan. Coming revolutions commonly
> thrust forward a numerous vanguard of pioneers, rebels,
> cranks, martyrs, saints and heroes. Some of these organize par-
> ties, sects and juntas. Some publish programs and manifestoes,
> or start demonstrations, parades, riots and secessions. They are
> the devoted band who would save the world without delay and
> build Jerusalem in their own time.[14]

It is of utmost importance to remember that the collective impact of
Puritanism, carried to wild extremes during the Protectorate, was to
call for changed government, changed tax laws, changed judicial
system, and changed economic policies, so as to give advantage to
the poor and disenfranchised. This was the horizontal dimension of
that religious revolution which said as well that every soul, poor and
brutish as well as rich and sophisticated, is equally dear to God. The
paradoxical effect of the common Calvinist doctrine of election, *pace*
Weber, was that social status is not a sign of virtue or salvation,
while brutalizing social conditions were recognized as the sinful
causes of sinful people. Puritanism was a great force for democrati-
zation in England and even more in America, not only because it
conceived of individuals as equal souls before God but also because

it understood that democratic institutions must be created in a struggle with sinful conditions.

Puritanism failed as a culture for many reasons, the most important of which was that its God died. The necessary living relation between deep divine historical passions and the historical growth of daily life could not survive the powerful forces of secularism.[15] Without the divine ground, the unique Puritan emphasis on responsibility in personal and public life lost its prophetic criticism. It also found the Protectorate a tragic disappointment; and with the Restoration, Puritanism was overtly retired from politics. Christopher Hill's *The Experience of Defeat* shows what this meant for the main representatives.[16] In America, the culture of Puritanism maintained its vitality, with ups and downs, until it reached its intellectual apogee in Jonathan Edwards, who died in 1758. Then even in America, the Puritan forces passed into those of Liberalism. Thomas Jefferson and his ideal of civic republicanism ennobled the moment of passage as combining, for a brief generation, the best in both cultures.[17]

The historical connection between Puritanism and early Liberalism is both complicated and controversial. Christopher Hill belongs to the group of historians that sees the rise of Puritanism and its Revolution to be a function of the dynamics of social class structure, as expressed for instance in his *The World Turned Upside Down*. The neatness of that view has been challenged by others, including J. H. Hexter in *Reappraisals in History* and more recently by Jack A. Goldstone.[18] In many respects, Puritanism provided the cultural background within which the personalities of the early Liberals were formed. John Locke is a primary example of the Puritan conscience, as Edmund Leites has shown in the book mentioned above.

For my own purposes of epitomizing both Puritanism and early Liberalism for the sake of remythologizing the former, it is important to stress their discontinuity. From this point of view, the coronation of Charles II delegitimated Puritanism as a viable political program and legitimated incipient Liberalism. The Hanoverian monarchy made this distinction a permanent fact. Liberalism by itself, however, is an inadequate ground for moral reflection, I shall argue, and nearly every one of the chapters below will develop a critique of some element of Liberalism in contrast with the Puritan's inheritance. Given the fact that Puritanism is dead and Liberalism has lived on to ramify itself in diverse and changed circumstances, it is important to take an historical and nuanced view of the latter.[19] The contractarian part of Locke's Liberalism was not shared by John Stuart Mill's Liberalism, and John Dewey's Liberalism rejected the individualism of the whole Liberal tradition up to himself. For the most part, my discussions of Liberalism below will focus on pre-Deweyan forms. Indeed, Dewey's own self-identification aside, he was really a throwback to Puritanism. Dewey was not the only American for whom Liberalism, a viable political identification, was really a cover for essentially Puritan sensibilities.[20]

IV. The Plot of This Book

The elements of Puritanism I want to emphasize and develop—its sense of responsibility and particiation, and its social definition of the individual—are surprisingly close to major themes in classical Chinese Confucianism. Chapter Two develops the similarities. Yet the two traditions are dissimilar in other respects. Puritanism is revolutionary where Confucianism is establishmentarian; this reflects the Puritan belief in transcendent norms on the one hand and the Confucian commitment to only-immanent values on the other.[21]

There are, of course, many elements of Puritanism that should be rejected over and above its theology.[22] The Anglicanism (and Catholicism) against which Puritanism set itself was the culture of sophistication and irony, of Shakespeare and Restoration wit, of compromise and mutual respect. These are values missing from classical Puritanism and without which it was and would be again a terror. It was far more pleasant to live next door to an Anglo-Catholic than a Puritan, I suspect. In our own time, we have learned again the cruel lessons of ideologically totalitarian revolutions of the fascist right and the Marxist left. Have we reason to believe a contemporary Puritan revolution would be kinder? Of course, we live in a postreligious age, we are assured, and I mean these references to religious traditions only ironically. Surely, none of us is a Puritan of any sort! My title is only a metaphor.

So the smile of the Puritan is that of a ghost. That particular ghost's smile, I think, has the proper irony to take a look toward moral reflection. Responsibility is the missing or misunderstood notion that requires, and limits, an ironic attitude. Chapter Two will make a responsible commentary on that irony.

One more remark needs to be made about the title, this time about the subtitle: *A Look Toward Moral Reflection.* This book takes no more than cursory look *at* moral reflection; it is not mainly a meta-ethical study. Rather, its focus is on considerations necessary for reconstituting, revitalizing, or maybe inventing anew, public discourse of moral reflection. Although the precise nature of moral reflection is itself a deep problem that the following discussion only begins to address, a preliminary definition of moral reflection is that it is critical inquiry into the affairs of personal and public life that identifies and evaluates the values involved. By values I don't mean people's ideas, the values they hold, but rather the real values embodied or achieved. And their evaluation requires imaginative comparison with what otherwise might have been or be achieved. Moral reflection is neither ideological in the sense of taking its values from a theory about what is valuable nor managerial in the sense of a technique of life or leadership in the service of unreflective values. The chapters below are efforts *toward* moral reflection.

Chapter Two analyzes a model of public virtue, deliberately moving outside the repertory of Western models to the Confucian in comparison with the Puritan. It also explores the ambiguities and ironies of the relation between the moral and aesthetic dimensions. Chapter Three asks how general social obligations — "someone ought to do something about that" — become the personal responsibilities of specific individuals. That they do is a presupposition of the previous chapter's interest in public virtue. My general and radical answer is to propose that everyone is responsible for all social obligations unless exempted by specific social structures. Thus, one way of measuring the moral health of a society is to examine how well its structures function to divide the labor of responsibility that fundamentally falls on all citizens. Chapter Four analyzes the goal of public action as aiming at a certain kind of harmony, a kind of harmony that is sympathetic to, but not reducible to, revolutionary chaos on the one hand and orderly totalization on the other. The point is that the goal of action is neither order nor disorder but a normative harmony mixing both. Chapter Five directly confronts the importance of suffering as a foundation for moral reflection in public life, and it presses a theory of experiential cultivation of moral sensitivity.

The arguments of the first five chapters presuppose that there are real values in things and that we can discover what they are with some degree of accuracy. Chapter Six makes these themes explicit and expands the metaphysical considerations introduced earlier to provide a theory of real value and of how it can be known. Chapter Seven then paints an expanded picture of a value-laden cosmos, with morally responsible beings such as ourselves. It asks in greater detail what forms science should take in order to be morally helpful.

I hope that the argument through Chapter Seven makes the point from many angles that philosophy has a social responsibility. The various choice-points of social life are in need of the wisdom that comes from taking the large view and critically assessing presuppositions. Puritanism was neither the first nor the last movement to demonstrate consequences. Certain social problems, though not all by any means, are caused or exacerbated by ignorance or confusions about the operative big ideas, and in certain respects the solutions to problems come through the achievement of better big ideas. At the least, philosophy, like history, criticism, the sciences and letters, is needed for understanding our social condition and moral life. This is not to say that all intelligent moral action has to be philosophical; nor is it to say that all philosophy has to bear on morality directly or indirectly. But it is to say that the whole of philosophy as a cultural enterprise is needed if we are to do well. If professional philosophers will not address that social responsibility, others will, and probably without the discipline the profession could contribute.

Chapters Eight through Eleven are moral reflections on structured dimensions of life: authority, freedom and privacy, and death. The reflections are not so much theoretical analyses as critical ruminations designed to display important normative considerations. They elaborate the critical integration of Liberalism, Puritanism, and Confucianism, and set the discussion of Western society in a somewhat more international context. The dialectic of topics is apparent as the discussion proceeds. Authority is the main problem that Puritanism, as well as Liberalism and Confucianism, failed to solve. In Chapter Eight, I cut the Gordian knot on the topic by rejecting any important sense of authority, and — in light of the positive emphasis on responsibility, participation, and the social definition of life — I defend a polity that impolitely could be called Big Government Anarchism. The danger of that polity, of course, is that it would amount to Lawless Big Government, and it is therefore essential to relate it to a doctrine of freedom. Since the view of freedom defended in Chapter Nine is freedom for responsible life, and the Liberal view of freedom from interference is qualified, the question arises as to whether there is any privacy. Again, the Liberal view of privacy is criticized, and the view, briefly introduced in Chapter Three, that privacy is an artificial creation by the organized public for the sake of creativity, is defended.

The remarks on authority, freedom, and privacy indicate an extraordinary stress on the social definition of human life, with every dimension providing responsibilities. God preserve us with a sense of humor! But that is not enough; because the responsibilities too often conflict, we fail them, and the resulting guilt is definitive of our souls and society. The Puritan smiles, triumphant! The contractarian Liberal solution of saying that private life has no real responsibilities, and that we can retreat to it, is no good. The Confucian view that the responsibilities all must fit together somehow is equally unhelpful. Ironic detachment by itself abandons the moral life at precisely the wrong moment. The answer I defend in Chapter Ten is that life defines itself as guilty and yet as resting on an infinite ground of obligation and satisfaction. Thus, the Puritans were right about the vertical as well as horizontal dimensions. If this is what life means, what does death mean for identity? Not to confuse the issue with Puritan theology, Chapter Eleven takes the form of a dialogue with Death's God in the Hindu pantheon. The intent in these topical chapters is to connect the most external and overt moral considerations (about authority structures) with the most intimate and personal (guilt and death). The connection is not a dichotomy, as it would be in the Liberal or Continental Cartesian philosophies, but a continuum with mutually interpenetrating positions.

My last introductory comment is a personal indulgence in nervousness. The course of these moral reflections lies closer to the Puritan heritage than to any other, and I rejoice in being able in part to re-create its critical stance. At the same time, there is much in Puritanism that is outmoded and impossible, and even more that is all too possible and utterly dangerous, particularly its authoritarianism, its fanaticism, and the totalitarianism of its right wing. Therefore, one of the major concerns of this book is whether the good parts of the Puritan heritage — its sense of responsibility, participation, and social definition of human life — can be complemented with well-grounded alternatives to its bad parts. Much of the argument is against the parts of Puritanism I wish were not there. I'm nervous about the attempt to cut and paste a tradition, because the coherence of ideas is not half as substantial as the coherence of solid history. The point is that we need a new tradition, drawing upon the Puritan as well as upon many others, especially non-Western ones.

2

Modeling the Moral Life

I. Models for Moral Reflection

T he popular understanding of moral reflection is that it is a kind of problem-solving, an intellectual technology that construes thinking as a technique for hitting upon the means to attain pregiven ends. The model was inspired by Aristotle with his claim in the *Nichomachaean Ethics* that deliberation is about means only and not about ends. In our own time, both philosophical functionalism and cognitive science agree that problem-solving is the basic paradigm of thinking in general, or at least the easiest to understand according to the paradigm of artificial intelligence. Because we understand much about problem-solving with fixed ends, it would be convenient were that popular understanding to be adequate to moral reflection. Moral reflection would then be a technical issue.

On the contrary, however, in an age when nuclear weapons are the means to defense, computers the means to communication, and spacecraft the means to travel, John Dewey's point that the value of the end is largely determined by the means to achieve it refutes the problem-solving model of moral reflection. The value of the end differs according to the alternate means by which it might be achieved.[1] Therefore, it is simply impossible to deliberate about the means only and not about the end; to attempt to do so is self-deceptive, because the end changes without being noticed. Moral reflection must continually reassess ends and their roles in context relative to alternate processes of achieving them, and this is not problem-solving in the technological sense.

But if we necessarily deliberate about ends, by what criteria do we identify that genuinely worthwhile? Twentieth-century Anglo-American meta-ethics has attempted to answer this question. Its results include the following: Good is a non-natural property we just know (G. E. Moore); the right consists of a set of rules that are intuitively obligatory (the deontologists); the good is what we strongly favor (emotivism); the good is the most efficient (and/or universal) distribution of pleasure (utilitarianism); the right consists of the rules that get the most efficient pleasure (rule utilitarianism); and the good is the state of affairs we would favor on utilitarian grounds if we were in the most disadvantaged position (Rawls). These and other meta-ethical answers too quickly reduce either to arbitrary feelings of certainty or to appeals to what we want, when the issues have to do with whether to trust our immediate feelings and whether what we want is worth wanting. The meta-ethical attempt to provide a quasi-deductive base for moral reasoning fails to serve moral reflection, whatever benefits it bestows on moral theory. Even if a perfectly satisfactory ground for moral reasoning could be found, it is difficult to see how reflection about the worth of things could be reformulated as an argument from normative premises to normative conclusions.

Popular frustration at this point yields to relativism, lauding tolerance of anything that does not harm others according to some quasi-neutral sense of harm. The metaphysical suppositions of such relativism are that objective values are illusions, that people are defined by their personal and group subjective values, and that they have these values by historical accident or by arbitrary choice. If the normative character of human life is defined this way, then there is no purpose for moral reflection. There is indeed a deep, if limited, truth in cultural relativism. But people do in fact question their accidental values and their choices, asking critical questions and wondering about good reasons for assessing things as they do; they cannot be told not to do this by a relativist argument. What shape can moral reflection take to guide their questioning?

A plausible response is to shift the question. Instead of asking how one can arrive at a correct moral judgment, we might ask how to understand the moral dimensions of life, the personal styles and social roles, within which moral reflection takes place. How can we model morally reflective living in our society? Alasdair MacIntyre has given an extensive critique of the failures of the   Liberal or modern Western moral tradition, especially of the twentieth-century attempts at meta-ethics, concluding with the suggestion that we need to reconstruct something like the Aristotelian conception of the virtues.[2] That conception proceeded from Aristotle's analysis of a social structure within which moral reflection takes place (Aristotle's moral philosophy did not limit itself according to its own prescription of deliberating about means only). Although Aristotle's answer is insufficient for our own social structure, as MacIntyre readily admits, the Aristotelian strategy of deriving a conception of virtue from social considerations is helpful. MacIntyre's approach is reinforced by the recent emphasis on *praxis* from Dewey through Bernstein, and particularly by the latter's critiques of the major European and American forms of moral and scientific thought.[3]

MacIntyre's is a good beginning for the task of appreciating a model in which moral reflection makes sense, a model that identifies the requisite activities (including problem-solving) and organizes them in ways appropriate to our social context. Our social context itself—determined by cultural, economic, military, and political considerations—includes a far richer mix than the European-American philosophic tradition alone. This has three immediate consequences. First, it is simply stupid to limit our repertory of inspirations to the Western tradition when we have the whole world to call upon. Second, "we" aren't just "us Westerners" any more; our conversation includes participants in all the world's traditions. Third, even the Western tradition cannot be understood only from the inside; not to know how the rest of the world views the Western tradition, and why, is like the man unaware of his open fly. Therefore, a beginning must be made to articulate, understand, and foster a context for moral reflection that fits the world situation. A beginning is all we can hope for, given the depth of our ignorance of one another's cultures relative to their true depth.

The model for moral reflection that I shall develop in this book can be drawn out of historical roots. In order to emphasize the breadth of relevant cultures, the place to begin the sketch is with the Confucian model, for reasons that I will specify immediately. The Confucian model compares in surprising ways with the Puritan, and contrasts in crucial ones. Both stand opposed to the model of moral reflection that has arisen out of Western Liberalism, the model of intellectual technology. The dialectical relation between these three— Confucian, Puritan, and Liberal—both constitutes the difficulties to be solved in conceiving moral reflection and provides important resources for the task.

What makes the Confucian model of moral reflection a plausible or helpful starting point? Even a quick study of Confucian philosophers (for instance, Confucius, Mencius, Hsun-tze, Chou Tun-i, the Cheng brothers, Chu Hsi, and Wang Yang-ming) suggests that their ideals for the scholar-official provide an extraordinary resource for addressing grave failings in Western philosophy.[4] The ideal of the scholar-official stresses the continuity of thought and action, thus surmounting the mind-body dichotomy. The scholar-official relates to the diverse values of many things at once in each action, thus circumventing the Western preoccupation with judgments about the morality of acts considered by themselves. The scholar-official is an individual person with a particular history and nature, and yet one who relates to the surrounding things strictly in accordance with their own needs, not in terms of self-interest; this acknowledges the universality in categorical imperatives without a Kantian denegration of the particularity of a person's nature. Moreover, the scholar-official is both a person of action and a contemplative inquirer after truth, an ideal combination lost in the West after Plato, perhaps recovered in part by pragmatism. If Mencius is to be believed, the Confucian scholar-official is obliged to be a social revolutionary whenever the government is unjust, which appears to be most of the time.[5]

Nevertheless, reading deeper into those Confucian and Neo-Confucian texts, one discovers certain grave limitations to the possibility of adopting the Confucian model in any literal way. When the philosophers stressed the "investigation of things," they mainly meant reading books so as to pass examinations; Confucianism is not a directly supportive philosophy for a scientific culture. Scholar-officials were presumed to be male and therefore do not provide a directly applicable model for moral reflection in a world where women are presumed to have some importance as moral agents.[6] It also appears that the scholar-official requires a lifestyle suitable for the agrarian gentry and unsympathetic to a technological bureaucracy in a world with a money economy.[7] Looked at from an historical point of view, contemporary Chinese in particular see the influence of Confucian philosophy to have been the bulward of social stratification, of the opposition to change and to science, of the denegration of women, and of the effete separation of cultured learning from real work and action. Far from being a revolutionary way of life, that of the scholar-official often has been to preserve the status quo. With his concern for grave demeanor and appropriately elevated social status, the scholar-official has been the epitome of the humorless and unspontaneous bureaucrat. This unflattering picture is, of course, an exaggeration. There have indeed been revolutionary scholar-officials. Nevertheless, by and large, to the Chinese the image of the Confucian scholar-official reflects a conservative, elitist, male-dominated society, exquisite in the refinement of an artfully crafted life available only for a leisure class. This is the opposite of the image of the democratic and revolutionary pragmatist, or indeed Puritan, to whom many, including myself, have likened the Confucian ideal.[8]

If the Confucian ideal of the scholar-official is a plausible contributor to the development of an appropriate contemporary model for moral reflection, it must be abstracted from much of the Chinese context in which it has been embodied and has shown its effects. What are the limits of de-Sinicising the scholar-official? Is there a coherent set of philosophic themes defining the Confucian ideal that can be divested of certain of its Chinese cultural embodiments and reinvested with cultural elements of the contemporary world, a world largely influenced by Western practices of economics, government, and multiculturalism? I shall address this question in detail in terms of only a few themes. I shall not ask what Confucianism really was in Chinese history nor debate with those who believe that its conservative, elitist posture is just fine. Rather, I shall pick out four strengths of Confucianism helpful in addressing some of our deep philosophic issues, explaining how they might be helpful. Then I shall discuss four Confucian themes that are weaknesses and require extirpation from the image of the scholar-official.

The "external" style of this comparative study is different from but not critical of the more "internal" developments urged upon Confucianism by scholars such as Cheng Chung-ying and Tu Weiming in their attempts to reconstruct it as a contemporary worldphilosophy; indeed, their approach requires that they address the issues I intend to finesse. Rather than develop Confucianism, my intent is to construct a contemporary model for moral reflection by finding inspiration in the Confucian model, among others. The emphasis on the Chinese tradition in this first chapter is meant to counter a Western bias and to stress the global range of the cultures that need to find their best elements incorporated in a contemporary model. Furthermore, unlike the Puritan model that burned with an intense flame for a brief period, the Confucian endured and developed for two and a half millenia. It holds serious promise despite its defects. Furthermore, the analysis of its weaknesses will reveal dimensions to an appropriate contempoary model that the Confucianism by itself cannot easily imagine.

II. Confucian Strengths

1. The first great virtue of the Confucian moral model is its insistence on the continuity of thought and action. Expressed as early as *The Doctrine of the Mean,* any personal event is located on a continuum between two poles. One is the absolute center of pure tranquility and readiness-to-respond-but-not-yet-responding. The other is the objective realm of other things as unrelated to the person. Both of the poles are abstractions, according to the Confucian belief. There is no absolute, unrelated center of a person, because the person is in fact always responding; strenuous attempts to reach one's center in meditation are always suspiciously like Buddhist escapism for the Confucian sensibility. Nor is there any wholly objective world unrelated to one's personal responses, from the standpoing of one's personal reality. This is not to say that there is no world where there are no people; it is rather that where there are people, their reality is made up in part of their connections with things, and there is nothing in their environment with which they have absolutely no connection.

Any personal event thus takes place somewhere on the continuum between those abstract poles that do not exist absolutely. The closer to the center, the more inward or internally personal the event. The closer to objective things, the more external the event, the more a public action. The whole identity of a person is made up of all the personal events on the various continua relating to the diverse things in the world. These events are connected by virtue of the facts that they are historical and that they are environments for one another. A person's body is ingredient in all the person's continua with things, and so are the person's basic traits such as family relations, relation to place, to education, and to the various structures that make up personality. One's social roles, such as being a scholar-official with a particular office, and personal affairs such as

career, homemaking, playing out a particular historical destiny, also
provide forms of integrity for a person.[9] But insofar as a person's
events are related to the external pole, the differences those events
make to external things are more important than the fact that they
arise out of the particular individuality of that person. In these cases,
the actions can be considered almost as if they were performed by
any someone. The essence of the continuum between thought and
action, however, is that no action is wholly public, unrelated to the
actual agent, and no inner thought episode wholly private, unstimu-
lated or unconditioned by external matters.

The terms "mind" and "action" may not have all the connotations in Western philosophy that they do for the model of the
scholar-official. Of great importance is that action is always toward
and with respect to the values of things acted on. Mind is not the
mere intention of the structure of the external things but also an appreciation of their values. Furthermore, the mind's appreciative enjoyment or revulsion at things' values is not passive aestheticism. It
is also an active response that begins action. From Mencius's doctrine of the Four Beginnings to Wang Yang-ming's theory of heart-
mind, the Confucian tradition interpreted experience and personal
reality as a valuative transaction. From the outside inward, a person
feels and appreciates the worths in the environment; and from the
inside outward, the person responds valuatively to those things.
Every personal event is a transaction involving both inward and outward movements. The moral task in Confucian ethics is to develop a
personality structure or character that neither distorts the appreciative perception of things' values nor impedes the subtle clarity and
rightness of the outward-tending intention and action. The special
difficulty in this task is that a person must develop complex structures that integrate all the continua relating that person to the world,
to family, fortune, place, future, and past; and these complex integrating structures can develop demands of their own that obscure
appreciative perception and frustrate righteous intentions. That is,
the continua constituting a person in relation to the world can be
structured with selfish desires.

I have articulated this outline of the Confucian notion of the
continuity of thought and action, emphasizing its valuative dimension, by using explicitly pragmatic terms. "Valuative transaction" is
a key notion for John Dewey. Even better than classical
pragmatism, process philosophy can make metaphysical sense of the

scholar-official's continuity of thought and action. According to process philosophy, a person in an environment is a society of events, events nested relative to each other in structured ways that make a difference to the events themselves.[10] The events closer to the center are those that, because of their nesting in the nervous system, are elegantly formed with the information carried through the nervous system; some of these events can be intentional thoughts, and they directly condition the events moving the body, especially in communicative ways such as talking and gesturing. As the effects of the thinking events frame the conditions for events in the wider environment of the body and larger physical world, personal actions take place. The great drawback of process philosophy is that its model does not register the essential continuities of a structured self developing through time, with a mind that thinks in time, and with actions the define personal identity through time. Process philosophy tends to identify the person with trains or societies of the individual events that have significant mentality, when in fact the Confucians knew full well that the identity of the human being lay in the broad continuum relating the more mental with the more overtly physical elements. A mental event is not human at all except for the fact it could not happen were it not for the environment of the broad human continuities. Recent developments in American speculative philosophy have addressed these issues directly.[11]

The conclusion with regard to the theme of continuity of thought and action is that the Confucians had the right balance and that we need to find contemporary ways of expressing it. For the practical role of the scholar-official, this theme means that prior to any particular action there is a weight of thought, including theory. And prior to any thinking, especially theoretical thinking, there is a weight of practice. This is to say, whether a personal event is more toward the inward thinking side or toward the outward action side it takes place in an environment formed of a host of continuities. Moreover, the character of the transactive continuity of thought and action is valuative—appreciative one way and responsively rectifying the other. The scholar-official is always in action, and each action should also bear the full resources of well-formed intelligence.

2. The second theme arises from the outer pole of the continuities just discussed. Every action a person takes affects a whole environment. Some things are affected in important ways, others in

unimportant—perhaps just in being left alone. For the Chinese philosophers, everything has its value, which in large measure is a function of relations to other things. So when an action affects many things, it affects their values. The cumulative worth of the action, therefore, is determined not only by its intended effect but by its whole range of effects.

Furthermore, we intend to affect something not just with one action but with a series of actions that deal with it in multiple ways. We don't just act upon it, we "treat with" it. Most important moral situations involve establishing an ongoing relation with the relevant people and institutions so that our own continuous behavior, which we control somewhat directly, can indirectly bring about the influence we want. As things change, we need to change our relations with them, and the relations are usually ongoing interactions.

Combine these two points—the multitude of things affected by an action and the necessity of ongoing actions if one is to do something—and the virtue of the scholar-official as administrator becomes apparent. Only on rare occasions would an administrator consider an action by itself, asking whether it is moral or appropriate. Rather, the scholar-official develops ongoing relationships with people. Better yet, the relationships are not so much with individual people as with the institutional and environing structures within which people live and interact. The function of an administrator is not so much to make individual people better as it is to affect the environment within which people exercise their own responsibility for creativity and excellence. Among the chief issues for determining how to affect the environment are determinations of how to acknowledge and respect the individuals involved, and this requires direct and personal relationships with other people. But the administrator's intent is to maximize the values of the environment for all those involved, and this requires direct and personal relationships with the other people. Since persons themselves are conceived as continua in the sense discussed earlier, administrative attention to the environment includes attending to person's own identities insofar as those identities are organized in environmental roles.

Because the administrative side of the scholar-official focuses on affecting all the values in the environment, the environment is in danger of being viewed as itself as institution. This is part of the Confucian emphasis on society rather than raw nature as the proper

domain of human concern. Of course, it is but a short step from
viewing one's environment as an institution to be managed by an administrator to a wholly bureaucratic conception in which the administrator is just one environmental role among many. I would
argue that the best, if not the only true, Confucian view is that no
person, no scholar-official, can be viewed merely as an institutionalized role. In fact, like the Platonic philosopher-king, the scholar-
official must stand above the regularities and roles of the environment precisely because of the responsibility to affect that environment always for the better. There is thus no situation within which
the scholar-official might not be obliged to revolution, transcending
legitimated roles. This is a dangerous position, with three possible
results. One is that the scholar-official might abandon true responsibility and become a bureaucrat defined by the role; this is what often
happened in China. Another is that, setting administrative responsibilities above the legitimate regularities of civilized society, the
scholar-official might become a tyrant; this tendency is apparent in
Western totalitarianism — think of Mussolini as a Confucian railroad
dispatcher. The third is that the scholar-official blend transcendent
responsibility with irony and laugh at the necessary pretentions; this
is an un-Confucian, Taoist, point to which we shall return shortly.

Supposing for the moment that it is possible to avoid the
bureaucratic consequences of the administrative image of the
scholar-official, the advantage of the image is apparent. Moral life is
displayed not as a set of court judgments on specifiable actions but
rather as the development of relationships, skills, and ongoing virtues that make it possible to affect things for the better at the right
time and in the right way. The power of this point derives from its
contrast with the usual Western mode of moral thinking. Perhaps
because of the pervasiveness of the juridical model, Western philosophers have looked primarily at the judgeable action as the proper
unit of moral worth. Kant expressed this attitude with the greatest
strictness when he demanded that actions can be judged regarding
their morality only when they can be formulated as maxims or uni-
versalizable cases. The attitude is exhibited as well in utilitarian
ethics that asks whether the action brings about the greatest good,
and in contemporary deontological ethics that identifies actions by
the rules that apply to them. If the Confucians are right, any
abstractly isolatable action affects an indefinite plurality of elements
in the environment and therefore falls under an indefinite plurality

of rules, each relating the action to a different context. No concrete act can have a moral worth by itself, but only insofar as it makes a difference to an ongoing relationship of the actor to the environment and of aspects of the environment to each other. Western philosophers such as MacIntyre have roused interest in the classical ethics of virtue because of the limitations in the ethics of acts.

3. The third strength of the scholar-official ideal is its publicness. Western philosophy, especially that influenced by Liberalism, sharply distinguishes the roles in social systems from the individuals who may play the roles. Some Liberal thinkers, such as Robert Nozick, have gone so far as to suggest that the relation between person and role is external, so that the person can choose to play or not. Within the Western conception, the publicness of life is defined by the roles. If a person can manage to avoid social roles with public obligations, public life can be avoided altogether; the disastrous effect of this view is a main theme of the following chapter and of Chapter Nine. Ironically, Chinese Taoism is popular among some Westerners because it appears to offer the wholly natural, non-role-playing, non-public, spontaneous, amoral private life.

The modern Western assumptions about the externality of role to person are not shared by the sense of publicness in the Confucian ideal of scholar-official. Precisely because a person's nature is located on the continuum between abstract inner core and abstractly external things, the person is internally related to the social roles of the context. Furthermore, because the social systems are not external to persons, the systems themselves are changed and shaped by the particular individuals operating within them, and therefore cannot be said to be impersonal.

The Confucian scholar-official is presumed to be ready, through personal self-cultivation and specific experience, to enter into or create the appropriate social roles in the context so as to bring about the good. Public service is not something added onto private life but rather is the essence of personal life. The historical Chinese context is especially to be separated off here. The "official" part of the scholar-official's life usually meant holding government office, earned by placing well on examinations in the classics. Clearly, however, the engagement in public life can take place wherever there is public life. Public life is care of the environment within which people can take personal enjoyment and exercise creative initiative, and the institutions of that environment include the home, workplace, neigh-

borhood, religious practice, and all of the social behaviors investigated by social scientists. [12] The ideal of the scholar-official is to exercise responsibility in all areas of public life. This makes the further
point that the ideal is applicable to everyone, since everyone plays
some sort of public role, simply by virtue of being in a family.

4. A fourth strength of the Confucian ideal, the last I shall
mention here, is its insistence on seriousness. Although the source of
the pomposity attacked by Taoists, seriousness is required in self-
cultivation and in attention to living right and getting one's job done.
The importance of this point can be seen with another contrast to the
situation in Western culture.

In the early centuries of the modern era in Europe, as noted
above, two ideologies contested for the cultural soul of the Anglo-
Saxon countries, Liberalism and Puritanism. Liberalism advocated
the essential externality of individuals to their environment, hypothesized that social relations are merely conventional overlays, made
morals a matter of self-protective due process for the exercise of will,
and shaped the capitalist economic system into the jungle-law horror
it came to be by the nineteenth century. Puritanism by contrast (1)
saw both nature and human affairs to be integrated according to
aesthetic models within the divine will and vision, (2) hypothesized
that social relations are the functional expression of the divinely
warmed internal heart of individuals bound into communities with
an ontologically grounded mission, (3) made morals a matter of
responding resonantly to the real values in theings, and (4) attempted an economic system of mutual help for all through the productivity of the capable.

In the contest, of course, Liberalism won out and Puritanism
was discredited. The failure of Puritanism is complex, but two difficulties are immediately apparent. As pointed out in the previous
chapter, it was too dependent on a theological mode of self-understanding that could not sustain itself within the cosmology of modern
science. And it ruined itself by the failure to solve the problem of
authority, both social and intellectual, degenerating into intolerance. For all its failings, the demise of Puritanism is lamentable
because it presented a social ideology stressing relation, integrity,
objective norms, and ontologically grounded meaningfulness to life.
And where Liberalism, by finally hanging all values on the contingencies of personal will, is cynical, Puritanism was serious. For the
Puritan, like the Confucian, life indeed matters. Self-cultivation and

righteous public life are matters of ultimate concern. Puritans and Confucians might be pompous and authoritarian, but they are never cynical or alienated; their metaphysical practice is the engagement of life.

After the Death of God, Puritanism in its classic forms has no chance of recovery. But Confucianism never had that theological history, and the ideal of the scholar-official returns seriousness to the engagement with life. Here is not the place to advocate the Chinese worldview to solve the problems of environmental ethics, of social relations, of distributive justice, or any of the other major problems facing contemporary society. But its fragrance turns our heads in new directions, and it can contribute to the development of a world philosophy surmounting the impotent dialectic of Liberalism and Marxism. The seriousness of the scholar-official, the insistent pursuit of responsibility, is an effective antidote to the alienation of late capitalism and bureaucratic communism.

III. Confucian Weaknesses

The above discussion has hinted at the difficulties associated with the strengths of the Confucian ideal of the scholar-official. Let me explore them directly.

1. For all the virtues of the continuity of thought and action, there remains the problem of establishing the integrity of individuals that allows them to stand over against their situation and say No! The fully developed theme of the continuity of thought and action is connected with the Confucian theme of being "one body with the world." Although this is too complex and nuanced an issue to explore here, let me suggest that the metaphysical imagination depicting us as one body with the world, defined thoroughly through the connectedness of our inmost soul with external things, undermines the possibility of basic negation, and hence of revolution. Of course, there have been Confucian revolutionaries, but they have run against the imagination of their culture. When Chinese society recently needed revolution, and the Confucian tradition could not provide the models, external Western models perforce were imported with results, we have seen, divisive for Chinese tradition.

Because practical possibilities are shaped by our metaphysical imagination, the corrective to the tendency of the theme of continuity of thought and action to congeal into the block universe is the elaboration of a different metaphysics that will be explored in this and the following chapters. Specifically, I suggest that we regard individuals as harmonies of essential and conditional features. The conditional features are those constituting the continuities of the person with all surrounding, past, and future affairs. The essential features are those originating through the processes of the individual's coming to be, which place the person determinately in each of those continuities. Conditional features are relational and essential ones are existential. Without conditioned features, the essential ones would be empty and have nothing to tie down to positions in existential process. Without essential features, the conditional features would be mere possible relations, possible positions in relational process. An individual is a harmony of the two, and the person's integrity consists in the precise *de facto* way in which essential and conditional features are harmonized.

Although two individuals are mutually connected by their conditional features, each has essential features unique to himself or herself. The norms for one individual to maintain his or her harmony in the course of changing events are those that apply to his or her essential as well as conditional features, and these norms may not be "one body" with other things. It is perfectly possible with this metaphysical imagination for a person to see that the essential way by which he or she ought to take a stand in the various connectives of the situation is to say No to the connectives, to break off connection, to disengage, to attempt to destroy the context that supports some evil. This is in no way incompatible with the thoroughgoing connectivity of a person with the situation. But it shows how the integrity of the person can take up a negating, critical stance. At this point, the "administrative" connotations of the scholar-official are exactly wrong. Although, indeed, sometimes we should attempt to manage the situation, reconciling opposing tendencies and redirecting the institutions to better values, at other times the institutions are just bad and should be changed. People sometimes are evil and must be stopped. Personal and social directions can be corrupt and need to be opposed. The scholar-official in these latter instances needs not to be one body with the world but to stand apart as a revolutionary and critic. There is a Chinese tradition of withdrawal from government office in protest and retirement to the mountains to await a shift in fortune. To that tradition must be added the negative power of conscience based on a normative integrity of harmonizing oneself over against a situation or against other people. This seems to me entirely possible for a growing Confucian tradition. It is at the very heart of the Puritan.

2. The second strength I cited of the scholar-official ideal is the richness of nuance in dealing with an indefinite plurality of values at once, a moral practice likened to an administrator's management of relationships. The weakness, of course, is that the complexity of the job can drive one to despair. Instead of the subtle, shifting sensitivity to changing values in contingently connected processes, a scholar-official can reach for a formula, a rule book, a set of fail-safe procedures so that he or she won't be criticized later for missing the critical trick. The cultural power of this temptation is what gives rise to highly codified societies, to formal rituals abandoning humanity for precision, to codified and predictable styles of behavior, dress, speech, and attitude. And, of course, relations of temporary advantage get transformed into legitimated relations of dominance. The rigidity of classical Chinese culture came as much from continuing despair at the possibility of living up to the infinite sensitivity Confucianism calls for as from the weight of tradition itself.

The antidote to this despair is the development of selective principles by which to give finite limitations to the demand of pure sensitivity and responsiveness to all things. We needn't retreat to Western rules, utilitarian calculi, or virtues conceived as predicates of substances. Chinese tradition, particularly through Taoism, sought to develop special selective sensitivities to what is important. Part of the deliberate "unlearning" of righteousness recommended by Chuang-tze is a putting aside of the strictures of intentions and sign-systems associated with language and ritual behavior, to let one's natural psychophysical taste go to play.[13] Confucianism too has emphasized the importance of clarifying all the depths of soul and action so that one's natural or "original" aesthetic selectivity can make the moral task a finite one.

As an underpinning in metaphysical imagination to this point, I would suggest that we regard our concepts not only in terms of their network meanings connecting them to other concepts, actions, rituals and other learned sign systems, but also with regard to their content meaning.[14] Content meaning is the actual set of signs, experiences, and real physical connections with things that are integrated under the rule-like form of the concept. It is possible to learn and use concepts according to their network meaning, but with great deficiencies in content meaning. That is, some crucial part of the content meaning is just another empty sign, not the real experience. Much of spiritual practice and psychotherapy is the remaking of missed or distorted experiences that are necessary building blocks for higher level experiences. True Confucian (and Taoist) self-cultivation should be the dismantling of crippling conscious and sub-conscious sign systems and the alignment of the layers of psycho-physical connectives so that the important values of things get car-ried over to the responsive self. To be a true person is to be so consti-tuted as to carry over into one's own experience and response the high values and important distinctions encountered in the world. To be a false person is somehow to misrepresent those values in ex-perience and response. There is nothing in this call for true experi-ence, for "truthing" our relations and things, that is incompatible with the Confucian position, especially the position on sincerity.

The purification of experience so as to have profound content meaning that is being true to reality was at the heart of the Puritan ideal, though expressed here in post-Freudian terms. In addition, the Puritan cosmology affirmed a positive grace from God working through nature's beauty. For intellectual Puritans such as the Cam-bridge Platonists, the purification of the mystical assent meant discovering how to conform one's will to the divine will, thus uniting the holy vertical and moral horizontal dimensions. But as Leites points out, the Puritan emphasis on the perfection of the personality required mastering an ideal of moral constancy that exacted a great price.[15] The price was that natural excitements and extremes of emotion need to be repressed, with the result that life can tend toward dullness. This was contrary to the Puritan intent, which was to har-monize all the affairs of life, including the extremes, so as to hold them steadily together in constant enjoyment, like God's bliss. In practice, steadiness was incompatible with excitement, and by the nineteenth-century Puritanism was, like Confucianism, a symbol of repression and self-righteous satisfaction in stolidity.

Perhaps constancy ought not be taken to describe seriousness. If being serious means being engaged with and true to the things of the world, and if there are aesthetic means of grasping and respond-ing to the intensities of things, then sometimes a truly engaged serious life will be rocked responsively from one extreme to another. This is a theoretical possibility for both Confucian and Puritan. But both would warn that volatility itself is dangerous to the purity of responsiveness.

3. The weakness associated with the virtue of publicness is extraordinarily profound. The initial force of the problem is that although public life is of the essence of the human, only a few can attain to it, those whom nature's grace and society's fortune grant places of power. For, without the power to act, participation in the public is illusory. So, for instance, women, the poor, the outsiders and foreigners, those of the wrong religion, and a host of other classes have been denied access to the public. This is not the complaint (worth making in its own right) that within a public structure some people are dominant and others subordinate; it is rather that some people simply are excluded from public structures. Sometimes differences between hierarchically related social classes are explained and partially justified as a function of reciprocal duties. My concern, however, is where the lower classes are not public or are deprived of public life.

The reason for the rare elite quality of public life is the difficulty in achieving public skills. One must have the natural talent, the educational opportunities, the support of the right family and social milieu, and historical advantages. Think of the exclusive group of literati in China, or those with the advantages of university education in the current world. In addition, there are a great many socially necessay tasks that don't require the refinement of publicness, and most societies have negatively relegated certain groups to those tasks. The effect of this elitism, coupled with the Confucian identification of publicness as an essential trait of ideal humanity, is that large groups of people, such as women and peasants, are treated as not quite human, though often romanticized. A large body of emerging scholarship is focusing on the anticulture or marginality of these privatized groups. We now understand that there have been countercultures always existing in the shadows of high culture. But the Confucian ideal of the scholar-official is a high culture ideal if there ever was one, and it cannot be asserted now unless transformed to become inclusive of those countercultures. (The Puritan ideal, particularly on the Puritan left, was anti-high-culture; or rather, the art of high culture had to be hidden in culture accessible to all, and active participation was the means of access encouraged. The Puritans were better on equality for the poor than for women, although they did believe in gender equality for salvation and in equality of mutual respect in sexual and domestic matters.)

The most penetrating weakness in the ideal of publicness is that its elitism requires authority, and our current culture has only an uncertain grasp on authority. In fact, in both East and West, the old notion of authority, deriving from the sovereign as the true author of all social deeds, has dissipated. We are left with authority merely as expertise. But expertise is only skill at means, not skill at determining social and personal ends, the very point requiring moral reflection. The virtue of the scholar-official is the capacity to be attuned to the shifting values of the situation, shaping human responses so as to achieve the greatest worth possible, appreciating the achievement. This is precisely the opposite of expertise. One of the enduring contributions of modern Western philosophy, both Liberal and Puritan, is the demonstration that responsibility for life belongs with the one who lives it, not with some other authority; expertise in others is helpful only insofar as it is an extention of one's own responsibility. Is authority then purely democratic, with each person responsible for his or her own self-interest? That question is answered affirmatively by modern capitalism — and also by communism, where self-interest is expanded to one's class interest. But as the Confucians as well as ancient Greeks have known, public obligations have to do with the needs of the real objective situation, not necessarily with any exclusively defined interest. Recognition of this point has underlain the polity of republican democracies, in which elected representatives act for the good of the whole rather than for their constituents. But this undermines the capacity of the constituents to exercise their own responsibility, and in practice often leads to the representatives serving their own self-interest while believing in bad faith that it is the best interest of the whole. These general remarks about authority in government polity apply as well to other public situations, whether in the household, the neighborhood or the workplace. How can public responsibility be shared without an authoritative distribution of responsibility? What happens when there is no accepted legitimate authority? This is a fundamental problem for our time.

Assuming that there is no adequate solution to the problem of authority at the present time, what limitations does this impose on the usefulness of the ideal of the scholar-official? The fact that publicness is an ideal practically limited to an elite does not mean that it is not also ideal for the others. At this point the Confucian tradition may do well to adopt the pragmatists' emphasis on universal participation in affairs. According to pragmatism, the most important lessons about the exercise of public power, indeed about public life as such, are learned through direct participation in events that influence the environment. To aid this, universal education is necessary, although we are far from understanding what this means when widely diverse groups are involved. The weakness of the ideal of the scholar-official with regard to the imperative to publicness is paradoxical. To claim publicness for the scholar-official seems inevitably to deny it to others; yet once others are excluded from the public arena, the publicness of the scholar-official is reduced to a mere assertion of authority, an assertion likely to be subverted by the giggles of Taoists, women, and other counterculturists.

4. The appeal to giggles brings the discussion to the weakness that is the other side of Confucian seriousness. The Puritan in the West is the very symbol of humorless, interfering, and restrictive authority. The Confucian has something like that reputation in East Asia. There is a large and pervasive philosophical issue at stake here.

Running through all the cited strengths and weaknesses of the ideal of the scholar-official is the specter of totalism. The continuity of thought and action might suppose the world to be whole enough to be one body. The overwhelming array of values to which any action is relevant threatens to freeze the agent into paralysis. The publicness of the scholar-official's life supposes an integrated world in which the divergent visions of the publicly disenfranchised are denied legitimacy. The seriousness that gives meaning to life can at the same time impose a limited meaning with the force of tyranny.

The metaphysical situation is this: The processes of life are infinitely rich in their multiplicity and relations, and our grasp upon them always involves an arbitrary cut, an arbitrary tonic note, an arbitrary order. The making of human life and culture involves a divinely arbitrary creation of basic steps. The fact that culture is at root arbitrary does not mean it is false — indeed pragmatic considerations alone guarantee that any culture that survives for a while has some truth in it. But it is always a limited truth, a partial truth that comes from going at reality one way rather than another. Some people of conservative persuasion perceive this tenuousness of culture in the fact that its infinite matrix is a threat against which we must guard by extending and securing the cultural system. A more relaxed attitude is to enjoy all the ways of going at reality that are possible to bring within our ken, and to use the inherent instability of any order as a friendly way of making improvements where we can, thus weakening the forces of evil and limitation.

The recognition that one's culture is just one among many possibilities, and that reality can be addressed, heard, and dwelt in
through many other orders, has led to cynicism in the West. The
only orders that seem to be universal are those representing the
world as dead, mathematical, and valueless. Nevertheless, contrary
to common "seeming," the cynical response is simply tired and
mistaken metaphysics. The very heart of human life and culture is to
find and create selective meaning in the midst of an infinite web of
possibilities. For this, a kind of infinite passion after the finite is
demanded. We think our way through philosophical systems,
through religious cosmologies, through histories, and into the arti-
facts of specific life that bear particular value. Without selective
order there is no value. But any valuable selective order is an arbitrary exclusion of any number of other selective orders. The problem
with Confucius was not that he failed to recognize that his human-
making conventions were indeed conventional but that he let the
conventions be imposed as if they were everyone's order; because of
this we need Great Robber Chih, Chuang Tzu's hero of de-
propertying.[16]

IV. Irony

What is the human way to comport oneself in the face of the infinite demand to comprehend reality with an order, a demand that is
infinitely frustrated? David Hall has argued that irony is the fundamental human stance.[17] It differs from cynicism and sarcasm
because it requires seriousness, the passion for order-building. But it
differs on the other side from popular Puritan or Confucian seriousness by recognizing the limits of any order. From the standpoint of
those not quite captured by the order, the order-making looks slightly ridiculous and giggle-worthy. Irony is the attitude that binds
together in a contrast both the insider's passion to bless an order and
the outsider's recognition of its arbitrariness and cosmic vanity.

Suppose we can, as a race, mature to the point of irony, continue the task of civilization and still laugh at ourselves as some kind
of divine play. Surely the model of the scholar-official has important
contributions to make to this project. But there is a limit to irony, an
ironic limit perhaps.

Irony is an attitude that accepts the metaphysical situation
regarding order and chaos aesthetically. It is a special order for how

we are to take things, how to feel them so as to keep on going. It leaves things as they are. Those excluded from public life and high culture are left with their laughter and capacity to undermine through gossip and ridicule, but without direct power of their own. What is also needed is a better order, one that does not abuse women, does not create poverty, does not demean or wrongfully privatize. The aesthetic attitude is dangerous without a conjoined moral commitment. The moral commitment of course is just the practice of seriousness applied now to the limits of our current world society, and the ironist will point out that any improved society will still be limited, and probably will spawn its own outsiders who splash funny water on its clay feet. I want to insist that the moral commitment is not just a partial appreciation of the metaphysical situation, myopically tied to the order side. Rather, the moral commitment, as much as the ironic attitude, is a serious contrast of order-building in the face of an infinite cosmos. The aesthetics of irony and the commitments of morality are two irreducible dimensions of true life and realistic metaphysics, and each entails the other.

A final comment is in order about the Confucian scholar-official. The tradition offers little hope that the scholar-official will ever develop much of a sense of ironic humor about life, and for this reason it remains important to cultivate Taoists cousins. On their side, the Taoists have generally been anemic at culture-building, and they have needed the Confucians for the serious side in the contrast of order and chaos. This partnership of incommensurables may in fact be a higher wisdom about the ideal of the scholar-official, namely, that it is a good and necessary ideal for the human spirit but one that needs balancing with other, incommensurable ideals. Such wisdom would require the scholar-official to abandon any pretense at an authoritative last word, and this might be what the Confucian tradition meant whenever it talked about the fundamental passion of "love with differences."

Many themes of moral reflection have been raised in this chapter that will be singled out for special development in those to follow. The singular conclusion at this point is that a proper model for moral reflection requires a recognition of the irony of serious commitment to a normative order in an infinite context. By themselves, Confucian scholar-officials tend to degenerate from moral reflection to deliberation about roles, unless they have the reminders of Taoist relativising humor. As to the Puritan ghosts, we might safely resurrect them in our pursuit of seriousness, responsibility, community, and social daring, but only if they are fixed with an ironic smile. Because they mixed their original passion for moral and spiritual order with an even deeper commitment to the contingency and radical dependency of the world, to its arbitrariness as an expression of God's glory, the current heavenly vantage point of the Puritan ghosts might give them a sense of humor about our necessary earnestness.

3

Social Obligation, Personal Responsibility, and Moral Identity

The Preacher said:

> Again, I considered all the acts of oppression here under the sun; I saw the tears of the oppressed, and I saw that there was no one to comfort them. Strength was on the side of their oppressors, and there was no one to avenge them. I counted the dead happy because they were dead, happier than the living who are still in life. More fortunate than either I reckoned the man yet unborn, who had not witnessed the wicked deeds done here under the sun (*Eccle.* 4:1-3).

I. From Social Obligation to Personal Responsibililty

The Preacher's vision was not new in his own time. Anyone who looks clearly today can see the same thing. What is remarkable is that the Preacher simply saw the oppression and did not say who was to do something about it. He wrote, of course, and his writing itself had the corrective power of a true witness. Indeed, in many respects the Preacher offers the first serious moral reflection from a standpoint appreciative of irony. But he did not write about who was responsible to do something about the oppression.

Philosophy has a problem, at least as old as *Ecclesiastes*, of determining how to move from a general social obligation—a good that ought to be done, or an evil avoided, or a situation changed—to the definite location of personal responsibility to address the obligation. Under what circumstances is a general, objective obligation binding upon an individual as a personal responsibility, a responsibility such that the person's moral character and worth are determined in the response? The question, "Am I my brother's keeper?" has no obvious answer.

Even if the question were firmly answered in the affirmative, there would remain the further question of what to do with him. What is the good for one's brother, for the public, for society, for its institutions? The question of identifying the proper norms is the traditional center of moral reflection, and subsequent chapters will address it with increasing directness. The previous chapter merely assumed both that the good can be identified and that people have some kind of responsibility to do it. The latter assumption is the focus of the present discussion.

Although there may be private or personal goods and responsibilities, the Confucians, the Puritans, and the Liberals all take themselves to be responsible for public life in some sense, and that is our own common assumption, if often unreflective and forgotten. That is, we take it to be our own responsibility to care for the health of the community.[1] What does moral reflection have to say about this?

In a somewhat stipulative use of words, I am calling the objective good of the community (however that is to be determined) a matter of "social obligation." As such, "obligation" is vague with respect to who is obligated to do something about it. "Personal responsibility" is the state of an individual being normatively bound to take on the social obligation, or some part of it, alone or in concert with others by virtue of membership in some asssociation. Our question is, how are individuals assigned personal responsibility for social obligations? Or, by virtue of what are social obligations able to command personal responsibility in a normative sense?

This question is close to the heart of the problem of finding a model for moral reflection. How does Liberalism account for personal responsibility for the public good? One of the elements of the Liberal moral tradition—for instance, enshrined in Hobbesian and Lockean social contract theory—is that morality springs from seeking one's own benefit as defined by safety (Hobbes) or property (Locke). Moral reflection then becomes calculative reason aiming at one's benefit (the reason operative even in the state of nature). On the one hand, the worth or justification of "benefit" is assumed without continuing critical reflection and, on the other hand, its content is left to be defined in detail by personal choice. Normative social goods are hardly more than contracts for the convenience of mutual individual benefit, in the Liberal contractarian view.[2]

The great strength of the Liberal tradition is that it has drawn a far richer picture of what fulfills an individual than those earlier traditions that took their definitions from socially determined roles. A second strength is that Liberal philosophy has demonstrated the great variety in kinds of fulfillment and hence has taught the fundamental lessons of tolerance of diversity and deviance. The current movement of consciousness to acknowledge and respect the different experiences of women and gay people, of foreigners and non-elites, owes its plausibility to the lessons of Liberalism. But the egoism, or pursuit of personal or local benefit, in Liberalism tends to reduce moral reflection to calculative technological reason. It corrupts the context for moral reflection on the worths of and obligations to things.

Kant had a far sterner conception than most forms of Liberalism of personal responsibility as duty. Duty for Kant defines those obliged actions without which a person would not be moral or free. He taught the point beloved of Confucians and Puritans that if something is really your duty, it is your responsibility whether you want it or not. Personal responsibility is categorical; it is not hypothetical in the sense that *if* you want a certain benefit, you should do a certain thing. Kant's position can be given a Liberal twist, which is to say that you should do your duty in order to be a free, moral person; this differs from Kant's own view, which was that even if you don't want to be moral or free, you are still responsible to do your duty and in doing so will be free anyway. But the Liberal interpretation reveals a weakness in Kant. He had no sense that personal responsibility is in the service of the public good to be done. There is nothing to define a Kantian person as responsible for a public life. Rather, a Kantian person simply acts for the sake of duty, which may be compatible with an extreme privatizing individualism.

To approach moral reflection by asking how social obligations become personal responsibilities is thus an unusual move in modern

Western moral thought. Its very strategic role is to suggest that neither the egoism of Liberalism nor Kant's emphasis on duty is sufficient. Moral reflection rather seeks to understand what is good and bad in affairs, and why; and what should be done, and who should do it. These have become unnatural questions for modern thought, though they were at the heart of Puritan social discourse. One reason for the Puritan now to smile is that to begin by asking these questions is to subvert, at least in part, the assumptions that have deprived the questions of a context.

Societies ordinarily have public officials to take care of general obligations or to organize others to do so. The careful understanding and "authorizing" of this point was the genius of the social contract branch of Liberalism. The social contract defines both the obligations attendant upon a social role and the conditions for occupancy of that role. But what if the public officials fail to address the issue? What if they themselves benefit from and so sustain the situation that needs amendment? The test of a social order that distributes social responsibilities to loci of personal responsibility comes when the actual operating system breaks down.

However slow some might be to invoke it, most civilized societies recognize a right of revolution, or at least of radical amendment of the regime. When public officials fail to address the issues, their legitimacy softens and threatens to dissolve. Who then ought to govern? Delinquent officials might stay in office until rebels dethrone them, and sometimes it is assumed that the revolutionaries themselves will take over the office. Is that assumption justified? Why? What if the revolutionaries go back home? Love of power and honor might be sufficient always to produce an abundance of candidates for powerful high office. But what would motivate even a disgruntled person to be a block captain, to organize a sewer district or a volunteer fire department, to raise money for a local symphony or agricultural school? And, of course, there is no guarantee that the revolutionaries or volunteers would be competent people for the job.

The fact that governments can break down, or be forced apart, or fail to do what is needful, demonstrates that we cannot define responsibility for public obligation simply in terms of official roles. Whether or not anyone is motivated or capable, is anyone responsible for objective public obligations? How is this to be understood? The question calls first for some formal reflection on responsibility; indeed, on the metaphysics of responsibility.

II. Personal Responsibility and Moral Identity

Responsibility involves a relation individuals bear to a situation in which something of the situation's good is normative for them. Several parts of this hypothesis need to be explicated.

The content of "the situation's good" may or may not bear directly on the particular individuals. Improvements in the judicial system, for instance, bear directly on those who go to court but not on those who never use the court system; responsibility for the improvements may lie with both groups. Kant was suspicious of those who stand to gain personally from doing their duty. John Dewey, on the other hand, was suspicious of those whose personal good is not bound up in their participation in public life. On both accounts, regardless of personal interest, responsibility has to do with some objective good being normative for individuals.

It is tempting to assume, with Dewey, that in a complicated social sense, personal interest itself gives rise to responsibility. For him, an active "public" is formed when people perceive that it is in their interest to exercise some control over transactions which otherwise seem to be private transactions.[3] He had in mind public regulation of commerce and also public regulation of government military policies (for Dewey the government is itself a system of transactions, and thus it is like a private realm that may need public regulation by groups of people outside itself). Dewey's insights into the formation of active public groups and into the motivations for participation in social life are extraordinary. Like Marx, he separated off the Liberal goals of individual personal fulfillment from the social contract theory of public authority, maintaining the former and rejecting the latter. But whereas Marx tried to write large the goals of individual personal fulfillment in the class solidarity and "species being" of groups, with dubious success and a total loss of Liberal tolerance, Dewey held that individual personal fulfillment develops out of complex social transactions respecting the uniqueness of each participant, hence valuing tolerance. And whereas Marxism radically distinguishes the people as public from the government — the latter being a dictatorship over the people in the short run, withering away in the long run — Dewey urged treating the relation between the people and the government as an interactive one: sometimes the government is the natural and neatly efficient vehicle of public action; and yet, in other affairs, government is the very thing the people as public needs to organize itself to control.

Dewey's subtle insights notwithstanding, his position does not account for personal responsibility. Public life, for him, is a vehicle for the defense of one's own interests, despite the participatory and interactive character he saw in the formation of interest. In this respect, Dewey did not go beyond the egoism of much Liberalism. Marx shares the same limitation, although he wrote "egoism" large enough to be the property of a social class. The pursuit of one's own or one's special group's interest is not enough to define either the content of responsibility or the having of responsibility as such.

What then does it mean to say that persons are responsible when something of the situation's good "is normative for them"? There are two levels of answer to this question.

At the first level, the normativeness applies to the individuals' potential actions. That is, among the things the individuals can do are actions that either benefit or harm the situation's good. That the situation's good is normative means that it contributes to the overall worth of those alternatives, making the beneficial ones publically valuable and the harmful ones public liabilities. The alternatives also have worth coming from other sources, including personal interest, the interests of others and special private groups, and also from intrinsic merit. At this level, the value one option has by virtue of benefiting the situation's good may be in competition with the value an alternative has for personal interest, or for aesthetic merit, and so on.

One must be careful not to imagine too simple a view of "potential actions" in this context. The relevant actions are rarely conceivable in themselves; more often they are matters of participation in large scale endeavors whose values can be assessed only contextually. Examples of alternatives include joining a neighborhood action group versus spending the time at one's own creative work, or participation in "dirty" politics versus remaining in "private life" in order not be be associated with compromise.

At this first level, the normativeness of the situation's good for people's potential action is just one of many kinds of normativeness that determine the aggregate comparative worth of options and does not by itself yet determine personal responsibility. At this level, all that can be said is that the person's potential actions have normative or moral content. As such, the decisions about what to do are moral

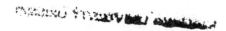

choice-points. Regarding content, there are many kinds of moral worth determined by the array of different values in the situation that can be affected by the alternate potential actions. These may or may not be compared easily and graded one to another; often moral deliberation, recognizing that the options are not directly comparable, seeks external grounds for deciding among competing claims — procedural grounds, for instance.

At the second level, the normativeness of the situation's good is an essential determinant of the person's moral worth. Given its atomistic and nominalistic metaphysics, it would be impossible for Liberalism to make the situation's good essential to the individual's moral identity; Kant's metaphysics of noumenal autonomy rather than heteronomy is similarly limited. To understand the axiological point, it is thus necessary to supply an alternative metaphysical conception of the relation between individuals and their environment. For a beginning, it is helpful to recur to the metaphysical distinction between conditional and essential features of things that was introduced in the previous chapter, generalizing beyond personal individuals to "thing" in general. Any "thing" is a harmony of essential and conditional features. The conditional features are the components that derive from other things, the "causal" conditions. The essential features are those that determine how the conditions are harmonized in the thing; they are what is essential to that thing without which it would reduce to the congeries of the conditioning things. As applied to people, the various options for potential actions are conditional features deriving from the fact that the people have actualized resources, a future, and an environment for action. Certian of those "future conditions" are also essential conditions, in that whether one chooses to act upon them determines one's own moral worth.

A person's moral worth is the special value that accrues from the conjunction of the moral content of action with the person's responsibility for that context. Most actions can be considered without regard to responsibility, and in this consideration there might also be an accrual of value to the person. For instance, one chooses to invest time in fund-raising for a local symphony orchestra; and by participating in this activity, one develops valuable skills as a fund-raiser as well as a more sophisticated grasp of music. These new skills and extra sophistication are valuable but not particularly moral as such. The moral dimension of the fund-raising

comes from the fact that the choice is a function of the person's essential features. That is, this choice is among the ways the person gives moral identity to himself or herself in this area and time of life. The person's character in this respect comes from the essential features of the person's past, present, and future as they impinge on potential behavior in this area and time. Responsibility is simply the fact that, however one acts, those actions determine one's character, and where the actions deal with matters of moral content, as they always do, that character has a moral worth. Responsibility is thus the interaction between one's actions and one's environment presenting options with moral content. One's responsibility is always *to* the moral content in potential actions; more realistically put, one's responsibility is always to make the best of the environment. One's responsibility is always *for* the moral worth or character one's moral interactions give oneself.

"One's own moral worth" is thus an additional factor to the various values that would be achieved by actualizing any of the options. How one chooses to actualize this or that option, each of which has its own aggregate value (some of what derives from how it stands with regard to the situation's good), determines personal moral worth. Only those choices are "essential" that determine the personal moral worth of the chooser. Those are the choices with respect to which the person has responsibility, rather than merely having the role of being the potential cause of this or that value. If there are choices that do not affect the agent's moral worth, they are not matters of responsibility.

The question of how choices determine moral worth, and are thus matters of responsibility, pushes the problem back to the nature of personal moral identity. Kant is typical of many modern moral theorists in limiting moral identity to a matter of whether one's actions are in accord with the right or good. It is the individual actions that count for Kant. But moral identity is cumulative through time, and it has to do with one's historical career. What is important is not so much each morally significant action—although that is important for the content of duty in each case—but how the actions cumulatively build character.

Moral identity has at least two dimensions. The one most commonly recognized is the development of personality structures and habits. Moral actions feed back to affect character in this sense. The other dimension is the historical uniqueness of a person's life, lived in a certain place with certain people and circumstances, determined sequentially by specifics of education, work, friendships, struggles, sicknesses, and the contingencies of historical social life. The cumulative quality of moral identity is what gives continuous moral identity across time. One is responsible in the future for decisions taken earlier, and is responsible now for the future consequences of decisions.

Moral identity itself is a normative affair in the sense that, as a person's potentialities are developed, norms apply to them. A newborn has no potentiality for speech until it learns to babble in the phonemes of its parents' language (an observaton made by Aristotle). Once it babbles in those phonemes, the parents reinforce certain strings of sounds and criticize others in accord with the norms of the language. Persons too immature to conceive of themselves as playing social roles may indeed have the norms of the roles apply to them, but they can't be held responsible as agents to play the roles; they must have the potentiality to conceive of themselves as agents, and thus to judge whether as agents they live up to the norms of the roles, in order to be responsible as agents. A baseline condition of responsibility, therefore, is the potentiality to conceive of oneself as an agent relative to the various goods one's actions can serve.

Whether and how an individual is personally responsible for social obligations thus depends on whether and how those obligations define individual identity. Wherever a person's potentialities bear upon the person's moral identity, the person has a responsibility to do the best. Any potential action bears upon personal identity when it expresses or embodies a relation of the person's identity to the values in the situation. The bottom line is that the values served by potential actions always bear upon a mature person's identity. And, therefore, such a person is responsible for the values resident in all potential actions, including those constituted in part by social obligatons. Moral responsibility is a matter of the interaction of the values affected or affectable by one's actions and the moral identity one accrues through a life of action.

What is responsibility to specifically social obligations? Persons are responsible for social obligations when the situation's good is not merely generally obligatory but defines the moral worth of those particular individuals. Whether or not they want to, whether or not they accept the obligation, the moral quality of those individuals is determined in part by the degree to which their actions serve the general obligation.

This is the heart of the vision shared by Confucians and Puritans, though not by Liberals before Dewey. A person's identity consists in and develops through participation in the social and physical environment. Most particularly, personal identity is achieved through social interactions. Because there are real goods and ills served by potential modes of participation, an individual achieves moral identity through cumulative participation. Participation lies under responsibilities precisely because how one participates has a moral content, especially a content relative to social obligations, and that moral content plays essential roles in determining personal moral identity. There are two inseparable factors in personal responsibility; that one's potential actions have moral content and that one's actual actions give moral identity to oneself. Without agents who have the capacity to give themselves moral identity by their actions, social obligations would be impotent to determine personal responsibility. Without objective obligations, moral identity would reduce to aesthetic identity, also lacking personal responsibility. Being responsible is having a relation to a situation with normative elements such that the relation in part determines one's moral identity.

Rarely is being responsible a matter of choosing to be responsible. Perhaps in some special cases — for instance, choosing a certain job, a particular relationship, or form of life — persons can be said to choose responsibility that goes with the choice. But in these cases it is because they choose the relation to the situation defining the responsibility that the responsibility devolves upon them. The basic fact of responsibility is that it binds individuals because of the situations in which they are positioned as matters of their own identity.

Of course, the fact of having a responsibility does not determine what the person will do in respect to it; but it does determine the moral worth of whatever the person does with reference to it. Nor does the fact that a person has a group of responsibilities mean that it is possible to fulfill them all. There are many kinds of responsibility other than to social obligations. In fact, it is usually impossible to fulfill all one's responsibilities, and one's moral character is thus inevitably flawed, even though perhaps one couldn't have done better. This is the topic of Chapter Ten.

The theory that responsibility is a defining feature of individuals deriving from their self-identifying interactions with the normative situations in which they are positioned can be termed an "axiological" theory. That it is axiological comes from the fact that it supposes the situations themselves to have objective goods and evils in them, values with respect to which something is obligatory to be done. It supposes also that individuals are defined in part by the values that give moral worth to their actions.

The axiological theory preserves Kant's insight that morality has to do with imperatives. Our desires and aversions put us into situations that have obligations, but they cannot determine anything to be a responsibility. Simply as such, our desires and aversions, though value-laden, are non-moral. To this extent, the axiological theory accords with Kant's. But the theory abandons Kant's attempt to define responsibility as the property of a person's act by itself; the nature of responsibility is relational, not autonomous. In this respect, the theory is Puritan and Confucian with its emphasis on the situational definition of responsibility; indeed, insofar as a person is defined by norms to which the person is responsible, the person is defined through situational relationships, not through any intrinsic selfhood or autonomy.

The question of how to transform general public obligations into particular persons' responsibilities can be reformulated now as a specification of the axiological perspective. Without specification to the public arena, the theory says merely that people are responsible for the goods in their situations. With such a general scope, responsibility must surely be overwhelming. One of the general goods of life, and hence one of its responsibilities, is not to be obsessive about always doing the absolute best; indeed, it is a often great good simply to enjoy the gratuities of life. And so there must be some principles for weakening, or turning down, and handling indirectly many of the general obligations that would bind us as responsible people.

How, we may ask, do particular individuals relate to public situations so as to have the appropriate responsibilities to fulfill the general obligations? The answer to that question depends in part on the meaning of the "public." The public is that which structures personal responsibilities for social obligations. Is the public situation defined by contrast to private situations in some profound sense, or is the distinction between public and private one of convenience that does not seriously affect the relational character of responsibility?

III. The Public

Let us examine the view, typical of early contractarian Liberalism, that there is a profound distinction between public situations and private ones.[4] On this hypothesis, derivative from the social contract, persons exist only in private situations except insofar as they have created a public situation by contract or participate in such a contract. Public obligations then would be the responsibility of public officials whose jobs define them to be so responsible; and those obligations might fall upon all people in the public situation insofar as they are citizens with the operational definition of citizenship (having to do with voting, taxation, and legal responsibilities).

The classically recognized advantage to this position is that it undergirds a very strong doctrine of liberty. One is at liberty within the private sphere, immune from public sanction, unless one's actions fall under a publically defined law. One has no public responsibilities save those defined by law. Business transactions in particular are private affairs unless regulated by law. The Liberal theory has provided philosophical intelligibility to growing capitalism.

If a general social obligation does not receive proper attention from the publicly warranted officials, and nothing picks out certain citizens over others to attend to it, then the obligation becomes no one's responsibility; that is, there is no responsibility beyond that assigned in the social contract. According to the extreme Hobbesian version of this Liberal contract theory, if some of the people rebel against the public officials in order to institute a public order that does attend to the obligations (or for any other reason), then, by definition, the public order has broken down and the situation is returned to the state of nature in which there is no distinction between public and private situations, and hence no responsibility. Of course, for Hobbes, there are no obligations that derive from the objective worth of things; all obligations derive from the social contract itself, save for the "natural" obligation to preserve one's own life. Therefore, if people rebel against the constitution of the social contract, for whatever reason (including a misguided belief that there is some transcendent obligation to be served), then all obligation save that toward self-preservation ceases.

A second great advantage of the Liberal distinction between public and private is that it allows for a public definition of persons to be given which in turn allows for equality before the law. Without having to look at the particularities of an individual, especially at those elements of life that are private and likely to trigger prejudice and special interest in the exercise of law and policy, laws relating only to legal persons exhibit clear fairness. It is fairness applied to individuals insofar as they are "legal persons," not with regard to their special nature and circumstance.

The disadvantages of the Liberal distinction between public and private have been well-marked in recent years. In the main, they come down to the following point. Whereas the obligations, and therefore the protections, of public life are equal for everyone, people are very unequal in private situations so that the strong, rich, or clever can use public equality to secure an unfair advantage. Without dwelling on this, in the present discussion I want to focus on a special disadvantage, that relating to the transformation of the public obligation into personal responsibility.

Where a strong distinction between public and private situations obtains, public office is voluntary. That is, there is no responsibility created by the public situation for a given individual to hold office. The law might enjoin certain nearly universal duties, such as paying taxes or serving in the armed forces. But these still are voluntary in the sense that the individuals can decline them by exiting the public roles that relate the individual to the public obligations; for instance, by relinquishing citizenship or residence.

We may assume that in a given polity, there is some public office charged with the responsibility of attending to any general obligations with which no other office is charged—the buck-stops-here-office. But suppose the omniresponsible officer voluntarily declines the office—resigns—and no one else will take it up if the office is responsible for a certain onerous or difficult obligation. (More likely, the incumbent will deny that the obligation is really obligatory.) If all public offices are effectively voluntary, then there are obligations that might perpetually fail to become anyone's responsibility. "Something ought to be done," but it is nobody's responsibility to do it.

That participation in the public situation is ultimately voluntary (if one is willing to give up the benefits of public civil society in hard cases) means that people are by nature in private situations.

Private situations, on the Liberal theory, might provide essential features definitive of personal moral identity, but these do not include any public social responsibilities, only responsibilities in private matters. As the contract theorists have argued, public life is an artificial construct. At most, according to contract theory, the public would define only an abstract part of one's identity, one's "legal" or "civic" identity, and hence one has personal responsibility for social obligations only insofar as one has that abstract identity.

The contractarian Liberal theory says that responsibilities to social obligations essentially belong to individuals as players of publicly defined roles. The transformation of public obligation to personal responsibility is effected by the social contract; insofar as individuals opt out of the contract, they opt out of social responsibilities. What they do in private situations might well be good or bad, but it cannot strictly speaking be a matter of public responsibility. Other factors in the popular culture of Liberalism make it difficult to define any responsibility in the private sphere. Since that culture takes personal identity less to be given or developed than chosen, who one is, even in private, is a matter of who one chooses to be. If responsibilities seem onerous, one can simply choose to be someone to whom they don't apply. Of course, not all Liberals go to this extreme of individualistic voluntarism. But it is an underlying theme of our Liberal culture. By contrast, in hard times the Confucian takes it to be his or her responsibility to go into retirement to plot an effective return, and the Puritan either redoubles commitment to the righteous cause or takes the whole set of responsibilities elsewhere.

The Liberal response to the Preacher quoted at the head of the chapter is that there might well be *no* responsibility to remedy oppression. In fact, insofar as oppression is the result of economic forces that still respect law and the abstract equality of persons, oppression is an unfortunate but morally justifiable fact of life.[5] We can do better by the Preacher if we observe that other principles distinguish the public from the private in more natural ways. Dewey would argue, for instance, that a transaction between specific individuals — for example, an economic one — is private if no one else is affected. But as soon as others not directly party to the transaction are affected, they have an interest in controlling it and the transaction is to that extent public. More generally put, public affairs are those that determine the environment within which individuals exercise their own creativity and enjoy life; insofar as individuals directly determine their own environment, they are their own officials; insofar as others determine it, the public has a structure partly independent of all the individuals, and responsibility for its care is problematic.[6] With this observation, we may turn to the specific suggestions of the axiological theory.

IV. Public Responsibility

In brief, the axiological approach hypothesizes that any objective public obligation is the responsibility of all individuals in the situation to which the obligation obtains. Being responsible for the public situation's good is one of the crucial elements of having identity in that situation. For, one's identity consists in being conditioned by the situation with the achieved, excluded, and potential values in its description. Since everyone in the situation is responsible for its social obligation, everyone occupies a public position. There is no natural private station one might occupy that fails to have personal responsibility for all the situation's social obligations. If one has a private station exempt from certain responsibilities for social obligations, that is because the public is so structured as to provide that exempt private station. This is the hypothesis.

Because the axiological hypothesis claims that everyone in a situation is responsible for every general obligaton, the fundamental task for an axiological polity is to find principles for limiting or deactivating responsibility. That is, an axiological polity must create artificial or contractual spheres of privacy in which one's personal responsibilities for public obligations are somehow put in abeyance.

Of course, there would be social chaos were everyone to pursue all his or her responsibilities at once, and no individual would be able to do it, anyway. Although it is natural to be responsible for everything that needs to be done for the social good, it is necessary to assume that in practice others will carry out enough of the responsibilities so that one's own responsibilities will roughly match one's capabilities. Cooperation regarding responsibilities is impossible without some limiting principles for relating individuals' responsibilities to each other.

The most elementary limiting principle is the division of labor. It has several forms.

Traditional role differentiation. Surely the most ancient division of labor is adherence to role differentiation by gender, age cohort, and other distinctions, assigning important obligations to each class whose members then have activated responsibility for them. Nonmembers of the obliged class have deactivated responsibility for the obligation, an artificial or publicly constructed privacy, though they may belong to classes with other obligations. In this way, food, shelter, clothing, and other important necessities are supplied to the group as a whole.

Official roles. Organized societies can establish official roles less general than whole classes but with specifically defined responsibilities. Systems such as government, the judiciary, and religion are defined by official roles. On the axiological hypothesis, an official role is a status whereby the office holder addresses the role-related social obligations as a substitute for all the other individuals. Those in such a private status are still responsible for the responsibilities actively laid upon the official role, but in a deactivated way.

Where traditional and official role differentiation do not work out satisfactorily — and efficiency in attending to the social obligations and integrating them with the other obligations of life is the only criterion for a scheme to organize the pursuit of responsibility — a further division of labor must be sought.

Recognition of readiness. Although all citizens might have responsibility for a public obligation, perhaps some are in the right place at the right time. Others might have a special talent or training to address the obligation. Others might have the appropriate wealth, or the right age or strength. In order to divide labor according to readiness at this point, two conditions must obtain. First, the ready individuals must recognize their readiness and be willing to exercise the responsibility on behalf of the group. Second, the other individuals need to recognize that readiness and accept a deactivation of their own responsibility, allowing or authorizing the ready person to act for them. These two conditions are not easily met, because the ready people might not want the extra burden of an activated responsibility and because the unready persons might be all too anxious simply to fail their responsibilities rather than accept the ready people as their surrogates. It is important, however, to keep clear the priorities as the axiological theory expresses them: First, everyone in the situation bears the responsibilities for the general obligations, and, second, the group can divide the labor so that all obligations are attended to and the group in general accepts those with activated responsibilities as representatives of the responsible activity of each person.

Within this theoretical perspective, public structures for the representative exercise of responsibility are recognized to be social constructs with particular merits and demerits. The responsibility to oversee them, to improve and correct them, lies with those whose delegated responsibility they exercise, namely, the citizens. Republican democratic polity usually conceives of the specific structures of government as aimed at overseeing the other public structures of distributing activated responsibilities. Although there may be division of labor with respect to higher and higher levels of structural responsibility, ultimately everyone in the situation is responsible for the public good. To the extent that public obligations are not properly attended to, it is the personal responsibility of each person to define the means to attend to them. Where individuals might prefer to remain within an unjust situation because of its benefit to themselves, they still are obliged with the personal responsibility to address the public good, and they are morally culpable for failing that responsibility.

In a situation, therefore, in which the established divisions of activated responsibility break down, or need support beyond their own means to provide, or are counter-productive, or unjust, or are insufficient for their tasks, or do not recognize or address certain social obligations, personal responsibility returns to those who had been thought to enjoy an artifical private exemption. The "return" of responsibility should not be misconstrued. It is not the case that those in the private sphere had no responsibility; it simply was not activated because others were exercising it. But to the extent that the others do not exercise it adequately, the people in private life are not as private as they might think; they are responsible anyway.

There is not then an either/or relation between activated and unactivated responsibility. Although social conventions, law, or other means might officially legitimate a division of labor regarding activated responsibility, that legitimation is not normative in itself. It is normative only insofar as the structure effectively addresses the social obligations; where it fails in effectiveness, the responsibility lies with all in the situation. People genuinely can be mistaken about where activated responsibility lies. Practically, one assumes that those in the legitimated structures attend adequately to the business of social obligations unless there is demonstrable reason to believe the contrary. But because responsibility basically rests with everyone in the situation, it is prudent to keep close tabs on the efficiency of the division of labor. Even though they might want privacy rather than public responsibility in some area or other, people should be in critical and dialectical touch with the official structures so as to know when their own responsibility is reactivated. In particular, it seems prudent for people to monitor the political situation carefully, and it is even more efficient to have a new division of labor consisting of *pro bono publico* institutions to watch all the others.

The metaphysical strategy of the axiological hypothesis is contrary to the intellectual habits of Western modernity. Descartes argued that the best way to keep knowledge on a sound foundation is to break things down into their simplest parts and to connect them progressively with relations that can be understood clearly. A Cartesian approach to responsibility for public matters would be to assume first of all that people are in a private state and then to add the increments of public responsibility necessary to account for the normative aspects of public life. This in fact is the strategy of social contract theories that view civil society as an artificial construct built rationally on top of a purely private state of nature. The fatal error of the Cartesian approach is that when the construction breaks down and the social contract fails to work, public responsibility disappears and all are returned to a state of nature. Social obligations make no sense and there is no normative drive to address the situation except for the egoistic drive for personal security or property.

The axiological hypothesis says that everyone is personally responsible by virtue of having identity within the situation, defined and developed through interactions with the normatively weighted elements in the social and physical environment. Social constructions are employed to make the exercise of responsibility efficient. Some people are given artificial private havens from the exercise of responsibility in order to let others do the work more efficiently, dividing the labor as efficiently as possible. When social responsibilities fail to be addressed adequately, the responsibility of everyone is activated. In times of crisis, public responsibility is generalized and made specific to all, with the demand that new divisions of labor be invented to address the obligations. Rather than collapsing public personal responsibility into a nonnormative state of nature, crisis collapses our artificial protections from having to exercise public responsibility and puts everyone in the normative state of having activated public responsibility. The first advantage of the axiological hypothesis is that it becomes more normatively rigorous when things do not work than when the conventional distribution of labor takes care of things without problem. Other advantages will appear throughout later chapters.

Most of what has been said about personal responsibility for social obligations carries over to personal responsibility for other obligations; for instance, to friends and family, to one's own health and well-being, to one's work, and to the excellence of culture. Because there are goods relevant to the way we live, we are primarily responsible to achieve them; only secondarily might we develop or abide in structures that deactivate those responsibilities. Where those structures are inadequate, the primary responsibilities are activated. In practical terms, holidays are an important part of life; but they must be prepared for in advance and sometimes things are so bad we cannot afford to take them.

Puritans, like Confucians, would find their instincts in the axiological hypothesis, knowing that in the most important sense we are not defined by our conditions but by our responsibilities to those conditions. Our identity is both relational and normative, and this is a deep metaphysical matter.

In response to the Preacher we should say that we all are responsible for the elimination of oppression, as we are for attending to all social obligations. The very existence of oppression demonstrates a failure of the constructed division of labor for public life. Whether we want to admit it or not, it is the responsibility of everyone in the situation to eliminate oppression, and our moral characters accrue unhappy identity to the extent that we do not address that responsibility. Of course, the chaos of everyone addressing his or her responsibilities without coordination with others is self-defeating. Therefore, there is a higher-level government responsibility to create new social constructs that divide labor more efficiently, circumscribing or eliminating the power of the malfunctioning structures. That is a true Puritan revolutionary calling.

The danger in Puritanism is totalitarianism, and in the present context that would mean the swallowing up of all realms of life into the political. Both fascist and communist totaliarian states assert the omnicompetence of the political realm, with everything else to be determined by the functions of politics. Is this not a danger with a view that says everyone is responsible for social obligations unless otherwise relieved? Does our view not entail that social obligations override all others, and that the needs or demands of the political realm subordinate all other claims?

In order to protect ourselves from this form of totalitarianism of the political, it is necessary to stress several factors in the analysis. First, the political realm is limited to the positive structures created to discharge responsibilities to social obligations. Where these work, they define responsibilities in limited ways. Where they fail, the unlimited responsibilities of the individuals are derived not from the political realm but from the public. Second, the infinite demands of public life are fully normative, but the norms are matters of personal responsibility, not of authority. Therefore, although one can be obliged to do something about "the situation," an obligation that can result in an infinite responsibility, nothing has authority legitimately to coerce someone into political action. As I shall argue in Chapter Eight, the notion of authority has very limited application, virtually none in politics except for conventionally established authority. Third, the responsibilities stemming from social obligations in no a priori way take precedence over those stemming from religion, family, personal career, friendships, cultural creativity, and the like. Where the responsibilities conflict, one fails the obligations ignored and hence is guilty. The responsibilities to social obligations, however, may be no more demanding than responsibilities in other areas.

Therefore, we may say that our axiological hypothesis entails a definition of individuals as wholly obligated to social as well as other values; we are inescapably public and are to be judged in part by how well we fulfill those obligations. Yet there is no authority in the public, as there is in the conventional political realm, to coerce public life. Because political authority is indeed a prudential convention, it should prudently be defined in limited ways respecting the definition of individuals in many spheres other than the political. Where political structures give such authority to the political realm as to abuse the nonpolitical ideal ends of life, those structures are in functional failure and are not normative. It then becomes a reactivated public responsibility of everyone to restructure the political realm so as to tolerate the full expression of the nonpolitical.

4

The Metaphysics of Chaos, Totalization, and Normative Description

Socrates: "The first, then, I call the unlimited, the second the limit, and the third the being that has come to be by the mixture of these two; as to the fourth, I hope I shall not be at fault in calling it the cause of the mixture and of the coming-to-be?"
— Plato, Philebus *27 c.*

I. Metaphysical Imagination

A lthough it is a fair start to discuss conditions of moral reflection generally, treating models of moral agency and the issues of general obligation and personal responsibility with the historical sweep of milennia, the problems of moral reflection today are matters of our own historical conditions. The purpose of this chapter is to deepen the previous discussion by reading it through an analysis of our sociopolitical situation.

By "our situation" I shall mean the 150-year "moment" from the apotheosis of capitalism and its dialectical Marxist critique in the nineteenth century through the spread of the Western economic system across the globe to the present interactions of the First, Second, and Third Worlds, particularly to the travails of modernization in the Third World. This may seem like a particularization of history only in contrast with the "moment" of "our situation" presupposed in the previous chapters, lasting from Confucius and Koheleth to the present time.

The salient character of the situation is that the result of the last 150 years of the formation of an international society is a terrifying and dangerous oscillation between forces leading toward political, social, and cultural chaos and forces leading toward totalization — totalitarianism when pushed to the extreme. What is missing is a positive middle ground that harmonizes those opposite forces. In metaphysical terms, our sociopolitical situation suffers from an acute disease of the One and the Many. The two poles are metaphysically opposed and tolerate no middle ground. A more profound metaphysics is needed that captures the insights of the poles, avoids their extremes, and unites them. It will become apparent in the argument that the epigraph from Plato's most metaphysical discussion symbolizes a political philosophy for the interpretation of our situation. In Plato's language, the end of the tendency toward chaos is the unlimited, that of the tendency toward totalization is limit; what is lacking is a harmonious mixture of those two, and to attain to that mixture we need to locate the cause of mixture.

For this kind of "political metaphysics" to seem relevant, it is necessary to appreciate the role of philosophical imagination in practical affairs. Human imagination shapes the world we inhabit. It determines as important for our attention a selection of natural and social pulses, and by implication it leaves out, suppresses, or transmutes the rest. Further, imagination guides our own sense of importance, forming our selective principles about the possibilities of response and action. Our tastes and intentions are captives of the bounds of imagination.

Having been formed over time by historical, cultural, and individual influences, human imagination is malleable. An individual's imagination consists in its particular versions of the social and personal elements entering into the makeup of sensitivities, sensibilities, orientations, needs, desires, social habits, mental structures, capacities for will, autonomy, and responsibility.[1] The developing formation of imagination can be influenced by all the elements entering into personal identity and into the sense of self and social belonging. Yet at any one time those elements themselves are constrained by the previously formed imagination that takes up and disposes them. People's imaginations are alike and dissimilar to the extent they share image-forming elements of biology, culture, history and particular social conditions. One can distinguish between the cultural imaginations of great traditions, for instance, China, India, and the European West. One also can note imaginative forms common to such traditions.

Imagination has certain deep and pervasive forms that, however they differ from one person to the next, integrate each one's imagination into a subliminal worldview. Or, if that suggests too much that imagination is conscious, we might say that each person's imaginatiion is a vague template for a world, a set of elementary forms selecting the important things to connect in order to have experience cohere as a world. Persons in a given society share these deep and pervasive forms, and individuals who deviate from them are thought to possess a kind of madness. As Plato pointed out in the *Phaedrus*, that madness is divine when, as in the case of poets, one's purpose is precisely to break the constraints of a given imaginative structure.

Philosophy, especially metaphysics, is the means by which people objectify, identify, reflect upon, judge, and call for the amendment of their deep and pervasive imaginative structures. As practice, metaphysics thus can point the way to new imagination, and hence to new actual worlds of experience, new cultural, social, and political structures. Mightier than steam or barbarians, great ideas give us, at once, distance from imagination, and new imagery.[2] Like poetry, there must be something mad about the great ideas. And like material inventions, they somehow must catch on and influence the effective popular imagination. When philosophy transcends and amends cultural imagination for the better, it contributes to the creation of a new culture. Stimulated so often in times of conflict and social decay — one thinks of the decline of the Chou Dynasty for the time of the rise of Confucianism and Taoism, of the collapse of Athenian democracy for the contributions of Plato and Aristotle — philosophy responds to broken imagination in order to heal with new forms. I believe we, both East and West, are in such a period of broken imagination, and that philosophy's task is to invent a new metaphysics with a power to heal. With this view of the purpose behind the present style of philosophical analysis of a social situation, let us turn directly to the task.

II. Liberalism and Chaos

One of the major roots of the unsettled dangers of our time consists in a world-wide social bifurcation — one line of forces tending toward chaos, the other toward strutural totalism that often amounts to political totalitarianism. Chaos is the end toward which the policies of Liberal capitalism are tending, and totalitarianism is the end of policies that seek to recover justice by means of increasing totalistic state control. The threat of chaos invites dictatorial totalitarianism, and totalitarian regimes call forth Liberal revolutions. Although there were many significant factors other than these, the oscillation between these extremes has been illustrated sadly in the fortunes of China, Japan, Germany, Italy, France, Latin America, Russia, Poland, Yugoslavia, and Czechoslovakia throughout the past century.

Classical Western Liberalism was born out of a self-consciousness of chaos that it called the "state of nature" and that was exemplified in the seventeenth-century Puritan revolution in Britain.[3] The idea of the "state of nature" was a philosophical construct, developed in contrast with the idea of a civil society resulting from the social contract. It was perhaps then an exaggeration to describe the English revolution as a return to the state of nature, but not much of an exaggeration. Hobbes's famous description of the state of nature expressed his fears for his own time.

> Whatsoever therefore is consequent to a time of Warre, where every man is Enemy to every man; the same is consequent to the time, wherein men live without other security, than what their own strength, and their own invention shall furnish them withall. In such conditions, there is no place for Industry; because the fruit thereof is uncertain: and consequently no Culture of the Earth, no Navigation, nor use of the commodities that may be imported by Sea; no commodious Building; no Instruments of moving, and removing such things as require much force; no Knowledge of the face of the Earth; no account of Time; no Arts; no Letters; no Society; and which is worst of all, continuall feare, and danger of violent death; And the life of Man, solitary, poore, nasty, brutish, and short.[4]

The evils of the chaotic state of nature were reinforced in the experience of the breakdown of the French revolution in the eighteenth century, a primary example within itself of the oscillation between totalitarianism and chaos, and in the several nineteenth-century revolutions in Europe and the United States. Liberalism's genius was to invent the notion of the social contract, a set of procedures for regulating some uses of force and for settling disputes between private parties. The genius in the notion is that it allows full sway to the claims of individualism. Even when an individual's authority is delegated or alienated to the state, it is done so by the individual's own will as embodied in the original or derived social contract. Furthermore, in Locke's contract theory the powers given over to the state for the purposes of regulating some uses of force and settling disputes are minimal. Classical Liberalism of the Lockean variety, so influential during subsequent centuries, particularly in the United States, was more concerned with limiting the overreaching tentacles of government than with giving to government an abundance of powers to make sure it did its regulatory and judicial work.[5]

The twin features of extreme individualism and minimal state structure made Liberalism attractive to growing capitalism. Capitalism counts all people to be equal before the law, protected by due process in the few respects that are relevant to government. It also counts all individual differences in wealth and talent to be private matters that are irrelevant to social equality, for it is in the investments and efforts of the fortunate that capital is accumulated, production expanded, and all people given places in the capitalist economic system. If relative wealth and talent were public matters, subject to social regulation, freedom of enterprise would be compromised.

There is an intrinsic instability, however, in Liberal capitalism arising from the disproportion between equality before the law and inequality in private means. As capitalism grows, so grows the inequality in private means, with an accumulation of wealth, power, and high culture among the relatively fortunate, and the deprivation of other people in those regards. Trade unionism, transfer payments, progressive income tax policies, and many other measures serve to moderate the inequalities in private life, but at the cost of compromising the minimizing of regulation of free enterprise. Within a given society, such as in the European and North American nations, both the rich and the nonrich can agree to such compromises because they allow the former to keep most of what they have and promise more to the latter. But when Third World nations are brought into the economic orbit of the world economy, and must adopt one of the systems to which that economy relates, the Liberal capitalist model has little chance of moderation. Social systems break down and violent revolution thrives on the margins of national life, if not at the center. This is the return to chaos.

Put in a somewhat more formal way, the social contract by means of which Liberalism seeks to separate civil life from chaos is not sufficient for its purpose, by reason of its very own principle. The tendency of Liberal polities toward chaos comes from the fact that they sharply distinguish public equality from private life; and with capitalism, private life develops highly unstable inequalities. By its own definition, the social contract cannot deliberately regulate private inequalities, and hence it is an inefficient distribution principle of public responsibilities.

III. Statism and Totalitarianism

The dialectical opposite of Liberalism is the family of polities claiming that individuals cannot be fulfilled individually but only in and through social structures. Rejecting Liberal individualism, they emphasize the solidarity of the nation or group and believe that personal isolation from the collective social structures is pernicious abstraction. As noted in the previous chapter, this set of views is no less egoistic in its definition of the motive for social action than Liberalism, only blessed by a larger sense of group ego. Hegel is the greatest theorist of the human importance of totalizing structure, although of course his own view is far too subtle to be summed up as totalizing. He wrote, for instance:

> If the state is confused with civil society, and if its specific end is laid down as the security and protection of property and personal freedom, then the interest of the individuals as such becomes the ultimate end of their association, and it follows that membership of the state is something optional. But the state's relation to the individual is quite different from this. Since the state is mind objectified, it is only as one of its members that the individual himself has objectivity, genuine individuality, and an ethical life. Unification pure and simple is the true content and aim of the individual, and the individual's destiny is the living of a universal life. His further particular satisfaction, activity, and mode of conduct have this substantive and universally valid life as their starting point and their result.[6]

Hegel's position was that a human being as a mere individual, as recognized in social contract theory, is abstract. The individual's very freedom to be able to do this or that means, in a crucial sense, that it doesn't matter what choice is made. Concrete life requires attaining to meaningful life, which is what Hegel meant in the quotation by "objective mind." Hegel's is not only a social definition of the individual but a definition of the social fulfillment of an otherwise unsocial and abstract individual.

Where this Hegelian kind of emphasis on the greater concreteness of social structures accepts a strong distinction between public and private affairs, which Hegel himself avoided, it becomes an emphasis on statism. Pushed to an extreme, which it is every time the uneasy balance of Liberal Lockean ideals and ineffective government tends toward chaos, statism becomes totalitarianism. Lockean social contract theory must be distinguished from the Hobbesian at this point. Because of the emphasis on limited government, Lockean polities are relatively weak in responding to internal (as opposed to external) dangers. Hobbes argued that the government has no justification unless it has sufficient power to keep the peace and, therefore, is authorized to have total control over power in the face of danger; a Hobbesean government should become frankly totalitarian in times of crisis. Hobbes did not believe that the state is the fulfillment of the individual; but he did believe that the state in principle has no limits to its powerful regulation of individual life should the sovereign want to exercise control.[7] Although the Fascists and Marxist revolutionaries had widely divergent analyses of the nature and goals of society, they agreed in the practice of giving ultimate authority to the state.

Several factors undermine statism and drive it to impossible totalitarianism. One is the fact that it simply fails to give expression to the aspirations of individual freedom, and this contradicts the imagination of most cultures, even traditional ones. But setting aside the direct appreciation of freedom as a bias, there are other factors. First, the nineteenth-century enthusiasm for social science overreached its accomplishments; the "science" of running a state is simply too meagre to do the job required. Second, the individuals in government are too richly human only to play roles in a state structure, and they fail at their jobs. Third, the purpose of the state becomes obscure when it is itself its own goal. Blindly the state treats itself as an organism, often a predatory one, with no way of measuring its virtues save in terms of power over other states. For these and other reasons, statist regimes find themselves increasingly forced to coercive measures and to more overdetermined policies until they reach totalitarian proportions. Totalitarianism is an unstable situation, inviting revolution from its own people, invasion from other nations it has to threaten, or a subtle reversal of government from within the ranks of its own officials.

Third World countries attracted into the orbit of totalitarian or statist polities are more vulnerable to instability than the developed countries. Statist regimes either try to reinforce a traditional social order that is incompatible with the contemporary world economy, or they educate the nonelites, which produces a middle class prizing individual freedom. In either case, a traditional culture is undermined but not replaced with an indigenously unified improvement.

Deep within the human imagination we seek to imagine how we can be individually fulfilled and socially harmonious, and the sophisticated development of that imagination is metaphysics. The images that underlie Liberalism tending to chaos and statism tending to totalitarianism are unsuccessful. However those images were themselves improvements on their imaginative predecessors, if they were, their limits have been reached in the twentieth century.

In the twentieth century, Liberal capitalism and Marxist communism have presented themselves as the competing options. Without minimizing the differences between them, differences that point the first toward chaos and the second toward totalitarianism, they are dialectically related. Both accept something of a common cosmological view of life and respond to it differently. In the West, the imaginations of both Liberalism and statism took their rise with modern science. The metaphysics of modern science supposes that individuals are something like atoms, each independent and externally related to the others.[8] Their connections are imposed from the outside by external structures such as regular laws that apply indifferently to all actualities they govern. Although both polities agree that one needs both the individuals and their connections, the external relations between the individuals and structures make for instability. Chaos results when structures are lost, and totalitarianism results when the individuals become inconsequential in their private selves. The very distinction between private individuality and public life in the integrating social structures reflects the metaphysical foundations of modern science: on the one hand, an uneasy balance of atoms in the void, and on the other, universal laws more real and true than any contingent atoms they accidentally might govern. That modern metaphysics and its culture need to be transcended.

When one sides with the individuals, forces tend toward chaos. When one sides with the connecting structures, forces tend toward denying the individuals save as they are defined by roles in the structures. As long as our metaphysical common sense supposes an external relation between social atoms and social structures, it seems necessary to side with one or the other.

The appropriate task for social philosophy, I believe, is the elaboration of a metaphysics providing a different imaginative form for the legitimate search for individual identity and social fulfillment. The modern imagination that bifurcates into chaos and totalitarianism was itself largely the product of the highly inventive metaphysics of Descartes, Hobbes, and their colleagues seeking to formulate the foundations of modern science. Perhaps metaphysics today can provide a similarly creative advance. I propose the following, a reappropriation of certain images of Plato, as a leading hypothesis that continues the development of the metaphysics of harmony introduced in early chapters.

IV. Metaphysical Suggestions

In his consummate dialogue, *Philebus*, Plato asked about the content of true virtue and was quickly led to formulatte a metaphysics, the summary of which is quoted at the head of this chapter. There are three principles, limit, the unlimited, and the mixture of these, he said.[9] All things in our world are mixtures. There also, as a fourth principle, must be a cause of the mixtures, by which Plato meant the aesthetic, moral, rational, or ontological norms that harmonize limits and the unlimited into finite mixtures, each mixture with a certain value.[10] His simple metaphysics thus contained (1) limit, (2) the unlimited, (3) the mixture of these, and (4) the cause of mixture.

In line with the remarks above about the practical importance of metaphysical imagination, the most wise and efficient way to understand personal and social virtue is with the aid of metaphysical considerations describing the very nature of the being which people have and to which they relate. More to the point here, the reason for much confusion regarding social life is the unwitting assumption of wrong metaphysical ideas. Because he so well understood the connection between virtue and metaphysics, Plato's philosophy was a "moral metaphysics."[11] I believe Plato was on the right road, and I want to continue down it further.

Without engaging in an exposition of Plato, let me expand his insights into what was called earlier an "axiological metaphysics." Beginning with the analogue to Plato's mixtures, let us suppose that every thing, event, situation, or actuality of any sort is a mixture or harmony. Without the harmonizing limits, its components are unlimited or chaotic relative to one another. Each component is itself a harmony with its own components, and so all the way down. Moving downward, as it were, from any given harmony is to approach the unlimited, pure chaos, although of course one reaches only more components of components, never something lacking its own limits altogether. Each harmony displays or expresses a form, a pattern, a Platonic "limit." Indeed, any harmony displays a great many such patterns, each uniting a group of components and all united together in more or less tight loops, systems, and hierarchies of patterns. The degree of regularity and order in the world depends on the kind and degree of these patterns of patterns uniting harmonies. In contrast to an atomistic metaphysics for which structures are external to the atoms they connect, this Platonic or axiological metaphysics integrates both structure or limit and the to-be-structured or unlimited in the nature of a thing as harmony or mixture. To be is to be a harmony.

This has a profound and unusual implication for the meaning of description, one which sets it apart from all phenomenologies and other positivist theories of description. According to this axiological metaphysics, description cannot be mere identification of the expressed forms or patterns, for these have no existential meaning save as they are patterns uniting some components. Therefore, the patterns in actual harmonies need to be identified with reference to the components they harmonize. No "formal causes" should be cited except as explicit abstractions that no longer refer to the harmonies. Translated to political theory, no laws, procedures, or other social connections should be described without reference to the particular groups and individuals that they potentially unite. As a corollary, as the components of society change, the normative structures should change too.

To describe harmonies through citing "material causes" is just as abstract because it would mean identifying the components without reference to the harmonies in which they occur. Components are harmonies in their own right and may have a career of their own outside the harmonies containing them; thus, they can be described on their own terms. But to describe them as components is precisely to relate them to the harmonies within which they are united with other things. The political specification of this is that no one is a mere individual but an individual identified in part by the many social relations and systems in which the person plays roles, as the Confucians and Puritans saw.

A Platonic description is not complete, however, or even rational, without "the cause of mixture," the reason why such and such patterns manage to harmonize such and such components. *That* the patterns harmonize the components can be observed, and analysis of the relation between patterns and components can display *how* the harmony works. To describe *why* the harmony is what it is requires showing how having the components together in the patterned way is the achievement of some value. To the Platonist, the Good is the ultimate cause of mixture, and the proximate cause is the value to be achieved by uniting the given components in some harmony rather than in none, or in one harmony rather than another. Politically specified, the axiological metaphysics asserts that things are to be identified by, and treated according to, what they are worth, not just what form they have or what they are made of.

Of course, in rational reflection on a harmony we can imagine alternate patterns that would have harmonized the components some other way, and with some other achievement of value. The reason Platonists tend to be so moralistic even when describing actual states of affairs is that they cannot think descriptively without thinking of alternate possibilities for the embodiment of values. Among the essential parts of a description are analyses of (1) what value is achieved, (2) what other values could be achieved given the same components but different patterns, and (3) what could be achieved given the same patterns but different components.

In the Chinese tradition, the axiological inspiration was in the very soil of the original culture, expressed in both Confucianism and Taoism. But each of those traditions was lopsided and needed the other. Confucianism, fearing that components could not sustain an integrating harmony, focused so much on pattern that the Taoists teased them to the effect that pattern by itself, even if pursued in the name of righteousness, is a departure from the tao that mixes the limited and unlimited. Taoism, fearing the positivism of an emphasis on pattern, focused so much on the pregnant chaos of a situation awaiting harmony that the Confucians thought the Taoists would never get on with intentionally virtuous action.

V. Moral Reflection and Normative Description

The thesis that description is normative has powerful implications for moral reflection in political, social, and cultural theory. According to the argument of the previous two chapters, individuals' actions take place within a situation that in turn defines the individuals. What is a situation but a complicated mixture of mixtures, a vast and changing collection of actual and actualizing harmonies, many of which have careers determined by distant pasts and headed toward futures far from the situation at hand?

The harmonies constituting relatively basic physical elements tend to have systematically integrated autonomous careers, only accidentally related to particular configurations of a given overall situation. The chemical elements, for instance, behave according to their own laws without regard for the prized patterns of human life. The harmonies constitutive of the patterns of human life—food, shelter, nurture, health, and many others—are highly fragile because they depend on the stability of their components as jointly making an environment, and those components may have independent, inhuman careers. A sudden change in atmosphere or in radiation could put a quick end to human life. The harmonies constitutive of civilization are so fragile that every age rightly worries whether it is on the edge of barbarism.

The precariousness of civilized human order is so great that many people, with Confucianists and conservatives, think that social action consists in renewing, reinstituting, and making adjustments in the components of cultured life so as to sustain the historical patterns of civilization. That indeed is a precious part of social action. But from the axiological perspective, any given cultural pattern is seen as the achievement of certain values at the expense of others. Perhaps certain components would flourish with far greater intrinsic worth if they were not harmonized with other components—such as the ideal of individual freedom stuck with mass organizaton. Perhaps those components would create a far more valuable harmony if united by means of a different civilizing pattern. And perhaps the civilizing pattern at hand does not include all it should among its components, as is the case when any group is subordinated to the interests of another. In these instances, the patterns ought to be eliminated or changed, as the revolutionary Puritans and Marxists have recognized. Normative social action requires both the protection of some patterns and the alteration or elimination of others.

The situation of social action, normatively described, exhibits the whole Platonic metaphysics. As to limit, one must be apprized of the patterns at hand and sometimes act to sustain them. As to the unlimited, one must be apprized equally of the components lacking for a place with intrinsic value, and sometimes act to discover and embody new patterns that give them a place. In all events, one must appreciate and weigh the values achieved, the values at risk, and the alternate values that might be possible.

By what model might we imagine social action? Certainly not the model so attractive in the West of isolating particular actions and determining whether they are right or good. For there are no isolable actions; each is a harmony within a multitude of harmonies, affecting many things in many respects with many kinds of moral content. Perhaps we should model social action with the idea of a virtuous person, replete with a paideia to produce virtuous characteristics. This model is more plausible than the "moral act" model because it emphasizes the obligation to get ready to make the right moral move; without the proper virtues we would be incapable of appreciating or responding to the values at hand. The limitation to the simple model of the virtuous person is that it assumes that the person would act habitually in a situation. Yet we know how important creative imagination and extraordinary effort are in moral action. So our model must include something of a situation ethics — a "habit" of reacting to novel situations with originality, being wary of generalized rules or previously fixed habits.

Perhaps the most appealing model of social action is that of the scholar-official discussed earlier. The "scholar" part focuses on the importance of investigating the true situation and determining the unique advantages to be gained or terrors to be avoided. We may now see that the scholar is a student of normative descriptions. In methods according with that theory of description, the scholar would investigate the patterns in things, the components of the patterns, the particular ways in which the patterns and components are mixed, and the values attained by those mixtures. In addition, the scholar would insist that any description limn out the alternate values that might be achieved with different patterns or different components.

The "official" part, despite a connotation of bureaucracy, indicates that an acting person is ministering to many people and institutions at once, never acting in isolation but always within a complicated context, never acting with one purpose alone but always with many cares. A scholar-official discerns and pursues the norms that balance many orders with many sources of chaos; this might be called "abiding in the highest good," one of the precepts of the Confucian *Great Learning*. Of course, the ideal of the scholar-official remains subject to the weaknesses noted in Chapter Two.

The alternative to the axiological conception, I believe, is an oscillating dialectic of public order stretched to the point of totalization, overturned by libertarianism stretched to the point of chaos, reacting in a renewed plunge toward order. Those polities that have turned from either extreme toward what is sometimes called a "pragmatic" position in fact are hunting for something like the axiological solution. Both the United States and the Peoples' Republic of China may be cases in point.

The potential contribution of moral reflection is a clear understanding of the middle ground. In particular, moral reflection can develop and clarify the axiological or value-oriented elements of social thinking, bearing in mind Plato's four modes of being; the unlimited, that by itself is chaos; the limit, that by itself is totalization; the mixture, that is the actuality of affairs; and the cause of mixture, that is the value embodied in achievements and ideals.

How can this metaphysics help our contemporary imagination? Two ways suggest themselves.

First, the fundamental habitual images by which we think of society should be those appropriate for analyzing societies with normative descriptions. We should view societies as harmonies, identifying their components, society by society, identifying forms of unity, explaining the interactions of these to produce situations embodying certain values while excluding others. Axiological philosophy suggests that moral reflection should not be ideological in the sense of importing preconceived categories for the basic components of a society, for instance, "individuals" conceived a certain way, or social classes. Nor should it be ideological in its conceptions of social unities, such as economic forces or government structures. Rather, both components and historical unities in each society need to be analyzed relative to their own historical constituent elements and the supervening harmonies of their environment. Hence, social thought should be contextual, thoroughly historical, and alert to how factors such as economic orders might be common to two societies but mean radically different things because of different historical constituents and different cultural frames within which they exist. Although, on this view, social understanding is a way of making specific an abstract metaphysics of harmony relative to social phenomena, it is still thoroughly empirical, more empirical than social theories that postulate social forms as components and structures prior to analysis.

Second, the axiological metaphysics suggests that social individuals are harmonies, to be understood with all the complexities of an harmonic analysis. The social components of an individual consist of all the systems in which the person plays roles—biological, economic, political, religious, educational, familial, associational, and countless others relative to geography, age, gender; of course, each of these is particular for the person's situation. The unities of a person's life are all the ways these systems are integrated in the person's life style, how the various roles are made important or trivial, how they cohere or conflict, how their relations change as the person matures, endures personal and social change, and responds to crises. Most important, social understanding of an individual will examine what values are achieved, what values are excluded, and what values ought to be achieved by having these social roles to integrate and these forms of integration. Great care must be taken to avoid overgeneralizing from ideal types regarding the social systems in a given situation. Equal care must be taken to avoid a dialectic of social conditions that neglects the diversity of forms by which they might be integrated.

As for the ideologies of Liberalism and statism, both illustrate social harmony degenerating into conflict and strife. Liberalism involves the abandonment of normative conceptions of social structure, throwing the metaphysical imagination of moral reflection back upon individuals as social atoms. Statism entails the eventual loss of normative conceptions of individuals and is forced, vainly, to describe human fulfillment in terms of social structure. Both ideologies run aground on the violence, oppression, suffering, and stupid numbness of the dialectic between social chaos and totalitarianism.

An axiological metaphysics transcends the positivist separation of fact and value that has characterized the European West since its Renaissance. It offers a method to recognize the normative elements of personal and social life, whatever their situation. Perhaps it points a way to a richer social imagination.

The heady idealism of this conclusion should bring an ironic warning from the Puritan. It is one thing to admit that our situation suffers from a disease of the One and the Many. It is quite another to say that a philosophical solution to the conceptual problem of the One and the Many, even applied to social affairs, will itself heal the diseased society. To expect that kind of power in philosophic ideas seems especially absurd in light of the strife and conflict marking our society. The interpretation of our situation in terms of a dialectical swing between chaos and totalization is philosophically neat. Even if it is true as far as it goes, however, it is insensitive to the brutal bluntness of suffering itself. Hobbes was right about the befuddled evil that comes from a state of war of all against all. Was he also right that the solution consists in a supremely powerful sovereign, not in the lure of philosphical imagination? Philosophers all too often combine naiveté about the power of ideas with arrogance about the worth of their own. To understand the limits of this chapter, it is necessary to reconsider its hypotheses and arguments from the perspective of suffering and evil, the avoidance of which is the primitive motive of normative reflection.

5

Suffering, Experience, and Politics

The massive habits of physical nature, its iron laws, determine the scene for the sufferings of men. Birth and death, heat, cold, hunger, separation, disease, the general impracticability of purpose, all bring their quota to imprison the souls of women and of men . . . Mankind has chiefly suffered from the frustration of its prevalent purposes, even such as belong to the very definition of its species. The literary exposition of freedom deals mainly with the frills. The Greek myth was more to the point. Prometheus did not bring to mankind freedom of the press. He procured fire, which obediently to human purpose cooks and gives warmth. In fact, freedom of action is a primary human need. In modern thought, the expression of this truth has taken the form of 'the economic interpretation of history.'

The fact that the 'economic interpretation' is itself a novel thought arising within the last sixty or seventy years illustrates an important sociological fact. The literary world through all ages belonged mainly to the fortunate section of mankind whose basic human wants have been amply satisfied. A few literary men have been in want throughout all their lives, many have occasionally suffered. The fact shocks us. It is remembered because it is rare. The fortunate classes are oblivious to the fact that throughout the ages the masses of mankind have lived in conscious dread of such disaster — of drought, a wet summer, a bad harvest, a cattle disease, a raid of pirates. Also the basic needs when they are habitually satisfied cease to dominate thought. Delicacies of taste displace the interest in the fullness of stomach. Thus the motives which stir the fortunate directing classes to conscious activity have a long-range forecast and an aesthetic tinge: — Power, glory, safety in the distant future, forms of government, luxury, religion, excitment, dislike of strange ways, contemplative curiosity, play.[1]

I. Suffering and Moral Reflection

That eloquent statement might have been penned by Karl
Marx, Mao Tse-tung, Ivan Illich, or John Dewey. In fact, it
was written by Alfred North Whitehead; it is something of an irony,
because his overall moral vision was the Whiggish one that civilization progresses as ideas become embodied in institutions. The statement brings into juxtaposition two important points: the "iron laws"
determining the scene of human suffering, and the protected, privi-
leged position of most of us who engage in moral reflections. One of
the themes of this chapter is what "reality" has to say about the personal and social context for moral reflection. Is moral reflection but
a superficial activity of the leisure class? Groans of Liberal guilt are
ruled out as an answer, as well as a pseudo-Confucian defense of the
privilege of the sage. Something more like Puritan commitment is in
order.

Whitehead's statement also lifts into relief the recognition that
there is a level of struggle with the "iron laws" far deeper than conflicts among moral systems, points of view, and cultural traditions.
Put another way, the conflicts among moral systems express differences between strategies concerning what to do about the suffering of the great bulk of human life. A cynical division might rank
moral systems from one extreme of total organized devotion to
alleviate the sufferings of others to the opposite extreme of protecting
the special civilization of the elite from dilution by efforts to help the
poor. A more telling division historically might rank moral systems
according to their views of what most efficiently mobilizes human efforts to cope with the iron laws: a maximization of individual initiative
(Liberalism), quasi-voluntary group organization (most religious
systems), or the identification and devotion of public resources
(socialist systems). Another theme of this chapter is the organization
of efforts to cope with suffering and the conflicts that arise about who
pays the bill. This returns to the theme of Chapter Three concerning
personal responsibility for public obligations.

There is a difference between suffering and knowing that you
are suffering, knowing how, and why. A tragic multiplier effect of
many kinds of suffering, particularly that which destroys culture, is
the blight it brings of numbness, denial, and stupidity. Furthermore, the suffering that arises from oppression by others is often ac-
companied by an ideology that disguises its nature and causes, as
Plato detailed in the *Republic* (Book II). If people are to do anything

about suffering, to eliminate its causes, to move away, to change opportunities for their children, even to help one another bear up, they need to understand suffering. That understanding of course is one purpose of moral reflection. Earlier, I used positive language about moral reflection — understanding what is worth achieving, prizing, and preserving. Negative language is perhaps more forceful — understanding the sources of suffering and, where possible, inventing steps toward its alleviation. The context in which moral reflection makes sense is a practical one in which thought issues in a action.

The thesis that moral reflection should take place in a practical context allows of several interpretations. The Liberal and Marxian alternatives are most obvious because they dominate world politics; understanding those alternatives has more than intellectual interest. Political theory, as a superstructure for moral reflection on social matters, has what first appear to be two distinct though necessarily conjoined purposes underlying its form: the purpose of knowing, and the purpose of guiding practice in some sense. Classical modern Liberal theorists from Hobbes to Rawls emphasize political theory as knowledge, however practical. Marxians emphasize its practical purpose, however cognitive it is in an instrumental sense. Perhaps at the end these two purposes can be integrated; in the meanwhile, they pull in two apparently different directions in conflict arenas such as the organization of professional meetings, academic departments, journals, and other media for moral reflection.

As to knowledge, the function of any theory is to know in whatever sense of knowledge is appropriate to the subject matter. It is an immediate and formal perversion of theory if some practical purpose directs the theory to recognize only those formal structures, facts, and variables that support the purpose, while those unfriendly to the purpose are relegated to theoretical limbo. There are common enough examples of how class bias, for example, dictates the preference of the rich for structural-functional rather than conflict theories. Therefore, to as great an extent as possible, political theory ought to be divorced from political interests, it seems. Those thinkers who emphasize this formal requirement for political theory would agree with what G. E. Moore said about ethics: "The direct object of Ethics is knowledge and not practice,"[2] and they would apply it to political theory.

On the other hand, a host of American and continental thinkers, including Marxians, believed that practical interests cannot be divorced from theory and, therefore, *should* be admitted, examined, and controlled for. The argument has been made in detail by Charles Peirce, William James, John Dewey, Karl-Otto Apel, and Jürgen Habermas. Against those who say the direct object of political theory is knowledge and not practice, these thinkers would argue that theory cannot pretend to cognitive objectivity unless its original orientation to practice is made central and is accounted for.

Because of the argument of the previous chapter, I suspect that the intellectualist cast of Liberal thinking feeds social chaos by disguising its own nature and that the practicalism of Marxian thought feeds totalitarianism. The divergence of theory and practice marks two sides of the same coin, much the way that Liberalism and totalism are a dialectical pair. An alternative to one tradition must be an alternative to both. Similarly, an alternative to moral reflection of theory is not practice, nor vice versa, but an alternative to the dialectical divergence of theory and practice. A directly political middle ground must be found as a context for moral reflection. Perhaps the pragmatists mentioned above can stop the emphasis on practice short of a perversion of knowledge by uncritical pursuit of political purpose. I shall argue, with Confucius and Plato, that political and moral reflection is directly cognitive and directly practical at once, and that these two purposes necessitate each other. The heart of the solution lies in the theory of normative description sketched in the previous chapter.

II. Praxis and Theory

Moral reflection includes an extraordinarily complex mixture of kinds of thinking, only some of which are theoretical in any strict sense. Of the theories involved in moral reflection, political thoery is only one. But it is an important one. The exact definition of political theory is, of course, biased by the theory in question. Some theories define it as the study of the distribution of power in society, others as the study of authority and legitimacy. Social contract theories define it as the study of the grounds, nature, and limits of the social contract. I define it as the study of the normative or obligatory aspects of participation in public life, as one would expect from Chapters Two and Three, a definition partial to the theory I hold. In the present context, the careful discrimination of political from other theories is not important.

The important point is what makes political theory theoretical. A theory consists of an interrelated set of categories marking out what the theory supposes as the important variables of the subject matter. "Marking out" means both defining and explaining on the one hand and giving criteria for identifying on the other hand. Social contract theory, for instance, gives careful definitions of actions bound by contract, how to discriminate them from others (the distinction between pulic and private affairs), the grounds for the normativeness of the contract, and so on. The earlier theory of the divine right of kings gave great weight to the intrinsic value of civic life (something of only instrumental value for most contract theories) and to definitions of authority recognizing the priority of the established social order over nature and modelled on the authority of parents. Marxian political theory relates its major categories to the dialectics of history, translating issues of authority and norms into those of historically determined power. The point to notice in these examples is that the theories differ according to what they enshrine as important in their categories and by what they relegate to triviality. On some now old-fashioned views, theories are supposed to mirror their subject matter. Whether they do depends entirely on what is meant by "mirror." Far more signicant than any kind of mirroring, theories select elements in the subject matter as important to respond to and take into account. Even if the theory has nothing to do with issuing imperatives or suggesting plans of action, its categories constitute a normative selection of what is supposed to be important in the subject matter, arranged so as to make perspicuous the important connections between important things. Acceptance of a theory is acceptance of its valuational worldview about the subject. To be in need of a theory is to be unsure, perhaps even at a loss, about what is important. And the differences between theories come down to disputes about what is important.

Understood this way, the quest for a proper context for political theory has to do with finding out what is important. The theory one begins with is indispensable, for it provides at least an initial purchase on the field. But it is also a prejudice that may reinforce blindness about what is important. Gadamer, following Heidegger, has romanticized prejudice as the cultural predispositions one carries into a situation.[3] If one has a culture at all, one has prejudices, he points out, and by a kind of crude pragmatism it follows that a culture cannot be totally wrong. The poignancy of political thinking is that some particular prejudice regarding importance in theoretical structures is so very often the question at issue, not a question to be begged. Therefore, attaining to the position of being able to question a political theory means transcending or partially neutralizing the bondage of one's culture's theory. Of course, there is no other theoretical place to stand, except perhaps in the illusory dialectic of ideas.

For this reason, the position for political theorizing needs to be in close touch with the phenomena whose importance is at issue. Indeed, it has become a commonplace now to say that theory needs to arise out of *praxis*.[4] Just as an experimental scientist's daily encounters with the subject under investigation provides a continual correction of habits of mind, as Charles Peirce saw, so political theory needs correction from close association with public life. But how does that work? How can one escape blind prejudice without falling into blind ignorance?

Answers to that question come on at least two levels. The first level has to do with the nature of categories. As Kant pointed out about concepts, a category can be viewed as a rule for unifying a manifold of contents. In particular, by virtue of its form a category supposes that it is worthwhile (for whatever purpose, theoretical or otherwise) to have this particular set of contents together this way and relating to other categories as one rule to another. The merit of the category depends on the importance of its way of unifying just that manifold. Similarly, each of the theoretical components of a category is itself an organization of other components, and so on down. The category of the contractually or legally defined person in social contract theory, for instance, unifies components of a distinction of abstract person from concrete person, of an individualistic and voluntaristic conception of human life, of the social importance of tolerance, and so on. Tolerance in turn has its own components. Each category, and component-category, has some value by virtue of uniting its components that way.

In actual practice, one deals not only with an overall political theory but with its components, often separated and subjected to stress in application. It was apparent after Marx's brilliant discussion of "the Jewish question" what price is paid in terms of human loneliness and thinness of publically recognized life by adherence to the contractarian theory of the civil person with equality before the law.[5] Recently it has been popular to extoll the contrary values of family, community and ethnic solidarity. But in practice, the price so often paid for concrete solid communities is intolerance and negative prejudice. Are those who extoll community solidarity in practice willing to accept its intolerance, particularly if it is directed against them? Or does practice reveal that abstract equality before the law, for all its burdens of privatizing life, is well worth maintaining because of its protection of tolerance? Or better yet, can a new conception be devised that unifies tolerance and equality of justice with more concrete and less alienated styles of public life than those characteristic of the Liberal social contract? Practice in dealing with the components of a theoretical category, as in this illustration, gives somewhat independent assessments of the worth of the category as a whole. This is the first reason for imbedding political theorizing in practice. It reflects the fact that the theoretical categories have a content-meaning as well as network-meaning.[6]

The second level of answer to the dilemma of having no place to stand while criticizing theory is that life itself is a critic of theories. If not in oneself, then in the larger life of one's culture the merits and demerits of a theory's selective representation of what is important are brought to light by use. In most humanistic theoretical disciplines, there are no precisely definable critical experiments. But there is the large experiment of whether life lived according to a theory is worthwhile, particularly compared to life lived according to alternate theories. The only question is whether returns on this larger experiment will be in soon enough for individuals and cultures to correct their serious mistakes. The best way to hurry the assessment is to be self-consciously theoretical. Political thinking willy-nilly takes place within a social context with political implications. It seems reasonable to require that, like any responsible thinking, political thinking should include the results of coming to terms with even the political interests of the theorizers.

None of this is to say, however, that participation in practical politics makes one a good theorizer. Like many fields, politics has many vigorous and "successful" practitioners who are utterly helpless when it comes to explicit representation of their principles. Because of the importance of theory for moral reflection, these people are not morally reflective. What else is required of theorizing within practice?

III. Perception and Imagination

In his 1937 essay "On Practice," Mao Tse-tung acknowledged Marx's point that knowledge arises out of work, through materially dealing with the forces of production.[7] What Marx had in mind is something like *praxis* as discussed in the previous section. But Mao developed his notion of practice with a subtle shift in conceptual framework. He argued that knowledge begins with perception, and that perception requires direct contact with the affairs about which one knows. He went on to argue that after perceptions are taken in, dialectical reason analyzes and reconstructs them, thinking creatively about them. The results of dialectical thought must then be tested in experience, which involves a new level of perception, and so on.

Now from the standpoint of Western philosophy, Mao's account of perception sounds like a crude Hobbesean materialism. It embodies none of the subtleties in Hume's, Kant's, and Hegel's criticisms of empiricism that Marx and his followers assumed as their cumulative Hegelian heritage. But from the standpoint of Chinese philosophy, Mao's reference to perception reflects an ancient and vital tradition. Beginning with the most ancient Taoist writings there had been a recognition of the importance of cultivating an intuitive perceptive sense of nature and society. Indeed, one of the meanings of being in harmony with the tao is that one's being is made up out of the perceptions one takes in.[8] From that standpoint it makes eminent sense for Mao to begin practice with perception and to call himself a materialist: as for Hobbes as well as Whitehead, for Mao the material of human experience is its perceptions.[9]

Furthermore, the Taoist tradition gives equal emphasis to a kind of spontaneity in experience. On the one hand, one takes in the world in cultivated attunedness; on the other hand, one responds (or should respond) with perfectly natural spontaneity. Creativity is immediate, yet fully responsive to the "ten thousand things" that antecedently condition it. With this as a background, Mao's emphasis on the creativity of dialectical thinking about perceptions is more than what Marx had in mind. For Marx, dialectical reason uses free imagination in pursuit of the implications and potential resolutions of the contradictions perceived; indeed, such imagination is necessary even for the recognition and analysis of the contradictions. But Marx did not have Mao's sensuous feel for the spontaneity of such thinking, nor the trust that common people could discover that dialectical imagination within themselves when set free from ideological fetters. Marx could not have written Mao's Taoist poetry, nor little of his own, I suspect.

Is Mao's view of perception and creative thinking naive? One could make the case that it is not by recalling his Chinese tradition. A case can also be made with respect to Western resources by recalling that Whitehead has provided a criticism of the Western rejection of intuitive perception and its relegation of imagination to transcendental functions alone. Whitehead provided instead a theory of experience that, like the Taoists', interprets the being of the experiencer as arising out of direct perceptions of antecedents; it is defended by an elaborate interpretation and critique of Western philosophy. Furthermore, Whitehead provided a sophisticated theory of creativity and imagination that can take Mao's expressions at face value.[10]

The importance of the Mao-Whitehead thesis for political theory is that it provides two corrective sources for theorizing beyond the ordinary direct engagement and the dialectical implications of the theory itself, two sources that are not tied directly to the intentions or interests of the thinker.

One source is cultivated intuitive perception. Although everyone's thoughts begin in perception, most people immediately express their perceptions clothed in subjective forms expressive of their own interests. Cultivated perception, like good taste, means a learned capacity to keep one's intentions from interfering with the perception. By "intention" here I mean both purposes and interests on the one hand and any judgment involving the form "that x." "That x" is not just the intuitive perception of something but the perception of it *as* something, where the "as" derives from previous interest-formed categoreal experience. Perhaps no *fully formed* conscious thought lacks an intentional subjective form; but perceptive thoughts have a nonintentional element appreciative of and registering the value of what is perceived. Although the inclusive intentionality might distort this, perceptions can indeed be cultivated by identifying potential categoreal distortions and neutralizing them, by developing categories that are sensitive to what is perceived so as to require least distortion, and by attentive practice at grasping things on their own terms.

An immediate practical result of cultivated perception for the formation of political theory is increased empathy, the perception of people's feelings and perspectives as well as ecological sensibilities. A political theorist with cultivated perceptions need never be ruined by being in the position of those whom Whitehead described in the epigraph to this chapter, protected by their own privilege and leisure from apprehending the sufferings of the "masses of mankind." The moral point hardly needs defense that the way people "feel" their social arrangements is crucial for any normative description of them, let alone any prescriptive political judgments.

A more general practical result of cultivated perceptions is that theorists would be in touch with a more naive source of values than those derivative from the implications of their theory. To anticipate the arguments of following chapters, I would agree with the Chinese and American traditions of philosophy that things in the world, both natural and human, are laden with intrinsic and extrinsic values, and that a pure perception of them includes acknowledgement of those values; expressed in judgment, this is a normative description. Without denying the great force of personal and social interest in forming our experience, especially that experience containing significant evaluations, it seems in accord with experience to say that there can be a cultivated perception of the worths of at least some things. Central to this cultivation is empathy with the way many different people value the things. Access thus is provided for the political theorist not only to people's feelings but also to the worths or dis-worths of some things in their experience, in social arrangements, and in nature.

The point about intuition ought not to be overemphasized, since there is little way to tell the difference between a relatively naive perception and an intentioonally formed judgment about a perceived object, except by the feel of practised experience. Cultivated intuitive perceptions of values are surely not infallible. Although certain early modern Western philosophers liked the idea of intuition precisely because it suggested infallibility, they were shown to be wrong by the analysis of intentionality as having the form of judgment. The claim to "perceived values" indeed can be perversely useful in a totalitarian way as a disguise for some special interest expressed as a perception.

Nevertheless, cultivated perception does provide an important check on ideological bias and practical interests in political theorizing. The discussion of the Confucian scholar-official in Chapter Two was deficient regarding paideia. What it should have said is that the paideia of both the Taoist and Confucian strands of Chinese culture focuses on cultivating undistorted perception of the worths of things, perception that triggers its own undistorted responses.

In addition to cultivated perception, political thinking in practical contexts can be corrected by cultivated speculative imagination. This is what Mao called "arranging and reconstructing" the perceptions.[11] Imagination moves largely through habit and under the guidance of the categories we have, and is thereby shot through with the influences of our interests; but not entirely so. Even in the Western transcendental tradition imagination is acknowledged to be a spontaneous faculty that operates with definite antecedents and that can be judged consequently by logical rules, but without being totally determined. The practical advantage of spontaneous speculative imagination is that with it political thinkers might be able to sidestep the pitfalls built in to their theory and its special interests.

Cultivated perception and speculative imagination are significan additions to require of the context for moral reflection and its political theorizing. The disadvantage of political theory arising out of *praxis* is that its interests may be tailored to too narrow a sphere of experience. Whereas the systematic formal requirements of theory may serve to universalize the descriptive categories, the values directing this also may be too narrow. Of course, it is impossible to get an experiential feel for all possible experiences. But through cultivated perception and imagination one can learn the difference between values really manifest in experience and those resulting from a close interaction of theory and activity in pursuit of a political purpose.

IV. From Normative Description to Political Theory

The theory of normative description sketched in the previous chapter rests upon the metaphysical theory that things are harmonies. As harmonies or mixtures they combine components according to patterns. The components are also harmonies. A harmony is an achievement of value, and the value derives from three sources. The components of a harmony, as harmonies, are achieved values, and so the harmony's value is at least the aggregate of these. In addition, there is the value of having the components together; perhaps if they weren't together they couldn't exist at all, but even if they could, their value as unified or summed up is over and above the aggregate of their separate values. Finally, a harmony is a new thing by virtue of the patterns actualized in its integration of components; even the components might attain new value by their juxtaposition.

Normative description then is the analysis of harmonies with a four-fold evaluation. (1) It describes the components of the harmony, and the components of the components, showing how these are themselves achievements of value and how their values are constituted by their arrangements within the harmony. (2) It describes the patterns embodied in the harmony, and the patterns in the components, showing how the actualization of each pattern is an achievement of the values in that possibility. (3) It describes the overall value achieved by this mixture of components and patterns, and in addition describes how alterations of either of these could give rise to other achievements of values, comparing them where comparable and articulating the best as idea. (4) The normative description shows how the value of the harmony relates to the larger environment, how it is centered there and what it contributes. Pragmatic considerations determine how detailed a description should be regarding components, patterns, actual and ideal values, and extent of environment.

Moral reflection engages in normative description from beginning to end, as it seeks to understand the worths of things, imagine alternatives, and give intelligence to action. But what should it describe? If we were to answer that it should describe everything, that would be no answer. What moral reflection usually describes is what its theorists say is important. This would be a perfectly adequate answer if we had perfectly adequate theories and were operating in the mode of logical exposition rather than discovery. Theories are fallible, however, and even the best of them are likely to be false in crucial respects. Furthermore, theories are always oriented to certain purposes and social contexts, and these might not be appropriate in the circumstance of the description at hand. Finally, when we look to theories for guidance regarding what is important to describe, the theories themselves stand to be reinforced or criticized by the results of description. Therefore, we cannot simply appeal to the theories.

Moral reflection differs from casuistry and other forms of deductive or applied reasoning precisely because it practises a dialectical mutual criticism of normative description and theory. Our intellectual situation at any given time is formed with at least the images of a theory that select certain things as worthy of description. The descriptions then help fill in the theory. Because dialectic is a rational procedure, one can ask how the phenomenon would be described under the leading strings of alternate theories. This in turn suggests that the alternate theories would pick out different ways of identifying the phenomena to be described, and these new descriptions can be examined.

The dialectic is not simply a relation between normative theory and normative description. Any theory is somewhat vague, and intermediate theories need to be supplied for it to be applied to concrete phenomena. A political theory, for instance, can say that all authority is determined by social contract. But what does this mean for the authority of the sovereign, of the citizen, of the foreigner? The vague theory will have to be specified with subtheories of sovereignty, citizenship, and alien status. Furthermore, people may agree on the vague theory but insist upon contrary subtheories; this is why theories are vague rather than merely general— their validity does not depend on the law of excluded middle applying to their specifying subtheories. Subtheories in turn are vague, though less so. Therefore, it is possible to view normative descriptions as theories at the lower end of vagueness. Whereas concrete phenomena include completely particular things — haecceities — descriptions of them always back off a bit to their "common natures," to the partially vague universals that are embodied in them. A concrete phenomenon such as an armed fight between factions may be filled with the haecceities of definite bullets striking particular flesh; an appropriate description would still rue the loss of the human lives as lives rather than the interruption of certain cardiac pulses.

By virtue of the four-fold structure of normative description, a description aims to bring out what is important in its phenomena, showing why it is important. Any successful normative description determines certain things to be important; an appropriate theory with which to understand that description must resonate with that selection of importance. Put the other way around, for the process of description to have an orientation to its phenomena, it must have theoretical suggestions about what is important to pick out as components, patterns, and so forth.

The result of this dialectic in moral reflection is a repretory of many different ways of looking at the situation, many slightly different ways of describing it and different theoretical ways of understanding, sorting, and connecting it. In practical moral reflecion, these different descriptions and theories often represent points of view taken by different agencies in the situation. Moral reflection is sophisticated to the extent that its repertory of alternatives is large and the levels of theories upon theories are subtle and nuanced.

The goal of moral reflection, however, is neither to arrive at a good theory nor to be able to give good normative descriptions. It is rather to know what to prize, actually and ideally, and how to respond to that. Or better yet, since moral reflection is not instrumental but is a practise of thinking that should be a dimension of life at all times, its goal is to be able continually to assess what to prize. The function of moral reflection is to keep the Confucian scholar-official alert and informed regarding the values to be affected by potential actions, and to temper administrative single-mindedness with the appropriate sense of irony.

V. The Irony of Normative Description

The dialectic of normative description and normative theory should be a potent stimulus to irony, particularly as it develops the diverse perspectives of many alternate paths of theoretical elaboration and particular specification. An individual needs to recognize many ways to understand a situation, ways that differ in what they value. But as I argued earlier, this appreciation of somewhat arbitrary particularity in the face of an infinite universe should not lead to ironic detachment. That would be an abandonment of the very commitment that makes particularity ironic in the first place.

Moral reflection is the intelligence of engaged persons, not detached ones. We have now returned to the opening quotation from Whitehead. What is the subject of engagement? First, the suffering of the world. Engagement with suffering entails a commitment to do something about it — eliminating its causes, alleviating its effects, or at least helping people bear with it. What is the content of the commitment to engage suffering? It is not a commitment to a political or other morally relevant theory; rather, theories should be investigated because of the light they throw on commitments. Nor is the commitment to a particular normative description of some phenomenon that bears on suffering. Normative descriptions are made for the sake of understanding the situation one is committed to alleviate. The commitment of an engaged, morally reflective person is to alleviate the suffering the reflection brings to attention. The context of the engagement is always the practice of real life in which one's cultivated perceptions and cultivated speculative imagination are fed by interactions with the ten thousand things, the·more direct the better.

Actually, that is an abstract partial truth, because one is rarely engaged alone. Rather, one engages through social institutions and personal relations that collectively define the contents of the social commitment. Similarly, moral reflection is only a partial activity when undertaken by a person alone. It is rather the practise of people in communal interactions. The dialectic of theory and description is all the richer when the reflecting community contains actual representatives of the various perspectives to be developed.

To say that the context for moral reflection is a social engagement with suffering seems to take a particularly negative view. Is not much moral reflection aimed at what to take pleasure in and foster rather than at what to avoid, avert, or endure? To be sure, it is; and there are at least two main reasons for the fact. First, the institutions, practises, instruments, and devices of cultural life that have arisen in response to problems of suffering usually have positive value of their own and need to be made the objects of attention. The economy, for instance, is a cultural institution for relieving the suffering of hunger; much moral reflection needs to be devoted to maintaining the virtues of the economy as such and to alleviating the oppressions and other forms of suffering the economy brings even as it addresses the problem of hunger. Maintenance of the positive values of the institutions of civilization is an intrinsically worthwhile subject matter for moral reflection.

But we must remember Whitehead's warning. If the positive values of civilization are considered in detachment from the functions they are supposed to perform in response to the iron laws of physical nature that "determine the scene for the sufferings of men," moral reflection degenerates to the leisure activity of the "fortunate class." Perhaps this is what happened too often in Confucian culture. "Delicacies of taste displace the interests in fullness of stomach," as Whitehead observed. The old Puritans were not tempted by this particular failing. They were revolutionaries rather than defenders of demonstrable virtue, or so they thought, committed to remaking conditions so that the divinity in all things might show through to the glory of God. For the Puritans, the response to suffering was indeed to avert it, avoid it, or bear up under it, but always with the sense that suffering and its causes, the iron laws, are themselves divine expressions. The Puritans sought the path, the tao, whereby the great harmony of God's creation could be brought into line after the corruption of the fall. What made irony so hard for the Puritans was that the order of creation with which they worked seemed so single against the infinity of the divine itself.

The second reason for the postive aspect of so much of moral reflection is that our feelings, spontaneity, and vigor of purpose exhibit a delight in life. Religiously put, this is the divine expression that in turn glorifies God in the Puritans' universe. It is what Whitehead called adventure, zest, and peace. We reflect on how to have life, and have it abundantly. We celebrate it in our arts, in our understanding, in our sports, in all our "activities in accordance with virtue," as Aristotle defined happiness. Of course, moral reflection should aim to promote and secure the profound enjoyment of existence.

But is not the real evil in suffering that it blights this joy? Death is evil because it cuts short the joy of existence. Pain is evil because it is intrinsically unpleasant. Nevertheless all cultures have noted with admiration the saints whose joy at life is so profound as to embrace pain and death as mere expressions of the iron laws of nature, glorious in their own way. Most of us can bear a little pain for the sake of a greater joy, and we can imagine when death would be a blessing. The real evil of suffering is when pain, hunger, misery, oppression, humiliation, and violence blunt the sense of life or destroy it altogether.

Shall we not then say with the Puritan, whose greatest joys and delights in God were never far from a tortured sense of the sins of the world, that moral reflection on the adventure, zest, and peace of existence requires keeping them in context with the suffering that would corrupt them? Of course, the Puritan is too serious. The preoccupation with suffering is itself a suffering. There are times when we need a holiday away from pursuit of the good because it degenerates into flight from the bad. In any case, obsession with the good seems not to recognize the vanity of struggling with a finite moral order in an infinite universe. But this is to recommend a holiday from moral reflection. That recommendation should be respected when it comes from ecstatic enjoyment, or from final loss to suffering, or from good moral reflection itself. A holiday from moral reflection cannot recommend itself, however, and we are therefore never far from the responsibilities of our commitments.

6

Moral Discernment and the Reality of Value

This moral sense — if the understanding be well informed, exercised at liberty, and in an extensive manner, without being restrained to a private sphere — approves the very same things which a spiritual and divine sense approves; and those things only; though not on the same grounds, nor with the same kind of approbation. Therefore, as that divine sense is agreeable to the necessary nature of things, as already shown; so this inferior moral sense, being so far correspondent to that, must also so far agree with the nature of things.

It has been shown, that this moral sense consists in approving the uniformity and natural agreement there is between one thing and another. So that, by the supposition, it is agreeable to the nature of things. For therein it consists, viz. a disposition of mind to consent to or like, the agreement of the nature of things, or the agreement of the nature and form of one thing with another. And certainly, such a temper of mind is more agreeable to the nature of things than an opposite temper.

—Jonathan Edwards

I. The Metaphysics of Moral Discernment

The arguments advanced in the previous chapters have assumed, as we do in practise, that there are real values in the world and that we can discern them with enough accuracy to dispute about them and to sacrifice our "life, fortune, and sacred honor" for them. Notice that the assumption has two sides, that things themselves have real worth and that we are to some degree appreciative of that worth. There would be no point to claiming that the values of things are real if that could not be appreciated, and it would be self-contradictory to say that we have knowledge or appreciation of such values if that were entirely fictitious or subjective. My argument now must defend that assumption in order to make sense of the practical discussion in the previous chapter about improving normative appreciation.

The nature of the defense, of course, should be metaphysical, that is, to sketch a conception of basic categories that plausibly describes the world and that shows how the reality of values and the comparatively accurate discernment of some of them are possible. But perhaps the assumption that I have claimed we ordinarily make in practice is not right at all, so that we should not attempt to justify it. Perhaps the positivists and skeptics are right anyway, and common practice is based on an illusion. We may begin by considering that possibility.

The nagging problem with all moral philosophies is that they pronounce on what is good and bad and on what to do about that. Puritanism is an infamous example. Yet this is so even for the philosophies that say there are no objective moral differences or that if there are, we cannot know them. Since all moral philosophies, the Puritan and Confucian as well the hedonic and Taoist, the cynical as well as serious, have been proved in one circumstance or another to be painfully wrong, perhaps the better part of wisdom is to avoid moral reflection altogether. This is especially attractive in light of the fact that any moral philosophy, even our own, particularly our own, is likely to commit us in the long run to something we don't want to do. Even the most cynical, skeptical, hedonic relativist finds it painful to stick to that philosophy in the face of a Hitler, and most other moral philosophies give us direct and sometimes unpleasant injunctions.

Nevertheless, it may be observed that the counsel to avoid moral reflection itself stems from moral reflection, at least moral reflection about the ethics of belief. Therefore, we must face up to the problem of how to tell, at least in minimal cases, the good from the bad, the obligatory from the neutral. The claim that there are no moral differences or that these cannot be known is minimally an injunction about the disvalue of certain beliefs. Is this enough of an answer to the skeptic?

I have argued so far that values do not attach to things or acts in isolation, but rather in systematic environments. Furthermore, I have argued that morality is not just a matter of determining the intrinsic worths of the various elements of the environment but also of determining how these relate to human action, specifically to individual responsibility. Therefore, moral discernment is the topic where a theory of value joins a theory of personal subjectivity. The former yields assertions about what things are worth and why; how they might be better or worse; what if anything can be done to make them better; or to keep them from getting worse. From these assertions, plus the principle that the best possibilities ought to be realized, seem to follow various assertions articulating, explaining, and justifying objective obligations; such and so ought to be done.

Not only have many philosophers dismissed metaphysics and history, becoming thereby not much good at the discernment requiring them, but there is little exactly settled public conviction about moral discernment of any sort. The most elegant situation for my case, of course, would be where there are common convictions on the topic. Then my arguments could take the form of showing that certain categories allow us to articulate those convictions fully, to express the diverse convictions so as to make them compatible (in contrast to other categories that express them partially, etc.). But since so many people in our culture believe there is no objectivity in obligations, they would take any attempt to "justify" objective obligations as a "transcendental illusion." A transcendental illusion is a bad argument of the following form: because our experience would be nicely ordered if certain conditions were true, therefore, we must presuppose the conditions to be true so that we may nicely order experience. This is a bad argument precisely because the conditions might not be true and the order imposed might be a fiction: What if personal responsibility is merely a fiction created by neurotic guilt? Being hoodwinked by transcendental illusion is not ironic, for irony requires that its finite commitments are indeed valid, as far as they go and relative to their perspective. Transcendental illusion is rather just pathetic.

For the real philosophic public of our society, the questions whether there are objective obligations or personal responsibilities, and whether there can be any significant moral discernment, are to be answered, if not at the end of inquiry, then at least pretty far along. And this is as it should be when something important is at stake in philosophy. The situation of cultural equivocation and ambiguity is devastating for all positivistic philosophies. For what the culture posits *de facto* as "given" is just the equivocation and ambiguity. Moral reflection cannot simply deny that fact in order to get going.

It is possible, however, to provide categories for moral discernment that are so abstract that they transcend our culture's ambiguities and equivocations. An axiological theory of value can be developed which, vague in itself, lends itself to being made specific both in ways consonant with prima facie experience of the worths of things and also in ways expressed in the initial observations about moral discernment. Furthermore, the theory is vague enough that we can see how some thinkers might conclude that there are no objective obligations or personal responsiblities, and that moral discernment is merely psychological, under special limiting conditions. The form of my argument here is to show that those who reject objectivity of values and the bindingness of responsibilities are special cases within a larger theory justifying those normative claims under other circumstances. Vagueness obviously is not a vice but a virtue; its virtue is that it allows conflicting opinions a neutral ground for confrontation.

Of course, there is a parallel set of suppositions assumed by those who do not assert the normative claims, and with those suppositions the assertion of the normative claims, contrariwise, is represented as a special case, usually of subjective projections of will. But even within the society embodying those antinormative suppositions there is a felt tension with deep-seated valuations, a dissonance between agnostic morals and fundamental repulsions and attracts. It is hard to reflect on the Nazi Holocaust and still psychologize moral discernment or relegate it to one among several language games. This tension, this dissonance, suggests that our culture should embrace and embody a different set of assumptions, one where the nonvaluative situations are the special cases interpreted by special limiting principles. But to justify this, I will refocus the theory of value that throws light on both objective obligation and personal responsibility. Part of the ironic stance recognizes the incommensurability of the two sets of suppositions; the other part of irony is to recognize that some suppositions are preferable to others.

II. The Harmonies as Contrasts

Recall that determinate things can be defined as harmonies, according to the analysis of the previous chapter.[2] A salient feature of being a harmony is that a thing is a "contrast" of components. "Contrast" is a term borrowed from Whitehead that means a unity in which things simply fit together. The immediate unity of components consists of a set of dyadic relations. Whatever triadic relations may also be contained in the contrast, their immediate or material reality consists of dyadic relations. Contrasts are perfectly definite according to their mode. The dyadic character of their inside relations marks this definiteness. By virtue of its dyadic character, a thing, including a process, is just so and not otherwise.

Harmonies contain their components in certain ways, and it may be that other ways of containing those same components would be better or worse. The word "harmony" connotes that things might be unified more or less well. But harmony should not be construed to suggest that any two components of a thing are integrated by virtue of some third component; for that would give the lie to the dyadic character of contrasts. Also, and this is a most important point, connotations of harmoniousness should not be taken to require that the togetherness be aesthetically pleasing in the popular sense, because a conflict, a fight, counts as a harmony, and indeed may be morally the best situation.

If anything definite is a harmony, then any component of a harmony is also a harmony, and so on down and around. Each harmony constitutes or imposes a level of order on its components that they would not have otherwise. Although harmonies might conceivably come about from merely random conjunctions of other harmonies, most come about because many of the surrounding and constituent harmonies are systematically interrelated and steady in that fact. The people and most objects in our world exhibit patterns of endurance, for instance, and many of the processes making up life have regular rhythms that interact steadily with environmental factors. But there are neither metaphysical nor experiential grounds for supposing that the components of a harmony and its wider environment are locked into a single self-sustaining system. Rather, many of the components of a morally relevant harmony seem to have careers of their own, subject to their own environmental reinforcements and tolerances. Because of the tendency of components to go their own ways, the unity of them in a harmony is a somewhat fragile affairs. From the standpoint of a harmony, to speak anthropomorphically, the constituent world may seem like potential chaos, ready to fly apart. The perceptible, threatening readiness of har-

monies to dissolve into their components is what Dewey so brilliant-
ly described as the precariousness of existence.[3]

From here it is possible to see part of the reason for calling harmonies intrinsically valuable. A harmony has worth in that it is a
way of having its components together. Without the harmony, or
without some other harmony, the components could not coexist.
Since the components are themselves harmonies, that which makes
possible their coexistence has the value of sustaining all their own
values. Do not most moral problems have the form of needing to
find a way for sustaining together seemingly incompatible valuable
things? For instance, the value of a fetus versus that of its mother;
the values of a large number of kidney patients with a dialysis
machine service for only a few; low inflation with high employment.

Furthermore, a harmony not only preserves the values its components would have by themselves, it sometimes enhances the values
in the components by the ways it fits them together, as mentioned
regarding harmony in previous chapters. For instance, Solomon's
threat to divide the baby not only found the baby its rightful mother,
which was Solomon's problem, but also brought about a moment of
honesty and revelation of character in both women, an added value.
Of course, unity is not necessarily good. Sometimes conjunctions
improve things, sometimes they worsen them. Partnerships sometimes bring out the worst in people. Some harmonies demean their
components, giving them individually less worth than they otherwise would have. All this is to say that harmonies can be changed for
better or worse by the ways they are together as components of other
harmonies. The variability in value stemming from different ways of
combining components cannot be accounted for by looking from the
harmony down, so to speak, to the logically antecedent values in the
components, for that would recognize only the summed values of the
components. Rather, the variability must be accounted for by
reference to differences in the form of the alternate harmonies.

Two kinds of differences are important, as pointed out earlier.
Alternate harmonies can differ in complexity, that is, in the diversity
of things they bring together. Alternatives also can differ in simplicity, in the economy by which higher-level orders in a harmony make
possible lower-level orders, facilitating the ability of the lower levels
to sustain importance in the whole. Maximum simplicity with a
minimum complexity would obtain when a harmony is virtually
homogeneous, with each part like every other part, no matter on

what level; this is boring. Maximum complexity with minimum simplicity would obtain when an indefinitely large number of different kinds of things are together by mere juxtaposition, with none of them internally influenced by the juxtaposition with others; this harmony would be trivial.

Value in a harmony consists in heightening both complexity and simplicity to some degree. The greater both complexity and simplicity, the greater the harmony's value. But a heightening of complexity might involve a trade-off in lowered simplicity, or vice versa. To increase value, a loss on one side must be more than compensated for by a gain on the other.

The fact that alternatives to a harmony change value as both complexity and simplicity are altered underscores a further characteristic of harmonies, namely, that values differ in nature as well as degree. A situation changed in complexity or simplicity is a different situation. If two harmonies differ in their components, or in their formal arrangements, or in both, they are simply different harmonies and each must be apprehended on its own terms. To conceive them as alternatives, as might happen in moral deliberation, is to employ a third standpoint that focuses on common components or common formal arrangements and that might relate the differences to possible processes that would bring about one or the other.

III. Intuition

Because harmonies as contrasts are immediate unities, they must be grasped intuitively in their distinctive natures. Since complexity and simplicity are incommensurable, increases and decreases in their jointly produced value also must be grasped intuitively.

Now the mention of intuition should always signal a stop in the argument to consider what is at stake. I have raised the topic of apprehending or grasping things as values in order to suggest that when we actually do value things, we suppose value to be something like what has been said. It should be possible to make this case even to people who think there are no objective values or veridical subjective discernments of them. My claim is that harmonies' distinctive nature and degree of value are apprehended in intuitive judgments. That claim itself is not presented for intuition but for consideration as part of the metaphysical hypothesis. To Charles Peirce's question, whether the recognition that a judgment is an intuition is itself an intution, the answer is no.[4] Neither is it intuititve to assess the worth grasped in an intuition; analysis and assessment of a harmony are always subject to further consideration, since the analysis might misidentify the complexity and simplicity, and the assessment might neglect proper comparisons. Normative description is always partial and incomplete, and intuition is always subject to the normative description at hand. But grasping the valuable harmony with appreciation is intuitive because it involves taking the contrast in the harmony as an immediate unity presenting specific complexity and simplicity. Analysis and assessment subsequently mediate the unity by stepping away from the dyadaic thisness of the harmony to the common natures it contains.

Because the claims about intuition are part of a metaphysical hypothesis, the hypothesis needs to be tested. The real test consists in noting over the long run whether the hypothesis is plausible and fruitful. But in the short run, consider the following examples (and here I am making a rough empirical induction:

1. In criticizing metaphysical systems, do we not (those few of us who criticize metaphysical systems) complain when a system leaves something out (a fault in complexity) and also when a system includes but buries something we think ought to be important (a fault in simplicity)?

2. Is it not the case that the things seeming most valuable to us — for instance, human beings — appear to be maximizations at the present time of biological and social complexity consistent with the simplicity required for individuality, consciousness, and deliberate action? Of course, a critic can retort that this is just coincidence, and that we egoistic selves just happen to be the most complex and most simple things around. Nevertheless, it stretches the credulity of the coincidence when we scale other things according to the same criteria we use for ourselves, or when we shift our evaluation of something because we find it is more or less complex or simple than we had thought.

3. When engaged in moral deliberations, do we not analyze alternatives into the range of factors that they reconcile (their complexity) and into the neatness with which solutions resolve things (their simplicity), struggling to get between the fact that complex solutions are not neat and the fact that neat solutions leave out or diminish items we think should be given importance? A critic might object by citing the role of preference. But preference legitimately

takes over in deliberation only in specifiable limiting conditions, namely, when deliberation comes up with imagined alternatives of indistinguishable degrees of worth, or when the situation is simply too confused for us to be satisfied that any imagined analysis has captured the important elements. When our understanding of complexity and simplicity makes us think that one thing is better than another, we call it (maybe tentative) knowledge, not preference.

4. As a final example, consider mathematics. When two proofs reach the same conclusions from the same premises, do not mathematicians say the more elegant is the better? Is not a mathematical system that reaches the same theorems from fewer premises taken to be better than one with more premises? Is not a system whose rules allow proof of more theorems judged better than one with fewer theorems from the same premises? The chief significance of this example is that it can hardly be denied even by those most loyal to the supposition that values are only nonobjective projections of will or liking. They might object that the example can be restated in terms of what mathematicians prefer rather than what they judge to be better. But in these cases there are objective reasons for the preferences, that is, fewer premises, more theorems, more elegant constructions.

These examples may be summed up in a rough induction to the effect that our valuational experiences value things as harmonies with complexity and simplicity; and where valuations are comparative or where we imagine alternatives, deliberations consist in varying the relevant complexity or simplicity and feeling the worths of the variant imagined outcomes. Even those who in other contexts deny objectivity to values, appreciate and evaluate values in much this way. If all this is so, and we have a metaphysical theory of value that represents it, then the burden of proof falls on those who say that valuation is not what it seems but instead is a subjective projection.

It is possible now to anticipate that counterargument by commenting on the limiting conditions in which the worths of things can be abstracted out and neglected. Those conditions are when the structures of harmonies and their interconnections are under analysis, as is the case in natural science. Natural science, in the form that lends itself to denying objective values, came to be in that remarkable Renaissance synthesis of Aristotelian qualitative thought with Platonic quantitative thought. The paradigm of knowing in mathematical physics, which legitimately prescinds from things' values, quickly became the paradigm for knowing generally, and valuation became either noncognitive or a matter of inference from structural or factual knowledge, as when we are supposed to have to derive "oughts" from "is's."[5]

With the wisdom of hindsight, however, we can see that this historical development resulted from a failure of metaphysical imagination. Instead of losing the great classical and medieval traditions of valuation, our metaphysicians should have conceived thinking and the nature of things in such a way as to make valuational thinking the inclusive and concrete paradigm, with mathematical physics a subcase that abstracts from questions of objective value. The slogan should be reversed: "is" can be derived from "good" or "ought" only by a careful act of abstraction in the direction leading to the language of mathematics. Even the concrete act of mathematical judgment is valuational in its way, as we have seen. Never too late, the attempt to provide a metaphysics of moral discernment is part of the larger axiological task of reconceiving thinking so as to acknowledge the value-character of things as things. Whereas the abstractions of things that appear in scientific analysis prescind from value, both the activity of scientific investigation and judgment, and the social practice of science, are freighted with objective worths and value judgments.

IV. Normativeness in Obligation and Responsibility

From the general comments on the objectivity of values it is pertinent now to move to an explicit discussion of the observation that obligations are objective and that persons have responsibilities to them. The argument begins with a move from value to ideals to obligations.

If a definite thing is a contrastive harmony with a value, and if there are other ways by which the component harmonies could be integrated, with differing values, then the better ways are ideal with respect to the given harmony. To the extent they are commensurable, they may be ranked with each other as more or less ideal. Let us hypothesize that the best of rankable harmonies is the way things should be, and is obligatory where something can be done to bring it about.

This hypothesis might seem to define obligation tautologically: obligation is what is best because it is what is best. But highest rank alone is not enough to make an option for integration obligatory. For a state of affairs to be obligatory is for it to be a possibility in a process to which obliged people have appropriate causal access. If the process contains alternatives, and a reason is sought for realizing one alternative over the others, then the only reason that could specify the obligation would be that one alternative is better. If no alternative is better, then decision regarding which to pursue is not made by reference to any reason in the set of alternatives, but rather by mere conditions of individual preference, by chance, or by acquiescence to ease. Without a reason in the set of alternatives for realizing some rather then others, there is no obligation.

Here is a deceptively simple characterization of obligation. An obligation is a potential harmony in a causal process to the realization of which human effort might be helpful and that itself merits realization because it is better than its alternatives. What makes it obligatory is that it is better than those alternatives also accessible to effort. Obvious variations on this include the following. Where a simple ranking cannot be achieved, obligation may fail merely on a class of alternatives that are better than others but without ranking among themselves. In a negative ranking situation, obligation may be to avoid the distinguishably worse alternatives. Since obligation obtains only when there are rankable alternatives, and the values of things in most situations are such that ranking is irrelevant or impossible, there may not be many situations with significant obligations. Preference, play, and convention make up the bulk of appropriate behavior in a world of valuable things.

Is not this characterization of obligation a sleight of hand? For how could mere ranking in worth be sufficient to produce obligation? Consider what has been claimed already, namely, that alternatives sometimes do differ in value, and that we can understand something of what that difference consists in. Much of the doubt that there are objective obligations comes from the belief that there is no real difference in value between alternatives. If there is a difference in value, then that constitutes a reason why the better should be realized.

Consider also what has not been claimed. I have not claimed that people must be able to discern the worth of an option for it to be obligatory; since moral discernment is so difficult, ambiguous, and confused, it would be very bad for a theory of objective obligations to say that nothing is an obligation unless it is discerned as such. But according to the argument so far, the only knowledge about the obligatory alternative required is whatever would be necessary for human effort to be relevant to realizing it, and that knowledge is mainly "how to do it," and appreciating what is done. This qualification accords with the common experience of finding that we were mistaken about our obligations and, on the opposite side, of discovering that we had obligations of which we were totally unaware at the time.

I have also not claimed that the objective obligatoriness in the option derives from people's accepting the obligation. The problematic of the move from obligation to personal responsibility addresses that topic. What I have claimed is that an objective obligation is simply an ideal option for which the situation presents an objective reason for choice. The problem now rests with the response of choice.

What about the move from obligation to personal responsibility? What is the subjective side of personal responsibility? By the metaphysical hypothesis that has been drawn since the topic was introduced in Chapter Three, suppose that a subject is a thing inheriting value-laden conditions from the environment, a thing whose essential features consist in the various ways it orders or integrates its conditions, and whose own definite nature and value is the complex harmony of those essential and conditional features. This is an extremely abstract metaphysical statement, more abstract than, but vaguely inclusive of, the Aristotelian view that a thing is a substance, or the process philosophy view that it is an event. A subject's own nature and value can take on other objective characters as it plays roles in other contexts. And its own nature and value may be relatively trivial in comparison with the larger processes and events of which it is a part.

At this level of abstraction it is appropriate to observe a distinction between the thing's nature and value in and for itself, and the thing's nature and value for other things in which its own final integration as one among many conditions. The latter is the thing's objective being, and it is known through locating the thing in various orders, for instance, in scientifically or artistically known orders. The thing's objective boundaries cannot be formulated objectively except in terms of the structure of the orders. Analysis of the former side of the distinction, a thing's subjective genesis aiming at its own definite integration, is important only when there is a reason to attend to the nature and value a thing has for itself.

Because the theory of personal responsibility is constructed in light of subjective genesis, it is pertinent to consider that some thinkers who would deny personal responsibility would also deny that there is any becoming or genesis of things, that there is any sense to people's aiming at achieving a nature and value for themselves. All nature and change, say these thinkers, can be accounted for in terms of the objective characters of things in their respective orders without reference to subjective genesis.

What might motivate this argument? One reason might be a defense of the integrity of scientific analysis. Introducing subjective choice or "self-constitution" factors into causal process seems to attack that integrity. But on the contrary, no objective order is denied or compromised by reference to the genetic process of self-constitution. Every thing arises out of a host of orders and constitutes itself as a definite objective fact in a host of orders. The degree of regularity and predictability is wholly empirical, a point essential to the integrity of scientific explanation; to assume a nonempirical determinism itself undermines the objectivity of science.

Another motive, though scarcely one to be admitted in public, might be to protect the status of scientific explanation as an ideal construct, separate from the ambiguities of the actual world. To refer to things exclusively in terms of their locations in orders is to prescind from the distinction between real and possible existence in those orders. Acknowledgement of subjective genesis, as opposed to appearance in an order, is at least tacit admission of that distinction. It is not my purpose here to consider whether science legitimately prescinds from the distinction between real and possible existence. But it is surely to the point to observe that for dealing with the vicissitudes of life, that distinction is of central importance; it is at the heart of doing or not doing. The rejection of subjective genesis is another case of reductionism abstracting from a richer reality; those who think of things as nothing but their objective characters in various orders achieve that abstraction by leaving out consideration of subjective coming-to-be.

Reference to subjective coming-to-be is necessary for defining personal responsibility. What specializes a human subject within the larger class of subjects is that part of the person's achieved nature and value are expressions of those epitomies having to do with moral value. Moral value here means both the worth of the motives lying behind the actions taken and the values justifying or failing to justify those motives. A human subject in a situation inherits a host of conditions with various values. Each condition presents itself, as it were, as something worth integrating into the subject. But the subject can integrate the host of things only by rejecting some and by finding patterns of integration that make certain things important and others trivial. The objective limits of the integration are found in the conditions that have to be integrated.

The subjective process of integration sometimes involves options between various ways of integration. These ways differ in what they make important because they differ in patterns of complexity and simplicity; different things are included in each way and with different forms. Then, since the result of the integration will be an objective condition for a host of future processes, some of the differences among the values of the various options arise from the consequences, and decisions are often to be viewed as extended actions. In the process of integration, a decision occurs when one integrative option is actualized over the others.

The values actualized as important in the components constitute the motives of the action; or rather, the essential features of that decision consist in the adoption of the relevant conditional values as motives. Furthermore, the components included or relatively trivialized by the decision constitute the element of moral character that disvalues those things, with the consequences that follow from the disvaluing. The difference between options is a difference between patterns of valuing and disvaluing things in functional relationships to one another. Each option, if adopted, has a complex moral character.

Responsibility consists in a person's being confronted with options for which there is a reason for choosing certain ones rather than others. The reason consists in the objective obligatory character, or real higher value, in the options that should be chosen. Where there is no real difference in value between the options, there is no responsibility, only preference. But where there are options with a reason for differential choice, the person is responsible whether the person chooses that way or not. The responsibility stems from the objective obligatory character of the options and from the person's being a subject that gives itself a moral nature by acting in a way that relates to a reason for acting.

The most perplexing problem here, however, is where the reason for acting lies. It is too strong to say that the subject must know the reason, for we often have responsibilities and act to fulfill them without knowing why the responsible action is better. It is also somewhat too strong to say that the subject could have known the reason if only attention had been turned that way, because we often, though not often enough, deliberate long and diligently about what to do, and only after it is too late discover what was genuinely most valuable and had the reason to be chosen. There is poignant tragedy in moral life that ought not to be denied in a theory of personal responsibility, and conversely, ought not to be allowed to soften responsibility to mere intentions. The reason for acting lies in the very differences between the options as they occur in the integrative process; to say less than this is to subjectivize objective obligations. But the reason for acting must occur in such a way that it is susceptible to being discerned for what it is. If it is not actually discerned for what it is, the fault lies in the activity of moral discernment, not in the objective reason why some options are better than others.

There exists, then, a higher level responsibility in every responsible person; namely, to be morally discerning. In fact, one can say it is an essential feature of every responsible person to have the responsibility to be morally discerning, whether or not one achieves much moral discernment. This is expressed even in such rudimentary epitomies of human activity as sociality, according to which there is a moral imperative to play roles well and to understand oneself as fit to play those roles. Both Puritans and Confucians agree that the high-level responsibility for being responsible is the central precept of morality and the key to human virtue.

Moral discernment is a deep and profound capacity, developed over a long time through many experiences of value, choice, and deliberation. It does not suddenly emerge, and if its intuitive aesthetic sources lie innate within deep human capacitites, as Mencius argued, the development of those beginnings into a habit of discernment requires an arduous education. Perhaps the deepest personal unity over time, over a lifetime, is that involved in the cumulative obligation to be a responsible moral discerner.

Before refocusing these remarks in a theory of moral discernment, three qualifications should be stated about the preceding argument. First, the discussion of personal integration provided an

occasion to point out another crucial character of harmonies, namely, that they integrate components as foreground and background,
or as important and trivial, relative to one another. This highlights
the complexity of valuation within moral situations. Second, the fact
that the valuable integration subjectively aimed at in a thing's
coming-to-be is the same value it presents objectively for other
things guarantees an irreducible objectivity for values. Whereas it
may be tempting to think of a thing's value as only that which it has
by virtue of its importance or triviality in another contrast, in fact it
has a value achieved in itself. One poignant perspective on existence
is to see the contingent discrepancy between a thing's own worth and
the worth it can bear as integrated in other things. This is the metaphysical heart of moral dilemmas. Third, these two points give rise
to the observation that the objectivity of obligations is not something
that lies indifferent to personal subjects but consists in the worthy
reality of things as potentially integrated within personal subjects.
For, the field of options itself consists both in the things presenting
their own values and in the synthesis of these things into such contrasts as constitute a field. The latter condition—that a thing constitutes something of the layout of its own world—provides the constant appropriateness of the ironic stance.

V. Dimensions of Moral Discernment

The themes of moral discernment can be summarized in theoretical form by classification in four dimensions.
The first dimension of moral discernment is the imagination for
forming options. Although patterns of integrating things are often
themselves among the conditions presented in a situation, the important ways things *can be* integrated are not necessarily given.
Rather, the synthetic faculty Kant called imagination forms and
reforms patterns of things so that the options in fact occur within experience. Within such imaginative options the operative elements
are the forms that make some things important foreground elements
and other things relatively trivial background elements, with various
functions in between. The complexity in the pattern consists in what
has a place in foreground or background and what is not excluded.
The simplicity consists in the form arranging foreground and
background, and excluding. The norms for imagination are not so
much moral ones comparing patterns of integration as aesthetic ones
of cohesion and intensity of contrast with the patterns.

The role of imagination in moral discernment is easy to neglect because typical cases of moral problems are typical precisely because the options seem preformed. But since the responsibility for forming the options is the subject's, even typical given patterns need responsibly to be adopted as relevant by the subject. Imagination in moral discernment should be responsibly trained much the way artistic imagination is trained, by practice in looking at things in new ways, by inhibiting routine visions, and the like. Whereas one perhaps should not be greatly blamed for lack of imagination in a particular instance, one can indeed be blamed for not having developed a free imagination over time, relative to one's age and experience.

A special focus of imagination is required by the social definition of the individual. Most things in our environment are socially meaningful. That is, their value consists in large part in the valuable roles they play in various people's situations, and in various systems. To discern their value, therefore, requires a multitude of imaginative projects into what they might mean for others in various contexts. At a rudimentary level, this imaginative practice is taken for granted, because the socially defined meaning of things makes us assume that they are what they are by virtue of playing roles for others and ourselves. We habitually interpret the world in terms of its meanings for the many interpretive perspectives we notice. Moral discernment specializes this projective habit of imagination, and it is intrinsic to any normative description.

The second dimension of moral discernment is the formation of choices. This is not the actual choosing but the construction of a ranking of the options with an articulation of the reasons that would justify the choice. From the perspective of each ranking, the alternate options have different values as excluded. In contrast to imagination, which is a relatively private affair, the formation of choices is public, requiring inquiry into how things fit together or do not fit, subject to the logical and empirical norms of reasoning in public discussion. Often the formation of choices results from actual deliberative discussion, although sometimes one talks to oneself about it. Within the formation of choices the operative elements are the objective values in the various components to be integrated and the ways by which the values in the highest-ranked option subordinate the values in the lower-ranked options.

A ranking of options is itself a complex pattern including more than one optional pattern of integration ordered from the perspective of the highest ranked. There may well be many rankings of options, however, each one of which presents its chosen action as having values which, if chosen, subordinate the other values.

Each ranking is only a perspective, however, and it is easy to end moral discernment when one has found a way of consistently ranking the options. Yet this by itself would be moral dogmatism. If the process of discernment does not go on to consider the claims of alternate rankings, one becomes fixated and asserts the particular perspective merely as a preference. To be sure, if the preferred perspective is well formed, the ranking respects the objective values of things; but then several rankings can be equally respectful. Or, since patterning the objective values into options requires compromises of importance, triviality, and exclusion at its heart, it may be better to say the several rankings are equally disrespectful.

Part of the objectivity of a ranking of choices comes as the result of the attempt to see how anyone in a given position would rank them. This is an attempt at rationality in ranking. It also illustrates again the social definition of the self, for the ranking is one that should be appreciated by the others around, if they were to be in one's place.

The third dimension of moral discernment is obvious from this last point; namely, the process of developing an inclusive vision that treats the various rankings as perspectives and finds some way of relating them. While there is no need to suppose that there is some surely true superperspective, there is always the relative task of compatibly envisioning the particular rankings of options that function in one's moral dialogue. Systematic philosophy is particularly helpful to this dimension of moral discernment because it presents maps for moving among various cultural perspectives, all of which include rankings of optional ways of patterning values. Of course, as itself a ranking perspective, the comprehensive vision is immediately relativized by the appearance of a ranking it cannot comprehend, and the task of envisionment breaks out again. Indeed, it may result that the best vision—best according to systematic criteria for envisioning—displays the rankings as themselves unranked; if this happens, the moral choice reverts to preference with no reason, and hence no responsibility.

The move from imaginative formation of options , to the ranking of options, to the envisionment of a set of rankings can be a dangerous tendency toward abstraction, however essential each step is for moral discernment. This danger points out another dimension of moral discernment.

The fourth dimension is a combination of what Plato called dialectic and the Confucians called sincerity. On the one hand, it is the process of moving back and forth to identify, articulate, and assess each of the previously mentioned steps in moral discernment, noting especially what values are distorted or dropped out in the process of discernment. Whether we like the conclusion or not, this dialectical practice is the ultimate self-referential check within the moral community and the last resort of honesty for individuals. On the other hand, the judgments involved in this back and forth movement, while criticizable after the fact, arise out of an antecedent formation of character. The judgments need to be sensitive, perspicacious, faithful in remembering what has gone before, and directed with an open hope for finding the best reason rather than a rationalization for secret motives. This is like Confucian sincerity in which relative judgments in analysis and decision are transparent to the depths of the heart. Whereas the dialectical element in this fourth dimension of moral discernment can be formed through discussion and politics, the cultivation of the sincere character revealed in, but antecedent to, judgment is akin to spiritual practice or what the Confucians called the Way of the Sage. It is also the aim of Puritan holiness. There is no obvious analogue in Liberalism.

The desired result of moral discernment cultivated through a lifetime and applied to a situation is an understanding of things displayed in reference to an array of optional responses on the part of the subject in which the reasons for choosing differentially are apparent. Or, if there are no reasons finally — after all the passions of moral commitment — that too is a vital conclusion of moral discernment.

7

Moral Science in a
Normative Cosmos

The first several chapters of this study focused on issues having to do with the models and context for moral reflection. To be sure, many "content" issues of morality were discussed along the way, and a beginning was made to the development of philosophical categories for understanding the world as subject to moral reflection. The purpose of this chapter is to continue developing those categories with reference to the ways in which other disciplines, particularly the scientific, articulate their subject matter so as to make it amenable to moral reflection. This continues the theme of normative description.

At least the following three projects suggest themselves as requisite for an adequate understanding of the moral aspects of the cosmos.

A conception of understanding, including natural and social science, needs to be developed that facilitates showing the carry-over of value from one thing to another. Ecology is especially interesting for moral reflection to the extent that changes carry value over from one thing to another within and among systems, modifying it in various ways. The ethical question for ecology is how value is altered by systematic changes.

An axiological conception of value needs to be developed that shows both value is an *achievement* in actual things and that it is constituted in part by the *relations* in which things stand. A conception of this sort is prespuposed in the first project.

A cosmological conception needs to be developed that displays how there can be enduring individuals with their own integrity that at the same time are internally related to some ecological systems. The theory must comprehend how both individuals and systems have value, and how value is transformed as it passes through a system to individuals and from the individuals to the system. In particular, the theory must show how an individual can belong to several systems at once, is determined in part by the roles played there, and, at the same time, how the individual mediates the effects of one system on another and might contribute some free effects of its own to the other systems, thereby modifying them.

I. The Carry-Over of Value in Change

Moral reflection always, willy nilly, prespposes and employs some notions of causal structure and change. The values and disvalues reflected upon are usually structurally and causally related to one another. Indeed, the point of moral reflection is often to discern what happens to the worth of things when certain changes take place or should take place. Therefore, moral reflection needs a cosmology, a critical view of natural structure and causal changes.

Usable cosmologies are not easy to find. Scientific cosmology is at an exciting stage of development, but its terms are framed by concerns so closely tied to the latest experimental and theoretical developments, expressed mathematically and identifying the very small and very large, that they are hard to relate to the scale of things involved in moral reflection. The new scientific cosmology has had a fortunate negative impact on inherited common sense, however. Our common sense moral cosmology until recently had been Aristotelian, despite the fact that Newtonian science had undermined its plausibility as a straightforward view of nature. As a result of the Newtonian subversion of the Aristotelian universe, the practical reality of modern moral reflection took place largely outside of official moral discourse and instead in the realms of politics and business.

Now the new physics and biology have undermined the Newtonian common sense. Liberalism, its Marxist flip side, *real politik*, and other voluntaristic or positivistic moral cosmologies have been subverted by the new, nonpositivist, scientific cosmologies (though perhaps few have noticed). Where do we go for contemporary moral cosmology if not to the moral traditions of antiquity and modernity, nor to contemporary scientific cosmology?

Twentieth-century Western philosophy has witnessed the rise of three rather related schools of thought centered on matters of moral reflection and directly employing cosmology (called that or something else): existentialism, pragmatism, and process philosophy. Each in its own way developed a theory of the temporality of the present, in which change takes place. Each attempted to understand how the past imposes conditions on the present, both enabling and limiting choices. And each discussed the problem of norms as they relate directly to decision-making. The genius of existentialism was to throw light on the subjectivity of freedom, that of pragmatism was to locate decisions within the flow of objective conditions, and that of process philosophy was to combine these with an elegant theory of value. Their common preoccupation with present temporality was a curse as well as a blessing, however. By neglect, both the past and the future were reduced, in their views, to the implications they have for the present.

Yet past and future have their own temporality not adequately recognized by existentialism, pragmatism, and process philosophy. The temporality of the past is that of fixed, actualized, achieved structures, with the values carried by those structures. Although those structures can enter into subsequent decisive "presents" as conditions for decision, that is not their only reality. The reduction of the past to its implications for the present might stem from a reductive metaphysical view that only present existence is real. Its moral consequence in contemporary consciousness is gross impiety toward achieved value, an overweening subjectivism, even a narcissism. The temporality of the future is the normative structure of possibilities that shift as the actual conditions for which they are possibilities shift. These future possibilities are of course normative for present decision-making, as existentialism, pragmatism, and process philosophy variously have elaborated. But they also are normative for future things and mark out a reality for the future that goes beyond mere reference to the consequences of present actions. Morality is concerned not only with doing the best thing now but also with care and respect for the world of the future. Whereas the reduction of past temporality to the present has tended to impious narcissism, the reduction of future temporality to the present has tended to amoral aestheticism.

Our need then is for a moral cosmology that recovers past and future modes of temporality without losing the sensitivities developed by existentialism, pragmatism, and process philosophy. The clues for this were dropped above in the fascination with the Chinese model of the scholar-official and assorted Taoist cousins. The Chinese tradition in its most ancient roots conceives of the elementary units of reality as changes from yin to yang and vice versa. More particularly, an identifiable unit of reality is a harmony of yin-yang transformations. A harmony is stable when all of its transformations repeat themselves; this can be called inertial change. A harmony is moving when some of its transformations are replaced by other transformations. Stability is thus a species of harmonic change. A harmony is always a harmony of harmonies. Though ancient, this idea was explicitly articulated by Chou Tun-i in his "Explanation of the Diagram of the Great Ultimate." Perhaps the best way for Westerners to experience the force of the Chinese approach is through extended practice of t'ai ch ch'uan.[1]

That yin-yang transformations can repeat themselves means that there are measures or patterns ingredient in harmonies—so much yin here relative to so much yang there, again and again. Differences between transformations consist in different measures of yin and yang. Thus, there are patterns that can be ingredient in a harmony, and over time those patterns can be repeated or exchanged for other patterns. Furthermore, there are relations between patterns such that some patterns can be ingredient in a harmony because they are sustained or tolerated by the ingredience of other patterns. Despite all the activities of one's body, the repeated general functional interdependence of one's organ systems is tolerated by all body movements; to move in ways that prohibit that functional interdependence entails death of the body. Because patterns ingredient in the same harmony mutually influence one another, changes in some alter the conditions for the possibility of changes in others. It is safe to say that all harmonies are constantly changing patterns, but according to different rates of exchange. The stability in our environment consists in the repetition of patterns. The greatest stability consists in repeated patterns that are tolerant of very great changes elsewhere. Perhaps the Neo-Confucian notion of *li*, principle, is a resource for developing the notion of pattern and pattern exchange.

The Taoist sensibility articulates a cultural aesthetic expressive of this conception of change. All present things are in movement, and the movements relate to one another so as to constitute a great flow. Harmonic processes show patterns coming together in harmonies so as to allow for more complex harmonies, such as Chuang-tzu's wife, and then the patterns change so as no longer to tolerate the complex harmony, returning the situation to more basic elements. The Taoists properly called attention within process to those elements making up the general tolerance of change, the feminine, motherly, womblike patterns that both survive the special changes and provide the matrix out of which the special changing harmonies can arise. For instance, t'ai chi ch'uan, as a Taoist exercise, cultivates those fundamental movements that, when practised and perfected, pull all the other physical and emotional movements into a reinforcing harmony, allowing for extraordinary—because fundamentally well-grounded—special movements.

By itself, the Taoist conceptuality might be likened to the recent Western emphasis on present temporality and change; indeed, the likeness of Taoism to process philosophy has been remarked frequently. It is necessary to remember, however, the existential and conceptual linkage between Taoism and Confucianism. Confucianism by itself might well be faulted for an inadequate treatment of freedom and choice, a fault regarding its practices in present temporality. Yet it is extraordinarily sophisticated regarding actuality and achieved value in past temporality, and regarding the objective normativeness of future temporality. It has a profound view of institutions as the bearers of past achievements. Confucianism knows as well that the future is never reducible to its implications for present decision-making and thus requires a commitment to continuing, long-term tending. Confucian ethics yokes profound respect and appreciation for the past with an equally profound recognition of the obligation in future temporality, but with a theory of present action that easily degenerates into routine—a projection of the fixed actuality of past temporality over present temporality. The Taoist criticism of Confucianism, on its positive side, has been to contribute a profound theory and practice of present temporality.

Our theory of change, therefore, need not be limited to change in present temporarity. Through the inspiration of the Confucian and Taoist sides of the Chinese tradition, we can appreciate temporally thick causation that is expressed in all three temporal modes. Causation involves the structured actual achievements of value that have past status and that set limits for the present. Causation involves change in the present. And causation is linked to a normative future that constantly shifts the possibilities it presents for changing values as potentialities for present actualization shift.

We can now inquire into how value changes. Suppose value consists — as has been argued — in achieving the ingredience of a pattern within process. If the pattern is reiterated, the value is carried over to the new stage of the harmony. The thing or event in which the value was first achieved of course continues to be itself, with its own value. It can be multiply located, however, maintaining the position of its original actualization and then also entering into subsequent things as a condition. Since many elements in the harmony are moving, the pattern may be exchanged for a somewhat different pattern, achieving a somewhat different value. Serious moral reflection presupposes a science that can explain how values are altered by the changes in their environment.

Some harmonies are environmental systems, which means that they exhibit diachronic patterns through which a series of exchanges of synchronic patterns is repeated, still tolerant of some unsystematic changes. Other harmonies are enduring individuals that not only have some important repeated patterns but also have diachronic patterns essentially relating their earlier and later elements of the enduring harmony. Many other kinds of harmonies lie between these two extremes. Environmental science should be able to trace how patterns are altered by changes moving around a system, from the system to enduring individuals, from earlier to later stages of the enduring individuals, from the individual back to the system, and from one system through an individual to another system in which the individual functions. This science is properly formulated for ethics when it can explain how patterns as achieved values are transformed as they move through these change points. Ethics is interested in the ways changes affect the worth of things, and it needs structural analyses that display changes in worth.

The result of this discussion is a call for two intellectual projects. One is the development of a philosophic cosmology recognizing past, present, and future modes of temporality as a basis for moral reflection. The other is for the development of a dimension of specific sciences that shows, each with regard to its subject matter, how given values are carried through and altered in causal processes.

II. Value as Achievement

Let us suppose, as in earlier chapters, that value consists in achieving an existential integration of things; the specific value is the sum of the values of the things integrated plus the extra value achieved by integrating them this way rather than that (if there are alternatives). Now there are two components of the integration. There are the "other things" entering into the process as the conditions that have to be integrated, and there is the existential process itself of fitting them together. A patterned harmony can be analyzed into its component parts and is related to the surrounding harmonies through those parts; its pattern is what it is because all those things can fit together. Because of this, a harmony is defined in terms of its relations, not in terms of any isolated nature. On the other hand, the patterned harmony has its own existential process of integrating things together, and this is its own essential individuality. Without the essential features of the process of integration, the harmony would reduce to its components and their relations. Without the relational components, there would be nothing to integrate, hence no definiteness of integration. Therefore, a harmony is a harmony of two different kinds of features, the conditional ones and the essential ones; neither is more important than the other. This conception differs both from atomisms that give too much autonomy to isolated individuals, externally related by somewhat unreal laws, and from idealisms or monisms that swallow up all existential differences in superunities.

If there are harmonies existing fully in a present moment, their existential integration is exhausted in that moment's present temporality. They are related to a host of past harmonies because those harmonies enter in to the present moment as conditions to be integrated. Even a fully present harmony thus is both relatonal through its conditional features and existential through its essential ones.

Most harmonies are not exhausted in any present moment, however, but have a temporal thickness, a growth and development. The temporal thickness of these "discursive" harmonies must not be forgotten. A discursive harmony is a moving thing. At any date in its career it has some achieved, actualized, past identity, and some future identity. The project of actualization at the present date involves existential integration of its own past and other past conditions within the limits of normative possibilities for its future and the future of the world. As discursive, such a harmony is an integration of conditional and essential features in all three modes of temporality — past, present, and future. When its whole career is finished and it has only past temporality, a discursive harmony can be analyzed in terms of the patterns it actually achieved, moment by moment. But precisely because it was a discursive harmony, a full understanding would have to include the options it rejected along the way, and the reasons why at each stage.

For discursive harmonies with interesting degrees of freedom, such as human beings, what is actually achieved is sometimes not as important as how the person faced choices among other options. Before the harmony is actualized at all — when it has exclusively future temporality — there is, of course, so much indeterminateness as to make speculations about choices difficult. But because the possible discursive harmony is a person, the future is structured so that first the person will go to school, then choose a career, possibly a mate, a place to live, and so forth. It is the very nature of discursive harmonies not to be complete at any date that could be a present moment of actualization. Rather, they actualize first this stage of affairs and then that, with the consequence that those harmonies are not fully real at any given date, even when they are fully actualized; as actualized, they still have temporally thick past actuality.

The Taoists and Confucianists have created a cultural aesthetic and morality for a theory of things in relations such as this. On the one hand, they emphasize the present inner spontaneity and individuality of things; on the other hand, they call attention and respect to the relatedness of things outside present temporality. They articulate the deference each thing's temporally thick existence pays to other things. (In our enthusiasm for Chinese temporality, let us not forget the ironies recounted in the second chapter.)

It is of utmost importance, morally and metaphysically, to acknowledge the depth of value and achieved intrinsic reality in a temporally thick thing. Part of the general culture of modernity seems to be a forgetting of this depth in things. Heidegger argued with great insight that the cultural effect of modern science is to lead us to assume that the world is made of things that constitute resources for our use.[2] Of course, it is possible to treat things, including people, as usable resources. But this is to be untrue to the depths of their reality and value. However we might, by right or obligation, employ things for our use, or think of them as possible resources, the more fundamental truth is their intrinsic achieved reality and value of which usability is at best an aspect. Persons, trees, mountains, stars, and seas all have depths for transcending any usable surface. These and other focal realities should be the orientation points around which we comport our sense of what is really important, orientation points that can tell us whether our own purposes are worthy.[3] The truth of our own being consists largely in how we acknowledge, represent, and make our way through the depths of the things in our world. The worldly natural piety of classical Chinese high philosophy, Confucian and Taoist, embodies that moral point. The metaphysics I have sketched shows how it makes sense in a world that is also scientific.

III. Enduring Individuals and Systems

The central practical problems for moral reflection have to do with those values consisting in the achievement of systematic environments, filled with valuable individuals, and with those values involving the special claims, if any, made by human individuals and societies. The values about which we need to reflect are those achieved in, or inappropriately failing to be achieved in, natural environments, social institutions, and people in their personal relations.

These problems can never be addressed adequately until we understand just what kinds of values are involved in both cases, in commensurable terms, and understand also what their relations are. More than that, we need to understand appreciatively the specific environmental systems involved, physical and social, with their specific values.

As an antidote to ecology, I would like to call attention here to the special kinds of values to be found in human life, values that are likely to be neglected when employing ecological models that treat people as species members and niche occupiers. These are the values focused on by Confucianists.

The temporal endurance of a human being is not just the maintenance of typical patterns through a long stretch of time, nor the growth of a maturing organism embodying a diachronic career pattern. It is also the case that at any time within a person's life, the existential process of integrating life's elements includes both past and future states of the person as essential, not merely conditional, elements. That is to say, a contemporary pattern does not merely integrate past and future states with present conditions, but does so essentially. Who the person is now depends in essential ways on that person's identity in the past and future. There are thus special patterns that a person develops over time, such as moral identity, rationality, ego identity, family and social role identity, building one upon the others. These discursively developed patterns must be embodied in each moment for the person to be himself or herself. Most of the structures of the social environment are designed to foster these epitomes of human achievement that need to be integrated across time into personal identity. These are the virtues that, although socially defined, must be individually developed and require the person to take a somewhat self-conscious position vis-à-vis the normative demands of life's situations. In order to understand that it is necessary to look more closely at human freedom and systems.

A human being, like any entity or discursive harmony, can to some degree value up or value down the things conditioning it at any moment, including elements of its own past. Within the limits set by its conditions, an entity might be able to integrate them in more than one way. The ways differ from one another not only structurally but in the values to which they give importance. One option might keep certain of the past values intact, perhaps even enhancing them by their surroundings, while paring down other past conditions with their values to subordinate instrumental roles, and eliminating yet another past conditions entirely from having any continuing influence.[4]

Process philosophers have sometimes overestimated the extent of this freedom. So far as natural science has determined, a great many actual entities are so rigidly conditioned by past conditions that there is only one way in which they can integrate their components to come to actuality. This rigidity is lawfulness in nature. Furthermore, it is a source of an important dimension of freedom for human beings, namely, the freedom to exercise control over the intended but distant future results of actions. If nature were at least partially rigid, we couldn't reach beyond ourselves.

The point to be stressed about choice is that although each conditioning element enters a harmony with its own intrinsic value, that value must be modified in order to be integrated with the values of the others, and the modifications might be diminishments as well as enhancements. Where nature is tightly organized according to rigid law, values tend to be transferred intact, because the conditions limiting one entity are pretty much the same as those limiting the other entities. But in human affairs, where there seems to be a wide range of free play and nonintegration, the values of the past can be transformed radically as they pass through agents and institutions. Questions of justice and morality often have to do with the transformation of values in process of transmission from one mode of integration to another.

A person can play roles in many systems at once, and he or she may value up or value down these roles, within the limits set by the past conditions. The heart of this idea is that a large group of things, including people, can be organized according to a pattern in which each thing plays a role unique to itself. A person may not have to play his or her role blindly, but might grasp the whole pattern, or at least a large part of it, and determine for himself or herself the particular role. Part of the solidity of nature is that whole systematic patterns can be "massively inherited," as Whitehead put it, and thus passed down from one generation to another. Of course, there are patterns within patterns, tissues within organs, organs within organisms, organisms within environments, structured environments within ecosystems, and so on. Systematic parts of larger systems may have something of a life of their own, only accidentally locked into the larger system and thus setting the larger systems at jeopardy of dissolution.

Systems can be described as more or less tight depending on whether the conditions that make their parts possible are more or less identical with the conditions that surround the whole. Social systems such as the economic, religious, or judiciary are not tight. They encompass subsystems of material artificats such as trade goods, church buildings, and so on, of ideas and images, of institutions that divide people into social roles by habits, by exercise of authority, by force, by human necessities such as hunger, safety, and the like, subsystems of the spread of natural and geographical conditions, and so forth. Each of these subsystems is affected by conditions other than economic and thus has a partially independent career. Furthermore, the large social systems sometimes, but only partially, interface with one another, so that economics is affected by politics and religion but not wholly determined by them.

An individual can play one or many roles in a social system such as the economic — for instance, as producer, consumer, manager, or "necessary victim" — and the roles themselves may be complex, producing many things, consuming some things but not others, and so forth. Each of these roles in all its nuances conveys values through the system to the individual who must accept them with the conditions necessary to play the role. Insofar as the role-conditions are accepted, the transmitted values partially define the person. Not only does the individual receive and embody the values in the roles, but the very playing of the role is to transmit back to the system the role's own contribution. So the system is affected by the individual. More important, if there is more than one way to play the role, then the system is affected by values that come from outside the system in question, the individual might make unique and novel contributions to the system.

An individual can play diverse roles in many social systems at once, and this fact is the source of much human freedom. Individuals value up and value down different systems, while playing acceptable roles in all. One person gives priority to job, another to family, another to creative pursuits. Not all social situations allow much free play here — one of the pains of poverty is that it does not. But in most social situations we can both value the diverse systems up or down and achieve greater or lesser harmony and resonance among them. Wholeness of life is not only playing all the important roles well but also bringing some mutual reinforcement to the lot of them, as differently played over the years of a changing career.

A theory that both traces the transmissions of values through patterns of social organization and understands how individuals integrate their multiple roles is true social theory. Human beings are not only integrations of diverse roles; they also develop their own character, layer by layer. Our discussion can now turn to individual development.

IV. Discursive Individuals and the Essentially Human

A human being is a discursive individual whose essential features determine integration through time. At any one present moment, there are not only spontaneous novel essential features, but inherited essential features of character, and future derived essential features giving long-term norms. These essential features cannot be conceived helter-skelter, however. They fall into classes that constitute specific levels of essential human reality.

What are the structures built up through growth, maturation, and learning that constitute the human? Although embodied at every moment of a person's life, once actualized, these structures exist only with temporal thickness; they build upon one another hierarchically, and they interpenetrate, affecting one another both essentially and merely conditionally as circumstances dictate. Let us call these structures "essential epitomes" of the human. The word "epitome" suggests both that they are universal structures essential to humanity, and that the structures are vague, requiring specialization in each person and allowing of many different embodiments and developments. To call them "essential" indicates both that they are essential to human life and also that their own identity requires essential features reaching discursively across a person's spread through all three temporal modes.

The essential epitomies I am about to mention are taken from Paul Weiss's book, *Privacy*.[5] They are intended by Weiss as the epitomies of an otherwise undifferentiated private power and are contrasted by him with public structures. I am not necessarily committed to that contrast. Nor do I want to claim that this list of essential epitomies is exhaustive, or that all are of equal weight. Nevertheless, Weiss's list is extraordinarily insightful and, at the very least, illustrates the general point about temporally thick human structures bound together by essential features reaching across time.

1. *Sensitivity* is the capacity to establish imaginative contact with what our bodies make available.[6] By "imagination" here I mean what Kant had in mind as the synthesis by virtue of which merely physical stimuli become formed into the stuff of experience.[7] That experiential stuff involves, within sensitivity, an ability to discriminate qualities. Sensitivity requires a temporal spread, because the body must be mastered and unified in experience to the point that it is revelatory of what is beyond it. The bodily qualities in sensitivity paradoxically are both termini of experience and gates through which the world is sensed. The more nuanced and mature one's sensitivity, the more one's physical feel of the world can sense moods, dangers, and other subtle qualities. A person embodies a cultivated sensitivity.

2. *Sensibility* is the organization of the person so as to be appreciative of values conveyed experientially.[8] Qualities sensed have af-

fective tones that may be registered in experience; but it requires a somewhat developed sensibility to appreciate those tones, to give them organized weight in experience, to seek out and nurture the good and avoid the bad. Sensibility refined becomes good taste; and when fully civilized, it constitutes the human activity of enjoying and cultivating the good. Sensibility is a sure prerequisite for the moral life.

3. *Need* is the organization of the person to seek out things not yet possessed without which one is incomplete.[9] Some needs are relevant to physical existence, but others, no less important, are relevant for the development and exercise of the essential human epitomies. There can be yet other needs that are wholly contingent. A need involves the identification of a lack and of the activities or structures appropriate for fulfilling that need. Some social systems, including the familial and the economic, are essential to human life because of their correlation with basic needs.

4. *Desire* differs from need in that its satisfaction is motivated and justified by the perceived merit in the object of desire rather than by the perceived lack or incompleteness in the one who needs.[10] Thus, while need is always, if justifiably, selfish, desire can be selfless. Weiss takes the sexual urge to procreation to be the elementary instance of desire. Although I believe this neglects the greater role that need plays in sexuality, it ties in with Plato's correct analysis of eros, beginning with biological attraction. Desire is responsive to the attractiveness of the object, and the organization of the personality around desire can turn it into a need. That is, a person is defined ecstatically as incomplete without the good desired. The objects of desire in the first instance, however, are selfless, such as beauty, justice, and the like.

5. *Orientation* is an epitomy of personal structure by virtue of which one relates to an environment, a milieu in which all the other epitomies can be exercised.[11] Constituted by activities that use the other epitomies, orientation is the developed organization of activities that takes into account one's body, place, basic relations with others, institutions, extent and terrain of movement, and scale of options. No atomic moment of experience has an orientation, which comes from relating one's enduring organism to an enduring environment, both through changes. Orientation organizes the values in the environment to be relevant to the other epitomies and to particular conditional interests.

6. *Sociality* is the organization of the person not only to interact with other people through niches in a social environment but to be accountable to oneself and others for the playing of social roles.[12] With sociality arises the elementary form of the trait that classically distinguishes the human, namely, rationality. Rationality is not cleverness at problem-solving but rather intelligent behavior that takes itself to be representative of any intelligent behavior. To play a social role is to act as a representative of the social group in the performance of the role. The meaning of playing a role in a society includes identifying oneself as a representative of the society, even if one is fit for only one particular role, and even if one is the only person in the society who can play it, as the son of the chief is uniquely destined to be the next chief. Sociality requires responding to oneself as a whole, interpreted as a type, and integrated into systematic connections with other people. The essential features uniting a discursive individual must convey this sense of wholeness and sense of being of a type. In most respects, the sense of wholeness derives from an appreciation of the type made reflexively relevant to oneself; my sense of wholeness comes from seeing just how I work out being a spouse, parent, teacher, and thinker.

7. *Mind* is the epitomy of the person that is explicitly representative, because it is the action in accordance with abstract or eternal principles such as those of logic or mathematics.[13] For mind, activity is normed by the principles that should norm anyone's activities, rather than being normed by its success at satisfying need or desire, for instance. There are, of course, many aspects of a proper account of mind that are not discussed here, including intentionality, memory, and consciousness. The point, however, is to stress the temporal stretch of mind and the fact that it is essential for any mental moment to take up a stance not only on the other moments of that mind but also on the relation between mental acts and the logical forms that make the acts mental. Of course, mentality does not require an explicit identification of the principles but rather a built-in criticism of potential mental acts according to their participation in the principles.

8. *Resolution* is that organization of the person capable of transforming the various values sensed, responded to with developed sensibility, needed, desired, oriented to one's life, socially structured and mentally understood, into goals, objectives, ends, and the good.[14] Weiss points out that goals are the objects of preferences,

other things being equal; ends are the objects of will in which complex behavior is organized in a commitment to secure the end; and
the good is the object of responsiblity which seeks to justify its objects
by seeing that they are the best. Resolution is the organization of the
multitude of habits and activities required for these voluntary
dimensions of life. Although some people are extremely irresolute, it
is essential to their humanity that they have some resolution and be
judged accordingly.

9. *Autonomy* is not merely separation of oneself from definition
by others but also the positive identification of oneself "to be deserv-
ing of rewards or punishments for what is publicly done," in Weiss's
language.[15] It involves taking over some of the causal processes in
one's action so that the constellation of one's own character and relevant choices is the morally effective author of the actions.

10. *Responsibility* couples a sense of autonomy with a sense of
obligation to what is objectively right or wrong.[16] Of course, the
determination of objective right or wrong is complicated. But
without some judgment of one's self-identity being oriented to norms
as objectively right or wrong, there is no taking of oneself to be
responsible. Without being responsible, one is not a self.

11. The *I* or *ego* is an ongoing organized activity coordinating
other activities with an intentional representation of the self. It is the
expression of the person in a self-reflective mode, contoured by its
representation of itself to itself. The representation may include not
only the particularized essential epitomies but also the particular
situation and historical elements of personal identity. The *I*, in addition, recognizes and represents the absolute particularlities, the
haecceities, of the person. In fact, a person doesn't really have a self
unless there is an *I* that represents these many facets as being the
self's. As soon as there is a capacity to represent oneself and to act
with responsibility toward what that self is and should be, there is
the normative responsibility to develop that representation.
Autonomy, responsibility, and the *I* are intimately interdefined.

Beyond these essential epitomies articulated by Weiss are the
essential interactions they entail with natural and social systems.
The natural systems are the necessary background, and the social
systems exist to make possible the development and exercise of the
essential epitomies of human life. Since there is a reciprocity between what culture has developed as the human and what the
human demands of culture, as both Confucians and Puritans knew,

it should be possible to define the social and human sciences in an harmonious way. In this discussion I have begun with the personal to make contact with social systems, but it is perfectly conceivable to work the other way.

A theory of a social system such as economics, in order to trace out the values in its subject matter, needs to trace the transmission and creation of values within the system and also the interaction of values between the system and each of the essential epitomizations. An economic system that does well in increasing the amount and quality of goods satisfying a given society's needs and desires might have disastrous effects on the sensibilities, resolution, and autonomy of its people. This is one way to interpret part of the Marxist critique of capitalism. Liberals criticize the ideals of Marxism for addressing basic needs, sensibilities, and resolution at the cost of the elements of the self. A good economic theory would build in to its very structure a methodology for paying explicit attention to all these matters.

The list of essential epitomies is, of course, hypothetical and provisional. So is the current state of the organization of the disciplines of social and natural science. If they are correlated and set in juxtaposition for mutual criticism, however, it is possible to envision the development of a unified common image for the sciences, geared to the display and explanation of the transmission of value. This would involve the quantified articulation of structures, but oriented to show how those structures bear and transmit value. Such a theory would be hypothetical and demand empirical, objective testing. But it would also be framed in such a way that issues of justice and morality would be stated directly. Valuational thinking would thus be reintegrated with the quantitative and qualitative thinking characteristic of modern science.

The argument has now been returned to the initial concern about the kinds of understanding of structure and causation required for moral reflection. The kinds of understanding range from the metaphysical through the cosmological to the empirical and scientific. In all these, it is crucial to be able to represent how values are affected by the kinds of causation at stake. In addition, we have traced out certain important structures for human life as such, structures whose values are especially to be respected. Having said all this about scientific modes of understanding, there are two important qualifications to be added.

The first is that moral reflection only 50% follows out structural and causal implications about the worths of things it appreciates. The other 50% of its effort is to objectify and criticize theoretical elements defining the structural and causal models used. This is the work of the "humanities" that ask about the relation between scientific models and their subject. The humanistic question is usually asked indirectly, because a direct questioning just presupposes another model. Its indirect methods include history, examination of rhetoric, and backing up to presuppositions. The humanities also use irony, which mentions the second qualification.

As I argued in Chapters One and Two, any conceptualization is but one finite way of articulating the infinite subject matter. There are better and worse conceptualizations, of course, and the point of this chapter has been to give some criteria for the former. But one still should maintain a sense of irony about the ultimate vanity, though necessity, of attempting to understand. It is not that one's understanding need be false; but it will always be limited and peculiar from a perspective across the limits.

V. Rudimentary Ethical Vision

Bearing in mind that irony, it is now possible to sketch a popular vision of the ethical problem. The ethical problem is to harmonize local things into a high level of value by means of being true to and resonating with the conditions undergirding them. Because of the metaphysical analysis of conditions, we now have a very broad vision of the range of conditions. Several points may be collected in summary.

1. With respect to ongoing structures, there are hierarchies upon hierarchies of conditions. The chemical, thermal, and atmospheric systems of the earth must be in a certain order for the biosphere to be possible. The biosphere must be in a certain order for human life to be possible. Human life must be organized in certain ways for civilized social order and literate culture to be possible. There must be civilized social order and literate culture for concerns with freedom and democracy even to be problematic.

Therefore, a dimension of ethical concern running throughout all problems is to attain attunement of the higher levels to the lower. The higher levels need to respect the nature of the lower and to achieve their own harmonies in consonance with the ongoing nature and activity of the lower. In the relatively deep levels of nature, lack of attunement manifests itself as instability, abrupt change, and decay of complicated structures that were only temporarily possible because the lower levels had not expressed all their real nature. Towns hanging on the slopes of volcanoes should not expect long duration, or blame divine malice or forgetfulness when the lava flows. On the relatively high levels of animal and human life, lack of attunement means suffering, as when the body cannot sustain a poison, or severe cold, or the trauma of a fall. To the extent people can modify various levels of the hierarchies making up their world, an extent greatly increased by scientific technology, they are responsible for living in harmony with the deepest powers of the universe.

There is a tendency in our culture to notice only the superficial layers of our world, those we name pragmatically. Yet the richness of moral sensitivity discussed in Chapter Five requires the cultivation of the capacity to appreciate the resonances of level after level, all the way down. Perhaps we have romanticized the capacity of "primitive" people, such as some Native Americans, to feel with the earth. But even if they did not actually have a deep ecological vision so as to apprehend the layered achieved values of things, we certainly need to develop it ourselves.

2. With respect to the passage of time and to change in structure, it is obligatory to be true to the values achieved in the past, arranged hierarchically, adventitiously, or intentionally. Being true to those values does not necessarily mean repeating them. But it does mean that we should comport ourselves in such a way that if we do not repeat them, we have good reasons for not doing so. Forgetfulness is an evil. Just as one can create temporarily a high level of order that is out of sync with its conditions, one can create a temporal present forgetful of its past. Without the attuned resonance with the past, however, the value in the present is mainly illusory. At least, it is reduced to an aesthetics of the moment, and it demeans the ongoing quality of human life.

3. With respect to the creative present, at the human level of organized harmony, the norms for integrating the contingent conditions may well be unique. Reality is in constant change, and so novel norms are always coming into relevance. Yet those norms govern not just the superficial, pragmatically nameable elements but also their historical and systematic depths. If we think with the prop-

erly imaginative metaphysical scope, our deliberations about what to do ought to be mostly about the elements of nature, and only a small part about the items of strictly human affairs. The most important moral justification for natural science is that it seems the best way to put us in touch with the real variables that give the human level of existence its suffering. This point has enormous importance for moral priorities. Respect for the environment has priority over improving diet; improving diet has priority over freedom; securing freedom has priority over the enjoyment of high culture. From the human standpoint, the operative moral causality goes the other way: A high culture is necessary in order to secure freedom, freedom is necessary in order to alter customs so as to improve diet, a good diet is necessary in order to exercise restraint on the environment. It is no contradiction that the order of conditioning and the order of human care should sometimes run opposite to one another.

A metaphysical vision of causal patterns along which value is passed provides an expansive corrective to the scope of most moral reflection. It also provides a vague form for making normative description methodic. That is, normative description should follow out the lines of causation sketched by the axiological theory of the cosmos. To make the vague form useful for normative description, however, would require that the sciences fill in the causal patterns, articulating them in ways that make the carry-over of value perspicuous.

8

Authority

T he fabric of this argument about moral reflection weaves the warp of inward personal development through the woof of outward social conditions, emphasizing the deep real values of things. The fulcrum of the inward considerations is responsibility, and the personal character needed to understand and fulfill it. The fulcrum of the outward is the obligatoriness of achieved value and its potential transformations. The concluding three chapters, on freedom and privacy, responsibilities in conflict, and death, will follow the inward direction beyond the instrumentalities of morals to the ontological dimension. Failure to resolve conflicting responsibilities, and the guilt of this, is the most inwardly essential definition of the human person; the Western language of guilt and responsibility finds Chinese counterparts in the analysis of selfishness and sageliness, however greatly the models of self differ. The inward part of the moral situation differs from relatively more outward considerations such as the conditions for moral discussion, the nature of value, and how value becomes obligatory. All of these themes, however, and the others discussed in this book, are of a continuous piece with respect to moral reflection. Moreover, all are important in the light of the Puritan's heritage.

But the heart of our moral confusion, and of the Puritan vision, its most intense light, radiates at the point of contrast between the infinitely demanding (divine) cosmos and the finite, failed, and faulted person. A sharply etched harmony, that contrast is more a tortured conflict than a benign unity, and thus the fundamental locus of Puritan irony. But how hard it is to sustain moral irony! The temptation is always to fall either down the slope of cynicism or over the brink of moral obsessiveness. Puritans have never been known for cynicism, although I wager that is because the cynical among them no longer identified with Puritanism. The Puritan nightmare is moral obsessiveness. No one objects when this takes the form merely of unremittant seriousness, although that soon becomes boring. The objection comes when the obsessiveness extends itself to other people in the form of assertion of authority. The great historic fault of the Puritan was authoritarianism.

Partly, the fall into authoritarianism was a function of the era in which the Puritan flourished — Divine Right and the English Revolution, the authority of science over witchcraft, the challenge of establishing a government for the Errand in the Wilderness. In larger part, the authoritarianism was a temptation to which the Puritan emphasis on responsibility is especially prone. If everyone is responsible for the obligations falling upon everyone, particularly in chaotic times, what possible limits can be imposed on the moral impulse to get everybody else organized? More treacherous yet, in those conditions what can limit the condemnation of those who don't comply with what one thinks is their place in the carrying out of one's own responsibility? In a monarchical conception, people should comply with their roles in the fulfillment of the responsibilities of the sovereign. In a Liberal conception, people should comply with the minimalist roles established by the sovereign, who is (for most Contract theorists) the people themselves. But in a Puritan conception, each individual is responsible for organizing everyone else — a plurality of sovereigns, as it were, each of whom can demand responsible roles for the others. A threatening conception indeed.

If the Puritan's ghost is to recover its sense of humor, it will only be because we can find a way to prevent the corruption of the Puritan vision into an authoritarianism of all against all. I pointed out in Chapter Two that both the Puritan and Confucian had failed to solve the problem of authority — the Confucian suffers the same liability to authoritarianism. I want now to reconsider the problem of authority in detail. The purpose of this chapter is to reconceive authority and reconcile the conclusions with the Puritan and Confucian emphasis on responsibility and participation. Actually, I intend

to attack and reject the notion of authority and to replace it with notions of responsibility and participation. The resulting polity will
surely draw the Puritan's smile: no authority but a strong emphasis
on public social action—Big Government Anarchism!

I. The Failure of Authority

"Authority," in its strong traditional sense, is the defining characteristic of a position in a social group such that the decisions made
from that position are the group's decision, in analogy with the way
individuals' voluntary choices are their decisions. Authority needs to
be more than the mere consensus of the individuals in the group
because it binds those who might dissent, as a personal decision
binds even those contrary interests and motives within one's personality. Authority is more than merely the "correct" decisions, because
responsibility for deciding is always lodged with individuals and only
responsible decisions are authoritative, as individuals must adopt
their choices subjectively for them to be their decisions. There is no
justification for political authority conceived this way.

A social group cannot be conceived by analogy with an individual without contradicting individual responsibility. Although
there are norms for social groups, as I have maintained, no individuals have such standing that those norms are exclusively their
responsibility; that is, no one has authoritative position. Individuals
may be "posited," in the modern sense of that word, as delegated
agents of the members of the social group, exercising direct responsibility. But such "positive" authority is legitimate only to the extent it
directly carries out the distributive responsibility of those positing; those
positions are not authoritative for people whose responsibility is to dissent or depose, and thus they are not decisions of the social group.

The safeguard to be erected against Puritan excess, therefore, is
its own emphasis on responsibility. Because individual responsibility
is inalienable, there can be no conception of an authoritative group,
and hence no authority for the group. The obligations for the group
divide into individual responsibilities. This does not diminish the
fact that individuals are largely defined by their responsibilities to
the group and those arising from social existence.

Political theory means, among other things, the exhibition or
demonstration of the normative ground for political authority. But

authoritative structures, being merely positive, indicate that the political community is merely positive. This is true of the natural-traditional polis of ancient times, of the divine community in either the ancient Hebrew or medieval senses, and of the contractual community of modern Liberalism. Individual responsibility contradicts people's allowing themselves to be contained exclusively within, or normatively bound exclusively by, a positive political community.

This does not mean that there are no objective norms, as modern Liberals sometimes have thought. Norms apply to any thing, person, collection, organization, or situation that could be better or worse. But only individual persons have a responsibility to norms such that the norms become binding obligations. Individuals may devote themselves to the norms of their social group; devoted or not they are bound by them. When devoted, they can be leaders perhaps, servants of the people, and they may obtain *de jure* legitimacy in their social roles by "positive" authorization from other members of the group according to some institutionalized scheme for dividing responsibilities. But they are not authoritative for the group as such, only for its posited political elements.

Nor does the theory of individual responsibility mean that politics is not a positive sphere of its own, that it is merely instrumental to some other sphere such as the economic or religious. On the contrary, politics is the sphere of social participation in which one sets the conditions for fulfilling one's social obligations. There are many positive positive (posited) political elements such as constitutional legislation, executive and judicial structures; and there are civilized institutional traditions such as the rule of law that undergird them. These elements are the reverse side of the positive or artificial creation of privacy for individuals; by virtue of these elements, everyone does not have to have active responsibility for everything all the time. According to their situation, these positive elements may be extremely worthy. They are outstanding achievements of civilization and are worth defending with the sacrifice of comfort, personal interest, and life. But they are not authoritative over individuals, however valid or good they are, except in the limited artificial sense. Individuals have the inalienable personal responsibility either to adopt them for their merit or to negate them and at the same time negate something of their own definition deriving from the positive political community.

By Plato's time, societies in ancient Greece were conceived to have "natural" positions of authority. "Natural" meant not "by birth" but rather what is needed for human life to be fulfilled as human. Just as, for Aristotle, people need to learn the habits of language from practice in order to be human, so societies need positions of authority.[1] Authority functions to decide matters both of utility for social organization and of political virtue; for the public life of people requires a decent polis in which they can develop and exercise political excellence. Although both Plato and Aristotle vigorously debated the constitution and forms authoritative positions might take, they did not seriously question the naturalness or appropriateness of such positions. Even the sophists who doubted the possibility of justifying norms for political authority did not question the need or appropriateness of it.[2]

The context in which this view made sense was that of the polis. As Jaeger and others have shown, the polis is a community such that people become human through leading political, public lives.[3] Life apart from the public is idiocy. How is it possible that individuals' responsibilities could set them at odds with the polis? The life of Socrates is the classic case. Socrates articulated and insisted upon most of the essential ingredients of personal responsibility. When this led to a contradiction with the possibilities offered for public life, he was given a choice between death and separation from the polis; he chose the former. In his imagined discussion with the laws, the Athenian authorities, he likened Athens to parents and said he cannot abandon filial loyalty.[4] How Confucian! He could not conceive himself to exist as a person outside the matrix of his polis and chose to make his martyrdom a testimony to personal responsibility within the polis.

From our perspective, Socrates' argument was specious. He could justify the life encompassing authority of the parent-laws only by representing them as gods. Yet the positive law, even the tradition, of Athens is anything but divine. It may indeed be the source, the matrix of life. But personal responsibility does not consist in being bound by one's sources. Unless the sources are indeed the cosmic origins of one's materials, norms, and responsibilities, one's relation to the sources is either through positive social roles or through personal commitment to the sources. The former is limited, and the latter supposes that one's personal will is authoritative and that the object of commitment derives its authority from oneself. Socrates attempted to *make* the laws of Athens authoritative by his own choice to bind himself to them. But this was only to acknowledge that they were not genuinely authoritative. Although he asserted his own integrity, it was but the prelude to the collapse of the alleged authority of the polis in the Hellenistic age.

George Allan has written an extraordinary book on Socrates' problem. *The Importances of the Past: A Meditation on The Authority of Tradition*.[5] His argument is that the achievements of the past, both of structure and value, are intrinsic to the past and help define and give identity to the present. In this light, were Socrates to deny his Athenian sources as the roots giving meaning and worth to his life, he would indeed be denying his identity. Allan is surely right about the importance of the past as the source of meaning and value. But it is also the source of contradiction and evil. The other half of Socrates' philosophy, the part affirmed in his choice to affirm his sources, is that responsibility requires taking up a critical stance toward the past. Sometimes one's inherited identity must be denied. There are limits to this criticism beyond which lies madness. But within those limits are the normative choices of everyday life, and of most of our cultural crises.

Both the ancient Hebrews and the medieval Christians thematized, in different ways, Socrates' suggestion that divinity is authoritative. In a cosmo-polis with God as head, the divine position could be construed as genuinely authoritative. This view was attractive in times when the particularistic polis was destroyed or eclipsed, as in the Babylonian captivity, the Hellenistic age, or the middle ages of Europe. If God is the Lord, then one cannot help feeling at home and fulfilled in the cosmo-polis; and, therefore, individual responsibility is part of the seamless cosmic whole. But God, on any of these views, has no finite position within the community and must exercise authority through something that does: through scripture, through an interpretive community of rabbis, through ecclesiastical leaders, or through divinely representative kings. Can an individual relate to any finite representatives as authority? No, not in a genuine sense, because each is authoritative only through being divinely posited. Only people's social roles relate to posited social structures, and individual responsibility stands over those roles and outside them. The European reformation of the sixteenth century asserted the priority of individual responsibility over religious authorities, and by the nineteenth century it had carried it over the alleged scriptural authority. Some theologicans of the hermeneutical tradition continue to assert the authority of scripture as within the hermeneutical circle; but the hermeneutical circle is merely an attempt to reassert the natural-traditional authority of a polis for scholars. Gadamer, for instance, argues as cited in Chapter Five that authority is a function of proper prejudices opening us to the truth. He is unclear, however, whether the authority involved attaches to the prejudices so that we can test it by discovering whether they do in fact open us to important truths, or whether it characterizes the beings to which we are opened, in which case references to the "truth" are beside the point. He says it derives from "reason."

Modern Liberal political theory began with Hobbes.[6] In the sixteenth chapter of *Leviathan* he wrote:

> A person, is he, whose words or actions are considered, either as his own, or as representing the words or actions of another man, or of any other thing to whome they are attributed, whether Truly or by Fiction.
>
> When they are considered his owne, then is he called a Naturall Person: And when they are considered as representing the words and actions of an other, then is he a Feigned or Artificiall person.
>
> Of Persons Artificiall, some have their words and actions Owned by those whome they represent. And then the Person is the Actor; and he that owneth his words and actions, is the Author: In which case the Actor acteth by Authority.[6]

In the succeeding chapter he defined civil society as the situation in which people agree with each other to give up their power and strength to one person or assembly who will act for them all; that is, they convey their individual authority to the sovereign who, having the multitude as the collective author of the sovereign actions, is authoritative over each. Locke was less generous in making the sovereign the actor who possesses all the authority of the people, claiming that authority could not cleanly be given to a sovereign but only delegated. Rousseau agreed that the sovereign's authority is delegated from the multitude of individual authors, though he insisted that the government is not sovereign; rather it is the peole acting collectively as the general will.

The Liberal theory rested upon the modern notion of position. That is, the authoritative sovereign is posited as such by the individuals who authorize its actions as their own. Modern Liberal political structure is "positive" because it is "put there" by the will of the people. But this is precisely the point at which positive political authority is ambiguous. If one says, with Hobbes, that the multitude bestows its authority on the sovereign *simpliciter*, retaining no authorship of its own, then there is only one author and actor in the state, the sovereign. Only the sovereign can have individual responsibility. The subsequent Liberal tradition rejected Hobbes's view because of its denial of individual responsibility and freedom to the citizenry. Furthermore, in Hobbes's contrast between the state of nature and positive civil society (one organism, the sovereign state), individuals are in one or the other but not both. Yet our experience is that personal responsibility demands sometimes that we negate certain of the positive dimensions of political society.

If one says with post-Hobbesian Liberals, on the other hand, that the multitude bestows authority on political positions in only limited ways, as representatives, with delegated authority subject to recall, and with explicit guarantees that certain authorities cannot be alienated from the multitude to positive representatives, in what sense can the authority be real? Since members of the citizenry may be in conflict with one another, the decisions with which some people disagree are not decisive as such for them. The locus of authority shifts back from those who occupy political positions to the system of government that gives them *de jure* authority. One says, then, that constitutional rule is authoritative. But at some point individuals may come to question the decisions made under constitutional rule to such an extent that they question the rule itself. After prudential arguments for constitutional rule have been found insufficient, there is no real authority left unless one can argue that everyone is bound ultimately by a civil contract. Yet who can admit to being bound ultimately by a civil contract while maintaining personal responsibility? Of course, one can choose to commit oneself to a contract of constitutional rule, but the authority here is one's own responsibility in the choice, and the question is whether the social contract is the proper content of one's responsibility.

II. Responsibility and Authority

The conclusion of the discussion so far is that the only authority sustaining legitimacy is the sense in which an individual is the

author of just that individual's actions. Authority reduces thus to individual responsibility, and there is no normative legitimacy to
claims for authority of or for the body politic. I want now to review
certain aspects of the theory of responsibility developed so far and to
restate it in political terms. Three these will be used for summary
purposes.

1. First is that there are better and worse ways that complex affairs might be organized, and that with varying degrees of thorough-
ness and accuracy as discussed in previous chapters it is possible to
tell the difference between them. Because the better ways are *normative* relative to the worse ways, there are understandable norms for
social and personal matters. The norms are always context-
dependent, since they apply to the organization of specific affairs.
Also, there is always a question about the scope or limits of the particular complex to be analyzed, because different norms apply to different scales of organizations. For instance, do the relevant norms
for a person's action in a particular situation derive from his or her
individual good, from that of the family, the neighborhood, the
state, the profession, the generation? Are these compatible? How
one identifies, as in a science, relevant organizational complexes
itself is a reflection of norms, for norms define the relevant components of things. From history we have learned a great deal about
where to draw identifying limits around potentially chaotic affairs so
as to realize the best norms.

Plato described norms as ways of measuring out the diverse
components of mixtures; affairs of social and personal life are indeed
mixtures.[8] One of John Dewey's lasting contributions is his articulation of the process of social deliberation by which we come to see the
value of one way of mixing affairs over another, how our norms shift
as affairs shift, and how our understanding of norms grows as we
come to appreciate previously obscure implications of the diverse
ways of mixing. Dewey perhaps did not stress enough the value of
self-understanding for fostering those ways of personal and cultural
life that themselves lead to authentic perception and responsibility;
that defect has ably been remedied by thinkers of the critical and
hermeneutical schools.

The thesis that there are objective and understandable norms,
as noted above, runs contrary to the grain of much Liberal thinking.
One, though only one, of the reasons many Liberals are ethical
egoists, is an underlying belief that values themselves are posited by

the will of individuals. This belief is the result not of moral analysis or deliberation but of meta-ethical reflections about metaphysics and knowledge. Classical Liberalism arose in the heyday of ambitious modern science. As pointed out earlier, the metaphysical supposition of that science was that only physical particles, not values, are real; and if the world has objective value, that value derives from the way God regards it, not from any intrinsically valuable character. The epistemological supposition was that knowledge has as its object "facts"; facts are what science knows, which is the paradigm of knowledge. If values enter experience, it is not in the form of knowledge.

Contemporary Liberals divide on the problem of the objectivity of norms. Nozick, for instance, in *Anarchy, State, and Utopia*, places such stress on the importance of individual autonomy that the objects of people's will seem far to outshine any claim for the morality of good social arrangements except insofar as it embodies individual autonomy.[9] Yet in *Philosophical Explanations* he provides a theory of value not unrelated to the one I have developed in earlier chapters.[10] John Rawls gives many examples of careful deliberative analysis of the prudential values of various social arrangements, with appeals similar to those of Hobbes and Locke about the advantages of the civil contract. But with his concern to maximize the minimum possible outcome, he argues that we should suppose that people will behave egoistically, regardless of the moral demands contrary to personal interest.[11]

The thesis that there are objective and knowable norms does not at all entail that people will act in accordance with them. Its practical moral, however, is that people *should* be concerned to discover what is worthwhile in their personal and social environment and to attend accordingly. This is vastly different from the moral attitude that follows from the thesis that there are no values except in the sense that people posit certain things as valuable, for my thesis accentuates the imperative to inquire. Indeed, it entails the responsibility to be responsible mentioned earlier. The thesis of value-objectivity differs also from the moral attitude of egoism that deflects attention from social affairs broader than the scope of one's personal interests.

2. The second thesis grows out of the problem raised just now. Regarding the relation of individuals to norms, who is obliged by norms? My thesis is that whereas norms apply to or measure the

situation for which they depict the better organization, they are *obligatory* only for subjects who have moral standing. That is, only moral subjects can have responsibility for realizing norms. The reason there is no real political authority is that the state has no position that is intrinsically responsible for social norms; political offices derive their responsibility from individuals.

This thesis emphasizes the distinction raised in Chapter Three between the rightfulness of norms to be realized in objective situations and the standing of individuals who have responsibility to realize them. Authoritarianism is perceived to be bad precisely because the person exercising the authority is thought to be other than the one whose responsibility it is to act; the authoritarian person acts without proper standing.

When does one have responsibility or moral standing? The question, as we have seen, has two levels. The general level refers to the problem of what it is to have responsibility or obligation as such. The more specific level refers to the problem of how to distinguish one person's responsibilities from another's.

Two principal conditions determine having responsibility. The first is that the subject of responsibility stand in some potential causal relation with the state of affairs for which there are norms, so as to be able to make a difference for better or worse. The causal contours of responsibility are complex, especially regarding social affairs, since so many responsible subjects may be involved as potential or actual causes and since persuasion is a kind of cause.[12] Without some potential causal relationship it makes no sense to say one has responsibility in the matter. The various kinds of causal relationship, from necessitated unavoidable involvement to heroic intervention, allow for classification of various kinds of responsibilty.

The second principle determining moral standing is that the agent have the potentiality to adopt the relevant norm as expressing an essential feature in the agent's own constitution, in the sense that the agent is determined then to act so as to fulfill the norm within the limits of the agent's direct and indirect causal powers. To adopt the norm is to set in motion the causal processes involved in acting upon it. The potential for adopting the relevant norm is one of the person's essential features. This contrasts with the conditional features that are the things given to the subject that it must harmonize in order to have a constitution. Essential moral features are the intentional potentiality of adopting the norms as ideal ends for action. The "adoption" has often been called freedom, or free choice, and Kant celebrated it as the autonomy to be a law unto oneself.

A person's potentiality for adopting norms has the same scope as one's potential causality. The obvious paradigm case of having responsibility is one who is conscious of one's choices and chooses deliberately; such a one is held to be fully culpable. We frequently allow excuses to soften culpabilty in other cases. If one is conscious of having to choose but misunderstands the options, we soften culpability if there are reasons why the person should not be expected to understand. Yet there is a moral imperative to understand one's options, beyond mere curiosity, and the person is responsible in the face of the options. If one is not conscious of being in a choice-situation, we sometimes soften the culpability; yet we say that people ought to train themselves to be conscious of these matters. If there are personality factors, for instance neuroses, that cause one to be unaware of the options, we soften the culpability if we think the person could not have overcome these factors; but the development of a character adept at fulfilling the responsibilities we are likely to have under ordinary social conditions is itself one of the most important responsibilities our civilization has recognized.

Only intentional beings, that is, persons, have responsibilities. Artificial persons, such as alleged political authorities, do not have responsibilities of their own, for they do not have the intentionality making them capable of adopting relevant norms. Rather, artificial persons have assigned to them from other persons responsibilities that they take on in an active way so as to allow the others to deactivate their responsibilities in the enjoyment of privacy. This reinterprets Hobbes's view that an artificial person is posited by an author to be an actor with the author's authority. An artificial person — for instance, the Food and Drug Administration — might be posited with responsibilities that allow for, even call for, the exercise of discretion; the exercise of discretion might involve adopting a norm. But, in contrast to a real person, that discretion rests with the responsibility of the society that posited the responsibilities of the FDA. If an official acts within the guidelines for discretion and makes a mistake, he or she may be called imprudent, incompetent, or a failure, but not directly immoral. Furthermore, in similar situations the agency as a whole can be judged imprudently established, incompetent, a failure, or badly justified, but not immoral. The charge of moral or immoral behavior relative to an artificial person is made only with respect to a real person who exercises the office of artificial person, and then only when the person can be distinguished from the office by exceeding the granted discretion, failing the responsibilities assigned to the artificial person, or perhaps misrepresenting his or her capacities and liabilities for holding the office.

Hegel's view in the *Philosophy of Right* is the grandest attempt in modern times to circumvent the above argument.

> The state is the actuality of concrete freedom. But concrete freedom consists in this, that personal individuality and its particular interests not only achieve their complete development and gain explicit recognition for their right (as they do in the sphere of the family and civil society) but, for one thing, they also pass over of their own accord into the interest of the universal, and, for another thing, they know and will the universal; they even recognize it as their own substantive mind; they take it as their end and aim and are active in its pursuit.[13].

Perhaps it is mischievous to tag Hegel with such a strong doctrine of state authority. After all, one of his most ardent disciples was the great English liberal T. H. Green. Furthermore, recent scholars such as John Findlay, Charles Taylor, and Quentin Lauer have shown that Hegel was far more nuanced than he was represented to be by those who launched all out war on absolute idealism. Nevertheless, the words above are Hegel's (as remembered by students who took notes), and they express at least one strain in his thought. For the purpose of my argument, I need only to find him to be a potent alternative to my denial of moral responsibility to the state as such. Individuals, according to Hegel, express their interest in the universal of the state through the legislature; and the executive branch of the government gives particular content to the universal in administering the laws. But since the universal transcends any individuals, and since the individuals themselves transcend themselves by willing it, the government has genuine political authority over and above the citizens. This authority resides in the crown, in which universality and particularity come together. The person of the monarch is the decisive will for the state in an even stronger sense of individual personhood than obtains for individuals in a mere natural situation or in civil society, according to Hegel. Short of a full state, individuals suffer a division between the private particularity of life and public universality of their citizenship; only by participating in the richer subjectivity of a monarchical state can individuals bring their own lives to personal unity. Marx made a similar argument, substituting the ideological interest of the proletariate expressed through the revolutionary party for the monarch.

The answer to be made to this argument constitutes another point referring to the relation between norms and the individual, and is my third main thesis in this section.

3. Individuals have a responsibility to all situations, the values of which are potentially affected by their potential actions. But it is clear that individual persons play roles in several ecosystems at once, and the ecosystems only partially overlap. In positive political structures the ecosystemic roles the person plays may have only partial and adventitious relation to roles in the production of artistic culture, personal friendships, and the shape of the person's own career. Because states of affairs measured by norms distinguishing the better and worse reflect groupings of causal cohesion, one's responsibilities will tend to be oriented toward different, partially overlapping and often adventitiously related areas of life. There is no a priori guarantee that any one system, such as the political, overlaps perfectly and includes all the others. The norms measuring any one systemic area, therefore, need not subsume norms measuring partially independent areas of life. It might be the case that the political norms in a certain context are more important than any others and should override them. But this must be based on an evaluation of the situation, not on the conception of politics as such.

Although one's ecosystemic roles are crucial for understanding one's life, the larger and more realistic frame is one's history, including the adventitious, nonsystematic relationships between relevant ecosystems and how one chooses to adjust the claims of each. In the context of responsibility, the context most essentially reflecting both the givenness and the intentionality of a person's life, individual histories are the best articulation of the entire complex sociophysical environment, over and above ecosystemic articulations.

Hegel's (and Marx's) argument misdefines the responsible development of persons by referring it to the rational demand for surmounting contradiction. For Hegel, the contradiction regarding the state is that the cleavage between the particularity of private life and the universality of public life is overcome in the authoritative sovereignty of the constitutional monarchy. But the allegedly a priori definition of rationality as the overcoming of contradiction is a mistaken reading of life, I believe. It asserts that there must be a unity to the normative fulfillment of life when instead experience itself points to a much more loosely integrated relation among norms. At base is Hegel's underlying belief that life is merely accidental and unreal without a unifying norm, individualized coordination in some sphere transcending the vagaries of individual life. Such rational necessity is a kind of "ought" on Hegel's view. But no such "ought" can be justified unless the empirical affairs of life do indeed belong to a single, completely organic whole. And they do not. Or at least there is little evidence that they do.

The real power of Hegel's argument comes from its criticism of the abstractness of the Liberal political conceptions. According to the underlying Liberal atomistic cosmology, a person is unique and complete in his or her particularity. Relations with other people or with social structures are comparatively abstract and external to the individual; consider such things as transferring property, for instance, and the legal-political systems that establish rules for transfer and protection. Individual political rights, on the Liberal theory, are abstract in applying equally to everyone; as Hegel—and even better, Marx—showed, the Liberal political states does not address or recognize what is concretely and particularly real about persons. In light of this, both Hegel and Marx were able to argue that self-transcendent participation in a higher state or revolutionary movement was a more integrated concrete form of life than the Liberal conception made possible.

Unlike the Liberal conception, despite its authoritarian drawbacks the Puritan view of individual life as constituting itself and acting in the sociophysical environment does not allow the sharp private-particular *versus* public-universal distinction to be drawn. Rather, individuals live by participation in the environment. Over time, people are constituted by taking up the environing factors into themselves. They have a necessity of conforming to the things and structures of the environment, within those limits alone freedom is possible. Furthermore, among the most valued epitomies of human existence is the cultivation of capacities for feeling the environment sensitively and purely. On the side of action rather than receptivity, people's choices at any time initiate complex waves of effects, determined by the causal contours of the various ecosystems in which their choices play roles. Nearly always, the consequences of action are recursive upon the individual. Furthermore, actions often affect not only other individuals but also the causal character of various ecosystems themselves. Responsibility regarding any sphere of affairs, therefore, is likely to have causal ripples in other spheres, and to affect responsibilities in other areas producing conflict and contradition. The best image for individual life with responsibilities is participaton. This is alien to the Liberal image that one is what one owns and that action is trading.

Against Hegel it is true to say that life can be fully concrete, though not necessarily complete or coherent, only by full participation in the various domains of one's environment. It is not necessary to grant transcendent authority to a sovereign body politic whose actions complete one's own. With Hegel, however, it is necessary to admit that the contours of total participation are fragmentary. Unlike Kierkegaard's disappointed Hegelian lament to "will one thing," participation in the fullness of life requires acceptance of fragmentation, partial stories, and inevitable failure to do full justice to any one responsibility because of needs to adjust to the demands of other responsibilities. Buddhism, Christianity, and Hinduism provide cultural testimony to the claim that life can be full while fragmented, incomplete, and in moral failure. If the world *must* make unitary sense, then perhaps there is a hidden ground for Hegel's argument concerning authority. But why must it make unitary sense? Is not the sense of the world rather that fragmentation, partiality, and moral failure are the case; and that this *is* the moral situation?

The emphasis on participation stands in contrast with another argument characteristic of Liberalism. Classic Liberalism assumes that if the only authority resides in individual responsibility, the only norms or interests served by individuals are their own. Coupled with the assumption that values are postulated by the valuers, this leads to the view that individuals tend to act only in their own self-interest, and that they serve the interest of the larger social group only to the extent that they see themselves as standing to profit by social participation. On the contrary, people's lives are participatory with each other and with the sociophysical environment in far reaching and intimate ways. As the contours of their causal participation go, so go their responsibilities.

How they recognize their responsibilities, however, is quite a different matter. It may well be that people first come to articulate and recognize those affairs very close to themselves. But ordinarily, as people come consciously to widen their actual social participation and the awareness of what is involved, the norms they recognize as binding on their own actions reach far beyond self-interest. People come to love one another; they adopt the interests of parties and institutions; they even are patriotic or act for the sake of the race. Indeed, as much foolishness and evil have been perpetrated in the name of altruistic interests as in that of egoistic interests!

In summary, the reason there is no authority in the full sense is that individual responsibility does not permit it. Individual responsibility cannot acknowledge the sovereignty of any merely positive sphere, since there are other spheres as well, each with its own demands on responsibility. At most, society can have delegated authority, and this is "authoritative" only for those who will it or acquiesce in it. Unlike Liberal theory, however, which infers a social individualism from the centrality of individual responsiblity, I follow the Puritan and Confucian in inferring both the constitutive and normative importance of social participation. So while there are no grounds for political theory in the sense of an *arche* for authority in the polis, there are many grounds for norms in social theory.

III. Social Implications

In this final section, I would like to draw out some of the implications for social theory from the above argument.

1. It follows from what was said above that the norms measuring various affairs of the social environment are the responsibility of all those with the potential to influence the affairs or with the potential to gain the potential. The nature of the responsibility, of course, depends on the potential causal involvements. But it depends also on the interpersonal social media by which the various individuals address their responsibilities or fail to address them. For instance, the responsibility for fair tax laws falls vaguely upon most of the adults of a given country; but the people agree to acquiesce in certain limited procedures, perhaps representative legislatures, for fulfilling this responsibility. A given citizen's responsibilities are always mediated by social structures at hand, structures that may shift direct responsibility elsewhere and that define a degree and kind of privacy for the citizen. This does not mean that the social structures take ultimate responsibility away from the individuals who could affect things if they would.

Social norms are effectively pursued insofar as that pursuit is built in to the institutions of the social environment. But the social environment itself is so deficient that pursuit of the norms falls upon individuals directly in most cases. Furthermore, since social affairs by definition involve many people, they usually can be moved only by concerted action. One's social responsibilities hardly ever are those relevant to one's causal potential acting by itself, but to causal potentials acting in concert with others. Concerted action itself requires that many individuals perceive common goals, reinforce their sense of responsibility through communicatoin, and coordinate their efforts.

The discussion so far lays the ground for pointing out the importance of three social norms.

The first and most important is that society should demand of and cultivate in all individuals the personal characteristics that foster the fulfillment of responsibility, in all the ways by which social structures and institutions can affect character. That is, not only are the higher-level essential human epitomies important for individuals, they are important for the society to develop; an essential component of social relations is that they foster the essential human epitomies. Although the American founding fathers saw the importance of an educated, participating citizenry for a democracy, American society has come by and large to take a *laissez faire* attitude toward the development of individual habits of taking responsibility. Out of a Liberal respect for individual privacy, our society has addressed personal responsibility mainly in the cases of its failure, in criminal and immoral behavior. But someone with a crooked or immoral character should be able to expect more help from society; society should have demanded, in small, learnable doses, that he or she learn to exercise responsibility properly.

From the perspective of the norm for demanding the development of individual responsibility, a thorough Puritan critique of contemporary society is possible, one more to the point than critiques of economic structures. Welfare systems, for instance, encourage dependence rather than responsibility. So do programs for treatment of drug abusers. New techniques for treating the mildly mentally retarded, on the other hand, offer unexpected options for increasing personal responsibility in persons who previously had been thought helplessly passive. These should be fostered at the price of abandoning some *laissez faire* freedoms such as the biological capacity to bear children if more important responsibilities might be learned through married sex life than would be possible if there were no threat of conception. Where social structure and institutions prove effective for developing responsible characters, they may well be allowed to be more coercive than they are when judged with *laissez faire* libertarian eyes.

The second norm is a corollary of the first, namely, that education is even more important than was believed on Liberal grounds. Not only is it necessary in order to keep reasonable control on delegated authority in positive political structure, it is necessary for beneficially affecting all normatively measured social and physical factors whatsoever. Education means not only political educaiton but aesthetic, physical, scientific, and professional as well. The recursive implication of this is that not only are schools important, but the procedures for distributing power and making decisions should be formed so as to be educational. Leisure, rest, and work should be educational. Sports, entertainment, and economic systems should be critiqued from the standpoint of their educational function. As Plato recognized, the entire polis is the individual's relevant educational institution. But there is more to life than life within the polis, and that "more" should be educational too. Social critique at this point is a glorious field day for the smiling Puritan.

A third norm is that people should develop leadership as a special characteristic of responsibility. Some people are more gifted than others regarding leadership, and such inequalities are likely to be inevitable. I mean to point to the fact, however, that responsible social participation requires initiative, and the exercise of initiative is leadership. By the argument spelled out in Chapter Three even the worst klotz has a special responsibility to take initiative where he or she sees others failing in various obligations. If initiative is transferred to more effective leadership, all the better. It is irresponsible to think of oneself as incapable of social leadership, for when the regular instituitons break down it is your responsibility, no matter who you are.

2. The fulfillment of social norms requires the development of elaborate and effective social structures. These include governmental offices and also a vast array of other institutions for the development of economic, educational, artistic, and personal life. In contrast to the main ("conservative") tradition of Liberalism, I favor

big government and organized institutions of culture. Otherwise, there will be ineffective fulfillment of many of our most important social norms. Precisely because people take their identity from their social participation, the media of that participation should be such as foster the most responsible people.

The status of these social structures, however, is not greater than their being valued by enough of the right people to maintain and enhance them. They are not authoritative beyond the derivate sense of being the products of those who sustain them. They have a moral rightness to them if indeed they are the arrangements with the best general effects on affairs; and they stand in moral judgment if they could themselves be improved.

As a consequence, established social institutions are always subject to a questioning of their legitimacy. The civil rights movement of the 1960s and the American Vietnam War, for instance, brought many people to challenge the responsible acceptability of rule by law in some circumstances. In a more constricted area, the possibility of grave dangers to health resulting from scientific experimentation on recombinant DNA has called into question the legitimacy, and remodeled our systems, of monitoring scientific research.

Because of the merely positive character of social structures, however truly valuable they are, people who object to them have an obligation to participate in the social process determining them. Indeed, because of the likelihood that any social structure is in need of improvement, a major portions of anyone's participation in social life should be that of the critic. If a social structure is perceived to be inadequate and improvable, people have an obligation to band together and change it. One of the implications of this social theory is that social institutions of criticism are extremely important. For instance *pro bono publico* law firms, critical think-tanks, news media, and universities in their critical function. It is through institutions such as these, as well as through more overt forms of political process, that responsibilities to improve the sociophysical environment might be met.

The ideal for social participation as such, I believe, is participatory democracy.[14] This is to say, at the most abstract level of social interaction, people willy nilly are in the process of shaping their social environment. The organization of social interaction is better to the extent that people have the knowledge, character, and accumulated controlled power for affecting the social environment in accord with their interests. That their true interests are their objective responsibilities, the Puritan would say, is an added dimension to the ideal. On the level of political organization, participatory democracy as an ideal stipulates the following. That people ought to have (as a norm for organizing the social environment) an influence on the process of setting the conditions under which decisions are made to the degree, and in the relevant respects, in which the outcome of the decision might bear upon them. Participatory democracy does not entail any specific government structure, such as majoritarian voting. The important point is that political life should be conceived in terms of ideals for participation rather than ideals for the distribution of authority.

That participation is an ideal does not entail that ultimate social unity is possible or that irreducible conflict may not be the last word. Non-conflictual social harmony may indeed be impossible if its achievement would require the abandonment of some real responsibilities. In practice, the distinction between someone's asserted interests and that person's real responsibilities is often hard to draw. Consider the claims both the Israelis and the Palestinians make to territory in the Mideast. The claims directly conflict, yet both are based on historic traditions, on demands for justice in the face of persecution, and on their respective will to survive as "peoples." It may well be that the ideal of ethnic integrity does not justify claims to territory nor justify warfare; perhaps only nonexclusive, secular states have any moral warrant, in which case both Israelis and Palestinians are wrong. But if there is no way of eliminating the validity of the interests of the "peoples," then the conflict is irreducible. No authority beyond the prudence of the respective leaders can draw boundaries. A more hopeful way of putting this is that the leaders, by attending to responsibilities all round, can tame the conflict by prudence. But for a long time the affair will be in process.

Responsibilities are not lessened by the fact that they are in competition with one another. The special point of this chapter has been to consider whether social groups as such have authoritative or responsible structures like individuals, and the conclusion is they do not. In light of this, individual responsibility must be given a public or social cast, and the conception of participation is the key. Like the exercise of individual responsibility in one's personal sphere, responsible social participation is fraught with conflicts and the marks of finitude, as the Puritan thought from the start and learned more deeply the hard way. The question that arises now is whether there are limits to participation. Or is this another obsession of the Puritan? After all, John Dewey, the Apostle of Participation, hailed from Vermont, a very Puritan place.

9

Freedom and Privacy

Authority is the chief stumbling block for a contemporary affirmation of the participationist insights of Puritanism and Confucianism. By denying anything like the classical sense of authority, and justifying that denial by appeal to a strong sense of Puritan and Confucian responsibility, that stumbling block is removed. The result is a polity with only the weakest kinds of authority, and this indeed is the historical consequence of Liberalism. The Liberal values of freedom and privacy make such a weak sense of authority necessary. The argument, therefore, has backed us in to the virtues of Liberalism as a limit to the vices of Puritanism and Confucianism.

The direction of approach may now be reversed. Does Liberalism in its turn rest on values that must be limited? Liberalism affirms strongly the values of freedom and privacy, but without a strong affirmation of responsibility. I shall argue that the institutionalization of Liberal conceptions of freedom and privacy, without responsibility or participation, are ultimately empty and require Puritan supplementation. What must not be lost in the Liberal conception of freedom is the importance of that exercise of creativity that is not a matter of problem-solving, of technology; John Stuart Mill rightly lauded the eccentric. What must supplement playful creativity is engagement. What must not be lost in the Liberal conception of privacy is the mostly negative protection of tolerance, the source of our salvation from pretended authority. What must supplement Liberal privacy is its function as the arena for creativity.

The argument will begin with an examination of freedom, focusing on freedom of inquiry as a central and self-referentially illuminating mode.[1] I shall look first at the Liberal tradition in its classic forms, then at its Marxist offshoot in the "Critical Philosophy" of the Frankfurt School, and I shall give a provisional statement of a reconciliation and supplementation of their insights. Finally, the discussion turns from the negative side of freedom-from to the positive side of freedom-to, or the rights of privacy.

I. Freedom in Liberal Philosophy and Critical Hermeneutics

The practical principle of Liberal philosophy was stated succinctly by John Stuart Mill.

> That principle is, that the sole end for which mankind are warranted, individually or collectively, in interfering with the liberty of action of any of their number, is self-protection. That the only purpose for which power can be rightfully exercised over any member of a civilized community, against his will, is to prevent harm to others.[2]

Underlying the Liberal principle are conceptions of personal agency and human reason. The classic source for the Liberal conception of persons as agents is John Locke, who argued that through acting, persons "take possession."

> Though the earth and all inferior creatures be common to men, yet every man has a property in his own person; this nobody has any right to but himself. The labour of his body and the work of his hands, we may say, are properly his. Whatsoever then he removes out of the state that nature hath provided and left it in, he hath mixed his labour with, and joint to it something that is his own, and thereby makes it his property. It being by him removed from the common state nature hath placed it in, it hath by this labour something annexed to it that excludes the common right of other men. For this labour being the unquestionable property of the labourer, no man but he can have a right to what that is once joined to, at least where there is enough and as good left in common for others.[3]

This question appears in a chapter immediately following a discussion of slavery, and the force of the argument there is that if it is wrong for one person to own another, that must be because the second already and inalienably owns himself or herself. Because people's actions are always through their bodies, their bodies are their most intimate possessions, so intimate as to be logically incapable of being "alienated" or sold. The more common meaning of action refers to work, and through investing one's labor in some material, one takes possession of that material. One then has title to trade it or legitimately defend one's possession of it. Although the analysis Locke gave is considerably more suble and complicated than sketched here, the upshot is a conception of human life wherein individuals inhabit their world by taking possession of it through their work.

The Liberal conception of reason is essentially technocratic, as I argued at the beginning. That is, the purpose of reason is to arrange means to secure goals. Liberalism is congenial to the use of science to solve social problems, and it has great confidence in the powers of reason. Accordingly, Liberalism views scientific inquiry, for instance, as far more than merely the private activity of scientists: it also serves a noble social purpose, and medical research is the paradigm of beneficent reason. Freedom of inquiry is not like other freedoms whose only justification is that their exercise harms no one. Rather, freedom of inquiry has a special value in that, as a pervasive cultural value, it generally enhances the social powers of reaching other goals.

The conception of reason as technology was first articulated by Francis Bacon and Thomas Hobbes, but it has achieved its most sensitive expression in the work of our contemporaries, Robert Nozick and John Rawls. Reason for them is conceived to determine only the means to achieve goals and not the goals themselves. Unless goals can be adjudicated by reference to other goals toward which they are means, neither of these contemporary Liberal philosophers considers reason to have much legitimate importance for the establishment of social values. Both Nozick and Rawls suppose an egoistic theory of decision-making in which each person is assumed to be deciding for the sake of his or her own perceived best interests.

Rawls has been extremely sensitive to describing the common intuitions of justice in a manner harmonious with the Liberal philosophy. He suggests that in designating advantageous and disadvantageous positions, the structure of a just society is one that any rational person concerned to further their own interests would accept. Therefore, in their enlightened self-interest they would want even the least advantaged positions to profit as much from possible social processes, lest they find themselves in such positions. Particular values are difficult to justify rationally save as instrumental to further values, and, therefore, persons should be free to pursue their desires within the limits of justice. Some values, however, seem to be composites of a variety of things that appear common to the pursuit of self-interest. Among these is health. If health is assumed to be a common social value, then medical research is justified by some aspect of the common good, as well as by the personal freedom of researchers. Safety in one's home, freedom from unnecessary exposure to disease, and freedom to regulate the activities in one's own community that might endanger that community, are other common social values to which Liberalism would offer an instrumental justification.

One of the chief functions of technological reason, in the Liberal view, is the reconciliation of competing values in terms of higher values. Therefore, the value of risky research—for instance, DNA experimentation—must be weighed against the value of protection from unnecessary exposure to disease, both adjusticated in terms of the larger value of health. The value of health in turn may conflict with that of community self-determination, and for this reason some higher-level adjudicating value would have to be found if the problem is to be resolved. Because technological reason does not deal with the intrinsic worth of the candidate values, the Liberal position is that some value disputes may be unresolvable and recourse must be had to purely procedureal settlements.

Thus, the Liberal problematic for freedom of inquiry has several levels. On one level, it is the question whether research is dangerous enough to warrant limitation in the interest of the self-protection of some part of the public. On another, it is the problem of defining standing to assert who is endangered and whose activity (i.e., whose private life) should be subject to limitation. On yet another, it is the problem of the social value of research compared with the various values that can be cited by those who do not want to be endangered by the research. These levels of the problem seem so obvious to us that it is instructive to go over the same issues from the standpoint of a neighboring alternative to Liberalism.

One of the most significant alternatives is the "critical" theory of Jurgen Habermas and, more generally, the Frankfurt school. The pioneers of this school were Adorno, Horkeimer, and Marcuse, who developed a sustained critique of Western culture since the Enlightenment based on reinterpreted Enlightenment and Marxist principles. More recent members of the school such as Habermas and Apel have been deeply influenced by debates about hermeneutics and by American pragmatism which they interpret in Kantian ways.[4] Like Marx and classical Liberalism, Habermas recognizes a fundamental human interest in controlling the material components of life.[5] He calls this a "technical" interest and believes that it guides the purposive-rational action. The riskiness of genetics research is a real conflict of technical interests. The conflict may or may not be resolvable by finding a more inclusive technical interest; for instance, the development of a social system of scientific research that adequately protects the community while delivering benefits, to the end that the communities have a greater technical interest in supporting the research than in blocking it. That is, the research would be supported within protective limitations that do not impair its value. A "critical" theorist would argue that this dimension of the problem is essentially a technical one, whose solution, if one is possible, would consist in adjusting the orientation of labor by diverse groups so as to be mutually compatible; the extent of the problem depends on technical knowledge of the nature and degree of risk, and so forth.

Habermas disagrees with Marx's view that labor for the sake of mastering the material conditions of life is the only fundamental human interest. Along with the technical interests, there exists what Habermas calls the "hermeneutical" interest, which guides the activity of developing the personal ego through the various symbolic communication systems of culture, the family, and other loci of personal interaction. Although obviously related to the material conditions of society, the ways by which human interactions build up or inhibit personal integrity and character have a logic of their own. The hermeneutic idea is a free communication system in which people grow by responding with understanding to the communications of other people, affairs, and culture. The hermeneutic ideal is frustrated by anything that impedes dialogue.

The hermeneutic interest, in its own way, parallels the Liberal theory's view of individualism. But whereas the Liberal model of the individual is based on the concept of ownership, the critical model is based on dialogue. Thus, whereas social interaction on the Liberal model tends to be viewed either as potential conflict over the integrity of personal ownership or as potential cooperation of otherwise independent individuals for the sake of material productivity, social interaction on the critical model is the source and necessary condition of individual growth; personal character is essentially dependent on social interaction, not merely contingently dependent on it. In this, critical theory agrees with themes we have found in Puritanism and Confucianism, and that perhaps were best stated by John Dewey. According to the critical theory, therefore, norms for social interactions are not merely negative ones defining protection but positive ones for fostering personal development.

The hermeneutic interest in critical theory brings out two more dimensions of the problem of freedom of inquiry in a field such as genetic research. First, there is a value to research far exceeding its potential benefits for the material conditions of life, namely, its benefit to dialogue and hence to personal development. Habermas analyzes this kind of point by reference to the psychoanalytic situation.[6] The patient and analyst engage in dialogue until the point is reached where prima facie communication breaks down (for example, the patient's real meaning is repressed and not expressed). The analyst then switches from dialogue to analysis of the mechanism of repression, and so forth, and when the patient comes to understand why he or she says something other than what is meant, open communication can be reestablished. (I doubt this is the way psychoanalysis really works, when it does; the account leaves out the role of transference. The point for critical theory is clear enough, however.) The mechanisms revealed by psychoanalytic theory are not the only ones that impede dialogue; there can be genetic, historical, social, economic, political, and other factors that distort communication. Only when we take possession of all the ways the world really is, will we be able to transform any human situation into a condition of open communicaiton. Freedom of intellectual inquiry is, therefore, valuable because it contributes to the understanding essential for the fulfillment of human communication. A critical theorist might say that the National Endowment for the Humanities should be as interested in sponsoring genetic research as the National Science Foundation.

The second dimension of the problem appearing in the hermeneutical perspective is that knowledge itself must be communicated to serve the improvement of communication systems. The social

organization of knowledg at the present time inhibits free communication. Understanding of the scientific results of the recombinant DNA research, for instance, is largely limited to the scientific
community and a few others who take pains to read the literature or
who benefit directly from its therapeutic consequences. This limitation causes those outside the scientific community whose lives are
potentially affected by the research to feel alienated. Putting aside
for the moment the aspect of power and control that comes with
knowledge of this sort, the plain value of research cannot be directly
appreciated by those outside the scientific community except insofar
as it is expressed within the realm of the technical interest in improving material conditions. If, however, the promise of material
benefits from research cannot be made clear and plausible, as was
the case in the early days of genetic research, then those outside the
scientific community will view any higher claim for the value of free
inquiry as only romantic self-assertion on the part of the scientific
community.

Beyond the technical and hermeneutic interests, Habermas
discerns a third fundamental interest whose function is to integrate
the activities of the first two, namely, an emancipatory interest.
Without the interest in emancipation and autonomy, the goals of
both material improvements and open communication are determined merely by the historical situation at hand. With the emancipatory interest, both of those activities can be turned to a critique
and a transformation of the historical conditions. Emancipation is
the interest that guides the cultivation and distribution of power.
Habermas insists that the character and distribution of powers at
any one time result from specific historical factors. Material conditions determining control of the means of production, for instance,
provide some groups with power to dominate others. Possession of
knowledge, or the illusions of ignorance, also distribute power so
that some people dominate others. Emancipation requires the
critical analysis of how both labor and interpretation serve to foster
modes of dominance in particular situations.

In light of the emancipatory interest, the problem of freedom
for socially risky medical research is essentially a political one. Given
our present system of research, advances in scientific knowledge
serve to strengthen the hands of the professoinals who dominate the
lay community both by defining the goals of health (and other professional services) and by controlling the distribution system. For

this reason, although it seems absurd to oppose an advance in knowledge that might bring great benefits to health, the interest in emancipation might very well determine that the overall power of the scientific community ought to be weakened by restricting research. Otherwise, the bondage inflicted by paternalism will remain. Furthermore, scientific professionalism in genetic research (and in other areas of research) tends to corrode an important area where democratic society has already achieved significant emancipation, namely, community control of local activity. Research is always done in some local community or other, yet control over research seems to be determined by factors within the scientific, industrial, and governmental organizations to which local community governments have little political entry. A critical theorist, therefore, would perceive the problem of genetic research as consisting in part as a challenge to local communities for effective control over what transpires within them. Even if the professionals "know best," the nonprofessionals are not emancipated until they control what happens to them.

II. Participatory Democracy

In one sense, each perspective discussed above brings out some legitimate aspect of the problem of freedom of inquiry. In another sense, the interpretation of the problem depends on the political theories providing the perspectives; here, criticisms can be made of both theoretical perspectives. The criticisms will serve to draw out once again the need to supplement the Liberal and critical hermeneutic observations with Puritan and Confucian themes.

The central difficulty with Liberal theory in this context can be exhibited by formulating an aspect of its position in three propositions: (1) There is no procedure for objectively ascertaining what things are valuable, ideal, or obligatory in the world; (2) therefore, morals and politics and must limit their value references to what individuals merely want, not what they can justify objectively; (3) in order to make sense of political theory, the authority of political norms can be derived by assuming that people are entitled to what they want and own, subject to the limitations of conflict over ownership.

The first proposition is simply mistaken, based on a bad metaphysics that separates facts from values, as I have argued throughout. Although knowledge of values cannot be demonstrated with certainty, some agreement and an understanding of why they are valuable can be reached through deliberation, assuming open communication of the sort Habermas advocates. In daily experience we find this to be so, and the skeptical attacks against the knowability of norms can be met by philosophic arguments.[7] Personal and social values are ideal constructs of states of affairs that harmonize various prized possessions. These ideal constructs are abstract, often metaphorical. Sometimes several such constructs can be applied to the same concrete historical situation, giving rise either to conflicts or to the mutual reinforcement or tolerance of compatible values.

The analysis of values, I have argued, is commonly practised on several levels, analogous to normative description of actual affairs. Abstractly, the values can be scrutinized to see what component values they harmonize. The ideal construct of freedom of inquiry, for instance, includes: the values of knowledge for its own sake; the adventure of discovery; the potential benefits of applied knowledge; the friendship, respect, and rewards of a community of inquirers; the therapeutic benefits of inquiring dialogue; and the historically conditioned value of resolving great tensions with religious authoritarianism, narrow patronage of learning, a system of education, and demands for social mobility.[8] The application of the value of freedom of inquiry to a particular case—for instance, the research involving recombinant DNA—reveals more concrete characteristics of its worth. The freedom to conduct that research depends upon establishing new principles of responsibility, putting researchers into new social roles, and providing contexts for scrutiny that hitherto were mere possibilities; such freedom has potential benefits and risks. From the standpoint of the historical situation, freedom of inquiry is but one value among many others, such as protection from needless exposure to disease, community control, and perhaps funding interests. Analyzed in conjunction with other values that might also determine the concrete situation, freedom of inquiry reveals itself to be valuable in some ways and not in others, valuable to some people and not to others. Although there are significant differences between large-scale social values such as freedom of inquiry and other values of a more personal nature, in principle it is possible to determine what those idealized states of affairs are worth both abstractly and in concrete application. We deliberate about them constantly and make decisions concerning them with varying degrees of confidence in our judgments. Because it is always possible — perhaps, to some degree, inevitable — that we do not understand all that is involved in some value, abstractly or concretely, our judgments should always be recognized as being hypothetical. They are, however, no less objective than scientific judgments that are also hypotheses with only some degree of confirmation. This point can be summarized under the title of the "hypothetical objectivity" of values. It contradicts the first proposition of Liberalism.

The second proposition of Liberalism is that human beings are egoists, that they merely value what they want for themselves, that they are essentially selfish although they sometimes extend their sense of self by identifying with family, neighborhood, professional group, or country. But on the contrary, despite the fact that most of us are selfish sometimes, and some of us are selfish most of the time, there are unselfish moments in all of us. Our first response to most things is aesthetic, picking up what values they seem to present; only later (though perhaps quickly later) are things related to their bearing upon ourselves. The rationale for emphasizing egoism is not because it is an observation of experience, but rather because it seems to be an analogue to the inertia or natural motion of physical things, and, therefore, can be used to explain other things without requiring an explanation itself. But is it not a fact that we differ in the values known to us, in how well we understand what they imply abstractly and concretely, in our beliefs and our interpretive schemes for recognizing the application of values, and in our identifications with those who benefit from or pay the price of the pursuit of the values? Do not our value judgments change as we alter our understanding of the meanings of the values, as we come to perceive others' points of view, and as we see how the situations to which values are to be applied parse out the costs and benefits?

Although the original sphere of a person's knowledge and familiarity is likely to be close to his or her own self, that sphere is expanded with experience, education, and, particularly, dialogue with others. If most of a person's values could be classified as selfish, it is because there is a limited sphere of his or her acquaintance with what might be valuable, as well as because of contingent psychological reasons. Habermas's view of the development of the self through social interactions is, in respect to the cognizance of what is worthwhile, far closer to experience than is the Liberal principle of egoism. This point can be summed up with the title, "the educability of evaluative sense," and it is Confucian in its resonance.

Liberalism's third proposition, that political norms are derived from people's entitlement to owning their desired possession, is mistaken in part because there are social values other than ownership that have been discovered to have a prima facie claim on our allegiance. More interesting for the moment, however, is the fact that it needlessly confuses a view concerning the nature and justification of political values with a view about authority. It is one thing to assert that certain values are worthwhile, that they are in fact known to be so by certain people, and that they are in some sense obligatory even to those who do not understand them. It is quite another to assert that a group of people or a government has the authority to coerce valued behavior on those who want to do something else. Each individual is the "author" or "authority" for his or her own actions; this authority can be delegated to others, but the original authors must retain responsibility for what the delegates do. It is misleading, in fact, to think of individuals' authority as being delegated to governmental agents. A better perspective is to see their authority as invested in the political processes in which they themselves take part. Their participation may be active in the sense that they personally press their values in the relevant decision-making forums; it may be less active in the sense that they rely on representative agents, though they do not escape responsibility for that reliance; or it may be negligible, as in the case of those who do not even vote or express views but remain responsible against their will or practice.

If the political process results in a decision that is contrary to one's views, it is then necessary to decide whether one's commitment to the deposed value is greater or less than one's commitment to the political process in which one participated. If one decides it is greater, then in effect one is denying the authority of the political process. Most people lend their authoritative support to a political process that follows the rule of law, although many balked when this process resulted in racial segregation and American involvement in the war in Vietnam. The authority of law resides in the fact that most people usually recognize its value and lend it their authority by active and passive support.

From this perspective, a serious dimension to the problem of freedom for genetic research is a confusion of authority. The great majority of Americans have lent their active or passive support to the social process that funds and protects scientific work. Genetic research in the mid-1970s posed a great apparent danger, with no obvious legitimated means to protect the public's safety; scientists' care and good will did not have the authoritative public approval. The subsequent debate, with restraint on the part of the scientific community and emerging institutions of criticism and monitoring, did supply authoritative support. The research enterprise is always in danger of losing its "approved" status as part of the generally legitimized political process, because the legitimating "authority" is really but a representation of the responsibility of all individuals. The question of legitimating authority in this sense is not easily interpreted according to the Liberal political theory that links authority to ownership.

Critical theory, however, is far more sensitive to the complex questions of social interaction than is Liberalism. Most of the important issues raised by genetic research are not those of conflicts of private interests but rather those of conflicts and confusions concerning realities comprising social interactions themselves. Interactions of work, communication, and the struggles for emancipation are important constituents.

If it is true that social values are objective and that people can come to know them through social dialogue, then Habermas's scheme supplies useful tools for understanding why various groups think of the values as they do. Where there are breakdowns in communications, there is sure to be a lack of consensus on what is worthwhile. Similarly, when there is an uneven distribution of material costs and benefits, there are sure to be real conflicts, whether recognized or not, in which a state of affairs is valuable to some but harmful to others. The critical pursuit of emancipation shows how values other than health or even free inquiry bear upon the development of social and personal contexts in which people can be autonomous.

But what is the status of Habermas's three interests, the technical, the hermeneutic, and the emancipatory? According to him it is "quasi-transcendental."[9] The "quasi" qualification probably means that these interests are empirical generalizations of basic goals that people pursue; Habermas tries to show that pursuit of these goals is part of the natural constitution of human life. But how do we certify that they are worth pursuing without raising the possibility that other goals are equally basic? And why should we assume that society is so cohesive that these interests express goals equally valuable for all people? If values are to be understood empirically, as argued above, then the justification of these three interests requires an extraordinary narrow interpretation of society and world history. It is hard to see, for instance, how important they might be in Chinese culture.

Further, critical theory's representation of the three interests as "interests" construes them as presupposed in the concrete processes of life, rather than discovered to be worthwhile. Yet, is it not the case that in situations such as that created by the revolution in biomedicine, where the most fundamental presupposed values are challenged, the worth of a person's interests themselves should be called into question? The critical theory imputes a normative status to the three interests that should be examined. What about people who dislike work and are willing to live materially impoverished lives? What about recluses who do not like dialogue and are quite willing to forego improvements of their interpretive egos? What about those who think the struggle for emancipation is not half as good as flowing with the social currents? Critical theory necessarily tends to regard such people as aberrations, nonparticipants in historical and social reality, perhaps deficiently human, and unknowing because not bound to the humanly constitutive interests. But perhaps those people know something interesting about the values of life, and even if they decline to talk about it, their perspective has an empirical bearing on our general search for the most worthwhile values around which to structure our society. From their perspective, the value of freedom of inquiry may be greatly overblown both for its supposed technical benefits and for its humanizing benefits.

If we say a participatory democracy is a polity viewing knowledge of social values as hypothetically objective and open to education, and viewing authority as responsibility resident in the persons who are the authors of their own acts (and resident in the political process only in the ways and degrees people participate), the following aspects of the problem of genetic research become important for freedom of inquiry. Until recently there has been a general social authorization of scientific research, meaning that the public generally identified with the social or political processes that supported the research and its technological spinoffs. But in the case of recombinant DNA research, for instance, as well as in other cases such as nuclear physics, the scientific activity has come to be perceived as having a direct bearing on the lives of all persons in the form of special dangers. This differs from the "direct bearing" in the form of technological benefits that had originally contributed to the general authoritaive legitimation of the scientific process. The public now finds it in its interest to limit the potential dangers, and at some point the limitations might impinge on the freedom of scientists to inquire. It is now necessary, as perhaps it has not always been, for the public to weigh the social value of freedom of inquiry. Before, the public needed only to appreciate the benefits of inquiry, and perhaps now the successful practice of genetic research, with its technological benefits, has restored this sense of complacency.

There are two problems that hinder such appreciation. The experiences of most people are such that they cannot identify with the perspective of the inquirers, and so cannot easily be educated to that point of view. This results in large measure from class differences. Further, the real value of freedom of inquiry is much greater to those who are inquirers or potential inquirers than to those who stand little chance of exercising that freedom. For the latter, the only value lies in the technological spinoff, and this is probably insufficient to persuade many people to take risks for the sake of freedom of inquiry.

In the short run, therefore, freedom of inquiry in scientific areas that pose special dangers to the public is not likely to have the authoritative approval of society unless public mechanisms can be developed and given social legitimacy for limiting that freedom. This has not happened, apparently, in the case of genetic research. In the long run, the social and educational class differences between people will have to be minimized so that everyone not only can appreciate the perspective of inquirers but can also realistically imagine himself or herself enjoying that perspective. Possibly, a step in this direction has been taken by those communities that insist on regulating the research that takes place in their environs. In this way, the researchers and the public engage in a common political process to which they might jointly grant their authority and from which they might jointly come to share values.

Nowhere in the discussion is there a serious challenge to the freedom of inquiry in the historical sense of freedom from a party line or freedom to express one's honest conclusions. Nor is there a challenge to the freedom of inquiry interpreted to mean freedom to pursue one's inquiry wherever it leads. The sticking point is when the pursuit begins to have social costs. The challenges always come at the point where it is recognized that the same potential activity, the research, is relevant to more values than freedom of inquiry itself.

The points made in criticism of Liberalism, including the hypothetical objectivity of values and the educability of evaluative sense, are part and parcel of the theory of moral reflection and practice I have developed in earlier chapters. The emphasis feeds in as well. The criticism of the transcendental elements in critical theory as needlessly a priori and exclusive of other important social values reinforces the empiricism of the position I have defended. The discussion here has reinforced the point that privacy, in any sense in which that term might be applied to scientific research, is a creature of the exercise of responsibility in public affairs.

III. The Virtue of Privacy

Some kind of continuity clearly obtains between the inward concerns of being responsible and the outward concerns with authority, freedom, and participation in public life. Whereas the Marxian sensibility would minimize the first and the Liberal would strictly delimit the latter, the Puritan and the Confucian would see them joined. If privacy is a creature of the exercise of responsibility, how can this be understood?

One necessary key lies in the nature of the distinction between the public and the private. I introduced that distinction earlier in pointing out that, from the standpoing of natural responsibility to public obligations, the private sphere is an artificial creation. That is, there is a public value in creating limitations to public demands, leaving a realm of privacy that is legitimate as long as the social structures function to fulfill the main responsibilities that devolve upon everyone. This view directly opposes the Liberal theory that sees public structures as the artificial creation of people functioning naturally as private.

It is not enought, however, to say that privacy is a special creation. Why is it created? What is its value? The argument I cited earlier was that efficiency is gained in the pursuit of social obligations if labor is divided, responsibility focused in those who are especially capable, and the others politely moved to the sidelines. This justification rests on its benefits to the public fulfillment of responsbility. Is there no other justification of privacy?

Historically, the concept of privacy takes it significance from its contrast with public life. In the archaic, preclassical days of ancient Greece, the aristocrats had only public life, no private life. The concepts of self and of legitimate activity had to do with the responsibilities, virtues, and rituals of the public conduct of affairs. Public life for them was not a public role that they played on certain occasions, but life itself. The nonaristocrats, on the other hand, had no public life. Except for the results of their work, they were irrelevant to public affairs and enjoyed little or no sense that public responsibility was basic to their identity. But neither did the common people have a sense of privacy, a domain of life free from the demands of public responsibility; they were not private, only unpolitical. I believe the situation was similar in ancient China until the popular successes of Buddhism in the second and third centuries, with the difference that the class of Confucian literati joined the aristocrats in the enjoyment of public life.

The Greek city states of the postarchaic classical period were significant precisely because they attempted to require public responsibility of everyone. The aristocrats' prime loyalty to personal virtue was superseded in the values of the city state by the loyalty of the citizens to the laws and welfare of the polis. Civic loyalty demanded of every citizen a portion of time and energy devoted to public deliberation and welfare, and thus it allowed a distinction to be drawn between that aspect of life and those aspects that had to do with tending one's own affairs rather than the city's. Werner Jaeger put it as follows:

> The polis gives each individual his due place in its political cosmos, and thereby gives him, beside his private life, a sort of second life, his *bios politikos.* Now, every citizen belongs to two orders of existence; and there is a sharp distinction in his life between what is *his* own (idion) and what is *communal (koinon)*. Man is not only 'idiotic,' he is also 'politic.' As well as his ability in his own profession or trade, he has his share of the universal ability of the citizen, *politike arete,* by which he is fitted to cooperate and sympathize with the rest of the citizens in the life of the polis. [10].

Plato and Aristotle, though imbued with the spirit of the polis, ran somewhat against the grain of its ideal in their belief that public life itself requires expertise. For clearly, if a statesman requires skills as a carpenter requires skills, then not all citizens are equally fit for the exercise of public responsibility. However we might evaluate the fact, Plato and Aristotle were practically right; politics does demand special skills. Or rather, those lacking the skills quickly lose out on the power to exercise public responsibility unless they learn the skills first.

The heritage of Greece regarding the public and private is therefore complex and somewhat contradictory. On the one hand, personal identity, at least for male citizens, consisted in both public life and idiotic or private life. Personal skills in one's work were idiosyncratic and belonged to private or nonpublic life. Yet the exercise of public responsibility required a special political skill or virtue, and the fact that most citizens lack this meant that it was something of a sham to say that they participated in public life. The reality, then as since, is closer to what Plato described when he noted that only one class of people rule, those capable of it in one sense of capability or another. For Plato, the rulers were supposed to rule by persuasion, not by the adroit use of political force; yet the effective skills have usually been those associated with force.

The social contract theorists who were the founders of modern political thought were self-consciously imbued with the classic Greek ideal (self-consciously neglecting the medieval world), and aware of its contradiction, that all citizens are supposed to be political, yet only a few have the skill to be. There was an important dimension added to the political thinking of the moderns, Hobbes and Locke. Instead of loyalty to the polis, the spring of political action for them was self-interest. They hardly could conceive of basic motivations other than self-interest, which seemed the analogue within intentionality of the inertia of physical theory. Just as inertia does not need to be explained, once understood, so self-interest is apparently self-explanatory, once understood. Individualism meant the fulfillment of personal interest. Political life, therefore, was explained not as an intrinsic part of personal identity but as a means for securing personal interest, a matter of self-serving prudence. Hobbes accordingly argued that the interest of all is best served by ceding the powers to cause violence to a sovereign. Through this ceding of authority, the citizens in a delegated sense are the authors of all that the sovereign does, according to the passage from Hobbes quoted above. But since they have in fact alienated their authorship to the sovereign, the sovereign is the only real author in the state regarding public life. Citizens have public life only to the extent that they act in accord with the dictates of the sovereign. But acting in accord with those dictates is being ruled by them, not participating in their formation. Personal life therefore has alienated its principal public responsibilities and retains only those of obedience to the sovereign's commands. The rest of personal life is private in something like our contemporary sense of privacy: whatever is not regulated by law.

In contrast to Hobbes, Locke emphasized a far greater public role for the universal citizen. Instead of merely being public through obedience to the laws of the sovereign, each citizen participates in the making of the laws (particularly concerning taxation) through the exercise of the voting franchise. Because of the vast and complicated scramble for public office, the sphere of politics was greatly expanded so that many common people could participate in ways more involved than mere voting.

The Liberal democracies derivative from Lockean political theory in one sense solve the Greek contradition by establishing a hierarchy of political responsibility through republicanism. Only those most skilled in political life make it to the top of a complex, bureaucratice political structure; but those with perfectly common skills can participate on the ward level, as it were.

A special problem arises in the Liberal democracies, however. Precisely because the state is seen as the agency of the citizens' own authority, its independent power is feared, and limitations on the power of the state, such as the Bill of Rights, were established in order to protect private life. Privacy then comes to be viewed as that area of personal life where the state should make no claim, at least not without passing through that due process itself designed to protect privacy. One of the strong connotations of privacy today is the negative sense that it is where others have no right to intrude.

Has Liberal privacy any positive value over and above its negative freedom from external infringement? If there is any value, it would be in the ways private affairs contribute to one's essential sense of personal identity. I suggest that, for the ideology of Liberal democracy, there are two basic factors that distinguish what is important in private life from what is trivial.

The first is that the important things are those that enhance our economic status and property. This is a function of the Liberal definition of personal identity as tied so closely to property. Whether society reinforces economic egoism because it is an important trait of human nature, or whether it is an important part of our nature because society reinforces it, I shall not hazard to debate.

The second factor for Liberalism in making private things important is their relative contribution to political power, or those skills that give one more public power than otherwise. Again, the most important private sphere is the economic, because with wealth goes political clout. But also education and in some circumstances, though apparently not in others, religion contributes to political effectiveness. The other aspects of private life—for instance, personal morality, religion in most circumstances, ethnic culture, beliefs about most nonpolitical things, the use of leisure, and a host of other factors—are relatively unimportant. Although we engage in them, they are relatively meaningless in terms of what counts in life.

Marx pointed out this difficulty well over a hundred years ago. Political life in a Liberal civil society involves an alienation of certain abstract and universal characteristics of people as citizens from the more concrete social life of private affairs. But precisely because society reognizes the public political sphere as the more important, the relative concreteness of private life loses its meaning. Human emancipation, said Marx, is not the same as political emancipation; the latter serves to alienate people from their concrete life while freeing them from political bondage.[11] The task of human emancipation requires the cultivation of what Marx called "species being," the potential character people have in association with one another by virtue of belonging to the developing human species. The species being of mankind includes common action and individual perspectives, but within the overall context of a common history regarding emancipation. The aim of the emancipatory process is the absorption of abstract universal human characteristics into the concrete social nature of all people acting together.

Attractive as the ideal of species being is, combining individual freedom with concrete social participation, Marx came to see that the conditions for its realization require serious changes in the Liberal social order. These changes in turn require a revolutionary period in which the need for group solidarity far overshadows the historical uniqueness of individual freedom. Indeed, the revolutionary government has the Marxist blessing when it restricts individual liberties to the absolute needs of the social revolutionary process. The dictatorship of the proletariate then turns back again to the very situation feared by the Liberal democrats, that in which their individual liberties cannot be protected against the public demands of the government. The Marxists, of course, argue that this is a temporary expedient and not at all a matter of pre-Liberal tyranny; but then any pre-Liberal tyrant would have said the same thing. At any rate, with the possible exception of China, the attempts of Marxist countries to transcend an abstract distinction between public and private life with the ideal of free species being in practice turns out to degrade private life without much apparent compensation.

IV. Creativity, Privacy, and Tolerance

That last remark, however, betrays a sense of what is important in private life extending beyond those items of importance listed above. The genuine central value in private life, I contend, is that it is the most beneficial arena of creativity. In contrast to the Liberal tradition, my argument makes the value of privacy a positive affair, not defined merely negatively as the sphere in which public determinations do not apply. Privacy is the life of creativity, made possible by public structures holding the private space open. In contrast to the Marxist tradition, privacy stands as an important norm for public life, not the other way around. A publicly demanding environment is good to the extent that it supports prized kinds of creativity. Whereas creativity is good in itself, still it ought not to be publicly detrimental and should be subordinated to public responsibilities when social structures fail to fulfill them.

Because the exercise of responsibility is a function of creativity, two kinds of concern pertain to privacy. One is the immediate concern of creating responsibly and well. The second is with developing the character that conduces to creativity. On the human level, creativity is not merely a requirement for existence; people can exist in many different ways, all creative, but some more creative than others. Values are involved in the very meaning of creativity. Merely to exist is to be achieving the values of coherence and definiteness relative to the limitations for integration imposed by the environment. Where the environment allows different ways of achieving coherence and definiteness, creativity is obligated by norms for higher values, relative to what is possible.

The Liberal tradition has tried through its doctrine of natural rights to resist the consequence that the distinction between public and private institutions is set by the public. If it could be argued that there are natural rights in the protoprivate domain, whose justifications is prior to the justification of public institutions such as government, those natural rights might provide norms for setting boundaries between public and private. Such was Jefferson's argument, for instance. But I believe it is impossible to defend the notion of natural rights as normative prior to an organized social life that is both public and private; here the Confucians were more on the mark than their Taoist cousins. Eighteenth-century theorists could appeal to our common sense that people are not reducible in their values to those bestowed upon them by the authority of the government, and that the irreducible core is more important and valuable than, indeed even incommensurable with, the values of structurally sanctioned social toles. But this is not to make sense of rights in a state of nature. It is only to note that the values of any action include those of private creativity as well as those of public worth. As a result of the failure to maintain a justfication for natural rights in a domain prior to social distinctions, Liberals frequently have been reduced to appeals to convention — for instance, to the United States Constitution — to justify the establishment of boundaries for privacy. Yet why, in a moral sense, are the constitutional principles valid?

How can the thesis that private domains are created by public political structures sustain the value of tolerance? It would seem that the body politic could legislate tolerance away. The key to the defense of tolerance, I believe, is the point that one has to have standing in order to interfere in the lives of others. The form of the justification of tolerance with regard to a person's behavior is that no one has the standing to interfere; it is not anybody else's business. to make this defense work, we must explain "standing."

The power in the Liberal tradition in this regard is that by denying means to the ascertaining of objective value, it could define standing solely in contractual terms. If one has the office to interfere, then one can interfere. Offices can be defined carefully so as to minimize interference in line with the protection of individual liberty. On the classical Liberal conception, there is no normative reason to interfere unless the behavior in question causes harm, in Mill's terms, or threatens property and other basic rights guaranteed by contract. Tolerance is justified by the absence of previously legislated standing to interfere in most cases.

I have maintained that the establishment of private spheres is a public matter, based on historical experience and justified by the real values discovered there relative to the structures needed to fulfill obligations. Within those private spheres, by definition, there is no activated public obligation and, therefore, no responsibility on the part of others to see that things go right. Perhaps much of what goes on within the private spheres has no moral obligation of any sort, a matter of preference, whim, leisure, plain rest. Even where there are definite values, especially those having to do with religion, sexuality and personal relations, and other matters generally deemed private in Western society, the responsibility for them is not a public matter but a concern only for those within the private sphere.

Precisely because those private spheres are created by public activity in fulfillment of social obligations to deal with social matters effectively, there is a public obligation to defend the boundaries of those private spheres. The grounds for determining the boundaries of private spheres have to do with the division of labor for fulfilling social obligations. As the needs for fulfilling those obligations shift, the boundaries of the private shift. There is no guarantee that the normative boundaries will be recognized clearly at any time. Nevertheless, there is a pragmatic factor that calls attention to inefficient boundaries. If no one attends to important social obligations, or too many people try to attend, the misdrawing of the boundaries becomes apparent. The classic cases of intolerance, in matters of sectarian religion, for instance, or in those of persecuting certain sexual preferences, consist in the assumption by some people that their beliefs about norms are matters of public obligation, when in fact they have little or nothing to do with satisfying public obligation. Sometimes a long history is needed for this fact to be discovered.

Furthermore, conditions can become complicated, as when activities have many meanings, some private and some public. This is the case with regard to abortion, for instance, contrasting the private right to sexual activity and the management of one's own body with the public obligation to respect all human life. Nevertheless, in those areas that are private by reference to the structures of attending to public responsibilities, there is a general social obligation to defend those boundaries and tolerate what happens within them.

This is by no means to suggest that, if there is no public standing to interfere, there are no norms obligating behavior within private spheres. One may be socially free, with defended liberties, to do what one wants in a certain area, and yet be morally bound to do what is right. The fact that it is not anyone's responsibility but one's own does not make it less one's responsibility. Establishing a large realm of privacy, ripe for creative action, does not diminish responsibility. It only highlights its personal locus. Individuals are responsible to do the better wherever their actions can make that difference. In this respect, responsibility is infinite because potentialities allow of alternatives, even though our capacities are finite because we can actualize but one of the alternatives.

10

Responsibilities in Conflict

A lthough Puritanism might be anachronistic to most aspects of the contemporary world, not so with regard to the conflict of responsibilities. More than ever, the world's increasing complexity puts people in situations with uncoordinated obligations and responsibilities. On a superficial level, this poses the practical problem of juggling tasks. On a profound level, it is the deepest problem of the human condition, at least for the identity of individuals. To explore the profound level it is necessary to trace through a heavy dialectic, for which I apologize. The form of the problem, of course, is the one and the many, the root issue of most basic philosophic problems.

From the standpoint of an individual, the fulfillment of a single responsibility usually requires complex organization of activities. In marking out the organization and allocation of resources in life, a responsibility focuses an ideal end or goal. Experience forces us to recognize not one but a plurality of ideal ends that are normative for an individual's conduct. Everyone has a destiny to fulfill, a culture to maintain and enhance, parts to play in the affairs of society, neighborhood, work or professional groups, and family, a life to mature through, a career to build, and a personal pilgrimage to make, as the Puritans would say. Having a destiny, individuals are historical and responsible to the goods of history and nature. Having a culture, they are civilized and responsible to beauty and moral excellence of all sorts. Having parts to play in affairs, people are responsible to others in their society and to the goods of the economic, political, judicial, religious, and other institutions and social relations of their society; particularly, in most cases, to their famiy and cultivated friendships. All of these parts bear upon the attention and care people are obligated to have toward the deep things in nature. Having a life to mature through, each individual has personal development on many levels, at least in the essential human epitomies, and is responsible to each stage. Having careers, people are productive and responsible to productivity. Living as on a pilgrimage, individuals are religious and responsible for relating all aspects of life to ultimate meaning.[1] These contexts of responsibilities, each organized according to ideal ends, are not unconnected with each other. Individuals' social responsibilities vary with their time of life; their productivity has not only social and economic significance but cultural weight as well; and the connection of religious pilgrimage with historical destiny is one of the most perplexing of all problems.

It might seem as if I have laid on the Puritan imagery too thick — how could we fail to be guilty if normed by all three ideal ends? But the truth of the matter is even worse. These ideal ends are but types, and responsibilities within each type uncover internally conflicting ends. The Puritan sensibility is right on target here.

At the same time, however, at least two factors, one theoretical and one practical, argue that the plurality of ideal ends should be reducible to one. The theoretical reason is that "a plurality of ideal ends" seems to be a contradictory phrase when it is said to apply to one individual. For, one thing comes to one end, and insofar as the end has a normative aspect, should come to one best end. This theoretical factor, however, has no real bearing, because what is at stake is *whether* a normative individual indeed is unified, or individual in that sense.

The practical reason for reducing the lot of ends to one is that experience delivers with equal force that conflict among ideal ends is inevitable. Society, family, career, religion, perhaps even culture and history, make insistent and simultaneous demands that our time, energy, and being are too limited to meet.

Exactly what the many ideal ends are is not a question to the interest of the present discussion. Whatever they are, so long as they are several, and conflicting when addressed to one individual, the problem at hand is to discern how this conflict formally can be resolved. It is no solution, as the Puritan would remind us, to take at the outset the monistic view of only one ideal end, though things may come to that pass in the end. Nor will it do to declare human existence inherently contradictory and tragic, though the outcome may be there too, and surely is for many. Instead, there are at least three hypothetical solutions that call openly for a pluralism of ideal ends, and I will consider these in turn.

I. Plurality of Ideal Ends: Three Hypotheses

The first hypothesis can be called aesthetic. It draws its cultural force from Modernism and Existentialism, and is perhaps best expressed in the artistic genius and popularity of writers such as Ernest Hemingway. Although not usually presented as a theory, its primary theoretical components can be discerned. Aesthetic pluralism holds that an individual can be excellent in any number of ways, from statesmanship to bullfighting. Each context of excellence is self-contained, and any one context is as good as any other. The excellence does not consist in an approximation to any external ideal but rather in the "style" with which one operates. A bullfighter may end up gored, but if he gets himself gored with a certain style of stoic courage, the acclaim of excellence is his due. It matters little what an individual attempts or to what degree attains success; it matters only that the attempt be made with beauty or style. The position can be called aesthetic because it judges people for their intrinsic beauty, not by any ethical norm; the distinction between the aesthetic and ethical was drawn in Chapter One.

Aesthetic pluralism is a plea for personal integrity. Despite its emphasis on the plurality of contexts in which excellence can be achieved, however, it amounts to no more than a monistic solution. For it comes to saying that only aesthetic values are objectively valid, and the only proper aesthetic object is a person's own self. Moreover, this solution to the problem of a plurality of ultimate ends is a degenerate monism, for it does not reduce all ends to one, or include them in a basic end, or rank them in a hierarchy; it simply denies the objectivity of all ideals but the aesthetic. Finally, it involves itself in a paradox of aesthetic judgment; a bad work of art is not, properly speaking, a work of art. But if a person fails to live and die with finesse, is that individual still a person in the normatively defined sense? No. Only if one has the integrity to attempt to have integrity could one be blamed for failure to attain it; but then one would have the integrity.

The overwhelming practical difficulty with aesthetic pluralism is that its notion of beauty or style or integrity is too abstract. It can be given content only insofar as a person takes some specific goal to be accomplished (beautifully) as objectively valid, but then the person either is in living contradiction with the theory or is deluded.

Some Kierkegaardians hold a variation of the theory in their view that a thing has value only insofar as it is willed. Here the value consists in the willing, and can be willed for no reason relevant to the nature of the things willed. Another variation of aesthetic pluralism is held by the mass of people in their view that "sincerity" is the only ultimate value. All of these views are a good step up from complete relativism; and they have the practical value of saving the disenchanted from self-defeating skepticism. But they dissolve the problem of conflicting ultimate contexts of responsibility by denying it outright.

The second pluralistic hypothesis is a standby of funded practical wisdom, and consists in assigning the different contexts of responsibility to different stages of life. Education is important to youth, the social roles of courtship and family life to the young adult, cultural and social productivity to the middle-aged, perhaps historical destiny or at least making it through to maturity, and personal religion to the elderly. Undoubtedly, this position is correct in saying that the different contexts of responsiblity have greater or lesser importance at the various stages of life.

But at best this solution is the monistic one of saying that a person should mature at the right pace and in the right order. And at worse it says that the other ends are important only because they are considered to be so at various times of life. This latter move has the virtue of tolerance, but only the kind of tolerance that costs nothing.

The difficulty with this as a pluralistic solution is that if the different contexts of responsibility are objectively binding, they are binding at all times, however much any one might dominate attention at a single stage of life. And this is merely to reinstate the problem. The hypothesis also presupposes a highly settled and discriminating culture, replete with "stations and their duties," to use Bradley's phrase. Our culture is not like that, nor was Confucius's, nor the Puritans', nor any other except that in the imagination of nineteenth-century British dons.

The third pluralistic solution is by far the most subtle. The position has two distinct steps. First, it acknowledges that a person's spirit yearns for a full life involving personal ethics, politics, religion, art, philosophy, science, and perhaps many other domains.[2] Second, since given individuals each can do but few things, the position says they should strive to realize themselves in at least one domain and share vicariously in the achievements of others who operate in the remaining domains.

What this implies is not immediately apparent. To begin with the first contention, the "full life" might be considered an ideal end that includes as its proper parts the various ends distinguished (ethics, politics, religions, etc.). However, the full life is the ideal end of an individual qua individual. The ideal of personal ethics is an end governing interpersonal relations; the ideal of politics is an end for societies and institutions; the ideal of religion is an end for all things other than the ultimate with respect to their relation to it; and so on. Therefore, the relation of the full life as an ideal to the ideals of the contexts of responsibility required for the full life is not that of inclusion; the ideal end for an individual does not include as a proper part the ideal end for what is more than individual.

Another interpretation of the involvement of many ends in the full life is that the ideal of the full life requires *participation* in the many other contexts of responsibility. *While* participating in politics or art, for instance, people ought to attend to the goals proper to those contexts; but *that* they participate is a requirement of the full life. This interpretation has the special merit of preserving in a strong form the plurality of ends, and it resonates strongly with the Confucian conception of the public life of the sage as well as with the Puritan conception of multifaceted responsibility.

But what kind of ideal must the full life be, if it is to require only participation in other contexts? Supposedly the full life reflects all the facets of the human spirit, and assigns that spirit to participate in the multitude of contexts necessary to exercise and realize those facets. This move, however, introduces a new relation between the ideal ends. For, if certain individuals participate in politics, for instance, only in order to lead a full life, then they strive for the political ideal end as a means for achieving the end of a full life. Therefore, the ideals controlling the plurality of contexts of responsibility are related to the ideal of the full life as means to an end.

This is a strange notion of means and ends, however. For the ideals governing the plurality of contexts are not means to the ideal of the full life, as, for instance, the ideals of building a plurality of good academic departments are means to the ideal of a good university. The *participation* in various contexts is a means toward living the full life; the ideals governing the contexts are not. Thus, the ideals governing the contexts are not related to the ideal of the full life in any ordinary sense of means-ends.

Care should be taken not to explain away the plurality of ideals, reducing the position to a monism; this would be done if they were construed only as means toward a single end. Rather, the irreducibility of each ideal should not be lost. Nonetheless, the various contexts accommodating the dimensions of the human spirit, each with its own ideal end, are subordinate to the ideal of the full life in a way other than as means. They are subordinate to the full life in the sense that people commit themselves to them in order that they might live fully; but once committed, they attend to them and them only. Those committed to the political ideal do not articulate that ideal by references to their own full life; nor do painters paint "fulfilling" pictures — they have the ideal of painting artistically excellent ones. An individual may withdraw from political life or stop painting in the interest of a full life; but in the context of politics or paintings, the governing ideals are those of statecraft and art, not the full life.

But is it the case that the one ideal end not to be denied is that of the full life? What warrant has it to dictate the timing and extent of a person's participation in the various contexts of responsibility? Surely, there are instances when a full life should be sacrificed to a nobler cause, as when a parent sacrifices his or her career for the family, a statesman his or her family for the state.

The mistake in our dialectic before, according to this new suggestion, was to suppose that the ideal end of the full life is an end distinct from the various contexts with their irreducible ends. The parent whose career was cut off is fulfilled in the family, the statesman in the statecraft. Moreover, even in cases where the price of participation in a particular context is not so extreme, it still is impossible to participate fully in all contexts of obligations. This raises as an issue the second contention of this hypothesis, namely, that people can fulfill vicariously their obligations to all contexts while participating actively in only one or a few. My recommendation above about dividing the labor of universal responsibility for social obligations requires some version of vicarious responsibility. How is this possible?

II. Vicarious Participation

The first method by which vicarious participation might be thought possible is by participation in all contexts via tokens. Certain people might not directly give food to starving neighbors, but they can contribute money to organized charities. Without being politicians themselves, they can still vote and pay taxes. They can worship the heroes of history from afar and hire priests to say masses. Most certainly, Solomon Guggenheim advanced the case of artistic culture with his museum far more effectively than most of the artistic denizens of Greenwich Village, and Andrew Carnegie the cause of learning more than many teachers.

One difficulty with this solution is that it is only partial. Few people can come up with as many tokens as Guggenheim or Carnegie. Moreover, tokens in some contexts, for example, family and religious responsibilities, are downright unsatisfactory. The chief difficulty with this solution, however, is that in a subtle way it gives up the obligatoriness of the plurality of ends. To show this requires three steps.

1. There is a distinction between an end and an ideal end. An end is a goal someone as a matter of fact accepts and employs to organize activities; an ideal end is a goal worthy of being accepted. The value of a mere end is subjective; the value of an ideal end is objective. Hence, two judgments can be passed on an agent: first, whether the agent lives up to the ends accepted, and second, whether those ends are in themselves ideal.

2. Participation in the various contexts of responsibility is required, according to the view presently considered, as a means for the many-dimensional human spirit to realize its full life. Now suppose participation meant submitting oneself to any end that might govern the activity of a context, irrespective of whether it be ideal; then the integrity of the ideal ends as many and different would be of no account, and the problem would be dissolved, not solved. If participation means only submission to an end as such, then this position is reduced to aesthetic pluralism. Therefore, for this third pluralistic solution to remain a live alternative, participation must mean submitting oneself to ideal ends.

3. Participation through tokens does not involve ideal ends, and is therefore inadequate participation for the full life. For, submission to an ideal end requires criticism of the actually articulated end as to whether it is in fact ideal. Further, in some contexts, for example, politics in contrast to art, the ideal end emerges only slowly in history as limited visions of the polis are criticized. Submission to an end through a token, however, cannot be critical, since criticism is an act of personal agency and a token by definition is not one's own person; therefore, one cannot submit to an ideal end qua ideal through a token. Moreover, one cannot adequately participate in contexts of responsibility through tokens. Certain people may participate in politics by paying taxes, but if their money is used for less than ideal political ends, either they are immoral or they are severed from responsibility for their money's use and hence submisson to the ideal end. Of course, we probably should be thankful that Guggenheim's trustees did not design their own museum, but hired Frank Lloyd Wright as a token. Nonetheless, insofar as they evaluated Wright's promise, they did criticize the envisioned end as to its ideality; and insofar as they did not, they deserve no credit for serving the ideal aesthetic end.

It is impossible, therefore, to participate passively in contexts of responsibility by way of tokens. As has been shown, participation in a context of responsibility requires submission to its controlling end as ideal, and this requirement is not fulfilled by a token. I admit that no sharp distinction can be drawn between active personal participation and passive token participation. In the most personal involvement we use tools (i.e., tokens), and in the most passive participation some personal selection of tokens, however uncritical, might take place. But just as far as people do not submit to the ideal character of their ends, so far they do not adequately participate in that context of responsibility. The problem remains, then, to understand how people can meet the demands of many ideal ends when they have neither time nor energy nor being to submit to them all as they should.

The second method of vicarious participation, by means of which people can attain goals that for them are mutually exclusive, is by making amends. Suppose an individual is confronted with a set of exclusively alternative actions, different values accruing from each alternative. On whichever action the person's preference rests, that person is committed, in choosing it, to the further end that would make up for all the values excluded by that choice.

The chief difficulty with this view is that it requires values to be commensurate; in several sense already pointed out, they are not. In addition, there are the following senses of incommensurability. First, a choice that excludes a human life is committed to making amends for that life. The problem is not to measure the guilt, justification, or forgiveness of the chooser against the killed person's life; rather, it is to measure the value of the person's life against the value the chooser must later bring about. Even were the chooser to do more public good than the dead person ever would, there is no standard by which to measure the intrinsic value of the victim's life. Human life is an incommensurable value.

A second and more relevant sense in which values are incommensurable is when the values consist in satisfying irreducibly different ideal ends. An aesthetic value cannot be measured by a political or religious value unless there is some ideal end that encompasses all as a third term. As I argued in discussing the relation between the ideal of the full life and the other ideals, there is no such overarching ideal for the position under consideration.

Therefore, however useful the principle of making amends might be in a limited context where values are commensurable, it will not solve the problem posed for it; that is, to satisfy vicariously the variety of different irreducible ideals by satisfying some one or few other ideals.

A third method for vicarious responsibility involves reconsidering the structure of the ends. According to this method, we should acknowledge that this ideal is specialized by the different positions from which we face it. The ideal end an Iowa farmer faces is different from that of a San Francisco ship owner; the ancient Greek had one specialization of the ideal, a twelfth-century monk another, a modern American yet a third. In each case, the ideal end must be schematized, so to speak, to the conditions from which it is faced. This solution not only shows how the end taken to be ideal must be relative to each culture, but also how within a culture its service is divided into separate offices. The ideal schematized to our society requires that there be firemen and mailmen, artists and politicians, philosophers and bartenders. An ideal fireman is not the same as an ideal mailman, but both of these ideal ends fit together as subdivisions of the larger schematized ideal.

It should be noted that the specializations cited by this scheme are of two kinds, though not often distinguished; they can be called schematization and subdivision, respectively. An ideal end is

schematized when it is initially vague in itself with respect to it application, and is then made determinate with respect to some case.
For instance, if neighborly love is an ideal end, it means one thing
when the neighbors are people, another when they are nations; yet
an analogy holds between them. An ideal specialized to different
cultures is of this kind. Subdivision, on the other hand, is simply the
marking out of various parts of a rather determinate complex ideal
end, as the roles of fireman and mailman in our society.

Neither schematization nor subdivision, however, solves the
problem of specializing an encompassing ideal end into the plurality
of ideal ends, each with its own integrity. The various ideal ends
produced by schematization depend, for their plurality, on the
diverse conditions to which the encompassing ideal end must be applicable; and their identity depends upon the ideality of the encompassing ideal end. The schematized end, that is, gets its distinction
from other schematized ends through the distinctness of the non-
ideal conditions to which the encompassing ideal end must be
schematized. And it gets its character as ideal end from the encompassing ideal it schematizes. A schematized ideal end, therefore, has
no integrity of its own, qua ideal, over against the encompassing
ideal end; and the position reduces to a monism. This is not to say
that the ideal end schematized to the conditions of ancient Greek
society is not somewhat different from that schematized to the conditions of American society, and that an American who tried to act like
a Greek at a point of difference might not be doing wrong. It is only
to say that the ideality of the two schematized ends consists in the
relation of the ends as schemata to the same encompassing ideal end,
and not in the fact that they are taken as different ends by different
peoples in different conditions. The only end whose ideality has integrity is the encompassing ideal end. All others derive their ideality
from that one.

Subdivision is in equally bad straits as a pluralistic solution.
Suppose the ideal end that is to contain limited ideal ends as subdivisions is not itself a schema of a more transcendent ideal, but is
the ideal itself (else it would have the difficulties of schematization as
well). To be sure, each subdivision will have integrity over against
the other subdivisions; but has each integrity over agains the whole?
As ends, the subdivisions are distinct in virtue of the complexity of
the whole; but as ideal ends they are ideal only in virtue of the fact
that they are parts of the whole. Apart from the whole, no subdivi-

sion has a claim to ideality. Subdivision as well as schematization reduces to monism so far as ideality is concerned.

But suppose that the ideal end of each subdivision did have its integrity. Then people either submit themselves to one subdivision only, or they must participate in a variety of subdivisions. If the former, the initial problem is again dissolved, not solved, for a single person has then only one real end to serve. If the latter, then it is just a reinstatment of the problem of how a person can serve many masters. If the fullness of the human spirit requires participation in many subdivisions of the one ideal end, and participation requires critical submission to the specific ideal end of each subdivision, the problem of how to do it all still remains. It is hardly a consolation to know that the many ideal ends are not mutually contradictory in themselves; for they surely put forth contradictory claims on our time, energy, and being.

III. A Puritan Regrouping

What are the conclusions so far? The problem was to reconcile to one person's life a plurality of independent contexts of responsibility, each with its own ideal end. The first solution claimed that a variety of contexts are open, but that what counts is the aesthetic style by which one does what one does; among other difficulties, this position denied the obligatoriness of the contexts and is reduced to a monism of "the good style of life." The second solution arranged the obligatoriness of the contexts in a series whose parts are appropriate to different times of life; but the principle for such an arrangement lies in the interest of the person, not in the nature of the ideals governing the contexts, and hence is ad hoc from the standpoint of the obligatoriness of the many responsibilities.

The third solution, much more complex, was developed dialectically. Its fundamental principle is two-fold: first, not only are there diverse, independent, and irreducible contexts of responsibility, each with its own ideal end, but also the human spirit must participate in them all to fulfill its many dimensions; second, since an individual cannot actively participate in them all, it must be possible to achieve vicariously the good not achieved by personal participation.

Focusing on the former contention, it was at first taken that the full life is an ideal end distinct from and transcending the various

ideal ends of the different contexts of responsibility so as to order
them. However, the various ideal ends cannot be included as parts
of the full life; nor can they be means toward it, although participation in the various contexts they goven can be a means. Still, participation in such a context requires submission to the controlling
ideal end of that context without regard for alternate ends; especially, the ideality of a particular end cannot be determined by reference
to the full life. Moreover, what gives the ideal end of the full life a
warrant to govern our participation in the other contexts of responsibility? Responsibility to self is but one responsibility among others;
and this difficulty must be faced by any self-realization theory that
takes the full life to be an ideal distinct from others.

The next move was to take the full life to consist, not in a satisfaction of its own, but in the active fulfilling of responsibility in one
or a few contexts with vicarious fulfillment of other contexts, thus
focusing on the second fundamental contention of the theory. Three
methods of vicarious participation were distinguished. The first was
by way of tokens; the chief (but not the only) difficulty here was that
a token accepts an end governing a context but does not criticize it as
ideal, and thus does not represent the person in a context of responsibility. One is responsible to true ideal ends, not just accepted ones.
The second method of vicarious participation was through making
amends in future action for the values excluded in choice. But this
requires the values to be commensurable, which they are not if they
are in different contexts, not subordinate to an encompassing ideal
end. The third method amounted to specializing a single ideal into
different parts; but such specialized parts do not have integrity as
ideals over against what they specialize. Even if they should, a person either is responsible to but one part, whereupon the problem of
plurality of ideal ends is merely sidestepped, or is responsible to
many, whereupon the problem is merely reinstated. The dialectic
comes full circle, finally, when the specialization theory is an
analogue on the cosmological level of the view that the various ideal
ends are either parts of (subdivisions) or means to (schemata) th
ideal end of the full life.

To go around the dialectical spiral again, this time on the
cosmic level, would be to uncover the same formal difficulties. For,
suppose it be said that any two conflicting ideal ends must be
mediated by a third. What is the relation of this third to the first two?
If it merely includes them, it shows them to be but parts of a complex

ideal end and to have all the difficulties of the specialization theory. Or if it is external to the first two, it decides between them on grounds irrelevant to their ideality, as ease of cooking may decide between two equally desired dishes. The first relation reduces to a monism, and the second provides a means for choosing but not a way of escaping the obligations of the independent ends and the concomitant guilt for failure.

What conclusions are to be drawn from these formal considerations of pluralistic solutions? Obviously, the pluralism can be be given up for a monism. But this is to admit that theory is irrelevant to our common and repeated experience that life has conflicting contexts, of responsibility. Short of resting in irrelevant theory, either a new pluralistic solution can be proposed or the problem can be acknowledged as unsolvable. If it is ineeed unsolvable, and if all monistic solutions are rejected, then people are necessarily guilty. It must then be right that the very conditions of human existence are evil, and existential humanity itself insures human guilt, however much choice people have in what they might be guilty for.

Two responses can be made to this allegation of necessary guilt. It can be accepted simply, and the human lot be marked as unalloyed moral tragedy. Most of us have felt pushed to this response at one time or another. But it finds little resonance outside Western culture; and even in the West, the better tragedians have known that what is inevitable in tragedy is not just a conflict of responsibilities but a fault. As simply as it is accepted, the response must be retracted upon presentation of a theory that does resolve the conflict of responsibility. The second response to alleged necessary guilt is to hand it over to God for redemption. Redemption might be by plain forgiveness, as many Christians believe; but this seems to deny seriousness to guilt. Or redemption might be through the attribution of vicarious merit that people cannot achieve by themselves. Some Christians also believe in redemption in this sense, with merit being attributed to Christ. Paul Weiss argues that God redeems by rearranging the cosmos, or the internal divine life.[3] These direct references to the intervention of God, however, suffer from the same condition that forces us to refer to the Puritan only with a smile. Namely, the God of whom we can speak this way is dead, and the death of that God's culture makes these redemptive appeals unconvincing.

Nevertheless, the Puritan was on to something. The third pluralistic type of solution began, it will be remembered, by asserting that the full life is an ideal end that directs our participation in all other contexts governed by other ideal ends. But the full life could not be maintained as an ideal end distinct from and on a par with others. Nor could it be submerged in one of the others with vicarious participation in other contexts of responsibility, as the consequent dialectic showed. The formal difficulties of the full-life theory hold for any ideal and which seeks to mediate the rest.

The resolution of these difficulties lies in recognizing that the mediating ideal end, that is, the full life or something analogous, is indeed distinct from the other ideal ends, but also that it is not on a par with them. On grounds that will come out in what follows, this mediating ideal end should be called the religious, in respect of the Puritan's contribution. I shall argue that all nonreligious ideal ends, whatever they are found to be, have their own integrity, as does the religious end. Moreover, we are responsible to them all and are guilty when we fail our responsibilities. Since conflict is inevitable, so is guilt. However, guilt for failing the nonreligious ideal ends is not on a par with religious guilt. Religious guilt cannot be amended by a future good, even when a God might do the good; whereas non-religious guilt can be made up that way. How is the position to be maintained?

Although the traditional God of Westesrn religions might be dead, the Puritan would remind us that the ontological functions once thought to be performed by God must now be performed by something else with similar functional powers. One of those functions was to account for the contingent actual existence of a world with diverse elements. Indeed, although only the Westesrn religions think of God as an ontological creator, all the major traditions of the world think the cosmos is contingent on some ontological principle internal or external to its existence—the Tao, Buddha-mind, Brahman. Of course, those other traditional religions are in trouble with modernity too. But modernity, like the rest, believes that complexity itself is what needs an account; the only thing that does not need an account is chaos, sheer lack of order.[4] Whatever accounts for the existence of the complex world cannot be another complex thing, for the relation between it and the world is just the complexity needing an account. So in some sense the world is contingent upon what is not finite or determinate, whereas the world itself is finite and determinate (at least in part). Actually, the contingent world might itself be infinite in the orders exhibited in it, so that any finite thing might be analyzed in at least an indefinite number of ways. There nevertheless is the stark contrast between the infinity of the ontological ground and the definiteness of individual contingent things. What one is in one order limits one's possibilities in other orders; to be definite is to exclude possibilities.

The clue to the character of the world's contingency can be seen in the categories needed to account for the determinateness of things as harmonies. Recall Plato's categories from the *Philebus* quoted at the head of Chapter Four above; unlimited, limit, mixture, and cause of mixture. Ontological contingency is contingency on the operation and cooperation of these four. In religious terms, the unlimited is the feminine principle, the Earth Mother, the diverse gods of vegetations, fertility, change, movement, cycles of construction and destruction. The limit is religiously depicted in the paternal principle, the Sky God, speaking the word, bringing order out of chaos, laying down the law, ruling through will and reason. The mixture is not just the combination of pattern and parts, but the actualization of the individuality of things, their haecceity; it is the reduction of material processes and universal patterns to definite existence. The problematic of creation appears here as the gound of existence, and the religious problem is not propitiating Mother Nature or making amends to the Divine Judge but rather reconciling oneself or one's group to the conditions of actuality. The cause of mixture, in religious terms, is the ideal end for the Tao, the Path, the way of sanctification and perfection; its religious problematic is the attainment of coordination of one's life and history within the overall matrix of nature and history, relative to existence itself. Although all the religious traditions develop these elements in different ways, with different emphases, we may summarize the four dimensions of the religious problematic in the following way: change and productivity, order and righteousness, harmony of essence and existence, sanctification and abiding in the Tao.

Now, part of proper human nature is to be finite in respect to all four dimensions, and a striking manifestation of this finitude is the inevitable failure to meet many responsibilities. But since human beings are created as finite, this failure is proper to human nature, and does not ipso facto constitute failure to meet religious responsibilities — responsibilities for being onself relative to the ground of being. How is this so?

The heart of religious sin is the attempt to overstep one's created nature as finite, to be infinite as is proper only to God, as the Calvinist would say; the root sin is pride. One of the most popular forms of this sin, especially among people sensitive to responsibilities, is the thought and expectation that one can fullfill all one's nonreligious responsibilities. As has been shown, such success is impossible when creation includes such a plurality of ideal ends relevant to persons. One of the most important features of the religious ideal end is the acceptance of persons' finite nature and their consequent guilt. But there is nothing in finite human nature necessitating that people must fail to accept this guilt and thereby fail to meet the religious ideal end. When the Puritan consciousness formed itself with the contrast, "Behold the infinite glory of God, and look upon us most despicable sinners," it was not a contradiction but a truth stripped of compromises.

The Puritan consciousness, not tolerating much spiritual privacy, said of its private intuitions, "behold . . . , and look . . . ." Moral life *presents itself* for judgment. Confucian morality also emphasized the appearance of good as well as its substance; in fact, for the scholar-official and the Taoist sage, proper behavior means doing good conspicuously. One's moral life consists in part in its positive influence on others. The Confucians, of course, would object to employing religious categories to interpret the mediation of the plurality of ends. They would say, as Anthony Cua explains, that the moral life consists not in following any particular ideal end but in bringing harmony to all the ideal ends that might bear upon a particular situation, in consonance with those particular ideal ends that have to do with personal virtue as an agent.[5] Nevertheless, the Confucian conception, no less than the idea put forward here in Western categories, holds that the fundamental harmonies of self and world are not mere cosmological arangements but the basic harmonies that make up the world itself.

IV. The Religious Dimension

What finally is the relation between the religious ideal and the others? At least five important contrasts can be made.

1. In the first place, the nonreligious ideal ends are contingent parts of creation, in whatever sense of creation satisfies the ontological question. There is no reason to suppose that normative

possibilities cannot be created as well as nonnormative ones and norm-seeking actualities. All the contingent things in the world have values and norms making them valuable and determining what variations might be more or less valuable. People are responsible to all the relevant norms, and each functions as an ideal end to define an organization of activity. The religious ideal end, on the other hand, is constitutive of what it is to be a creature as such. It is thwarted and becomes problematic only when people try to overstep their created nature and to assume the powers of the gods. To be a good creature and rightly related to ultimate things is simply to realize one's true given nature. To make this contrast in technical terms, with respect to one's harmony as a creature as such, the non-religious ideal ends are conditional, and the religious end is essential because constitutive and definitive. Recognition of the essential finitude of human life in the face of the infinite demands of the universe is the moral ground for irony in the Puritan smile.

2. In the second place, people face the nonreligious goals by means of their conditional features, whereas they face the religious ideal end as individuals with unique and personal identities constituted through harmonizing those conditions with their essential features. People face ideal ends such as statecraft or art in the appropriate medium of accomplishment — e.g., politics or imagination — exactly as would other people in those circumstances. Responsible circumstances vary in particularity, some being highly particular. Responsibility to care for the parents of an only child falls upon just one person; but the character of the responsibility is what anyone should do is they were that only child. This follows from the universality involved in those higher essential human epitomies that consists in being a representative role-player, thinker, actor, and so forth. Responsibilities in this sense stem from the patterns or orders, the limits, that constitute our nature. The specific individuality of persons is of no relevance to nonreligious ends over and above the positions they occupy relative to those ends. On the other hand, people face the religious ideal end with the fullness of their being; the ultimate ground of persons' contingency is the source of individuation and of their integration in all respects. Although people have nonreligious responsibilities because of their predicates, as it were, their concrete being is more than the sum of the predicates; it is their predicates harmonized essentially and individually. The religious goal is finding the path for coming to terms with that whole individu-

ality. What is true of personal individuals here applies as well to individual groups, although the degree of unity in a group may be problematic.

To face the religious ideal end as an end, people must have put their status as creatures in jeopardy; the religious ideal end is faced as one's own jeopardized individuality. In terms of the Western tradition, only people who have fallen have a religious end problematically to be pursued; and what they pursue is their own proper creaturely status. A nonreligious ideal end is an end for a counter or character "of a certain kind." The religious ideal end is an end for whole personal harmonies, requiring the personal, whole, individual responses for its accomplishment.

3. Since only universal characters of people are relevant to nonreligious ideal ends, and since people are specific individuals, the nonreligious ideal ends are obligatory only on the condition that people are identified with their relevant universal features. The problem here is that people can be alienated from their universal characters, hiding their existence from their "essence." (Paul Tillich, in a different use of "essence" from mine, expressed this point as the alienation of essence from existence.) There is nothing psychological to prevent people from choosing not to identify themselves as responsible, because of their nature, to some ideal ends; people often do reject that responsibility. But to choose not to identify with that nature is simply to deny the nature one has. The obligations bind responsibility whether one wants them or not. The religious motive for denial of these responsibilities is to deny one's finite status. Those responsibilities are at once indefinitely many in extent, determined by one's finite nature, and productive of guilt; hence, the motive for denial. But that finite nature, with its infinite context and inevitable moral failure is the human condition. To deny it is to alienate oneself from one's created status as a mixture. To accept one's finite condition is to accept the actualization of that essence with its guilts.

The upshot of this contrast is then two-sided. One side is that all responsibility, even that to nonreligious ideal ends, comes from the religious, the created status one has as a finitely normed person. The other side is that failure to accept a nonreligious responsibility is not only a wrong against that nonreligious end but a sin against the religious end as well, as the Puritan would put it. For, to deny a responsibility, not just to fail to meet a responsibility already accepted, is to deny the finiteness of one's given, obligated nature.

4. The fourth contrast can be brought out by drawing a stipulative (and temporary) distinction between aspects and dimensions. Both aspects and dimensions are pervasive through experience, but pervasive in different senses. An aspect is the relevance a thing has for a nonreligious ideal end. Thus, a painting has more or less political relevance, and persons' careers have relevance for their family, a domestic aspect, so to speak. The important thing is that, whereas every ideal end may touch a relevant aspect of every thing, there are degrees of relevance. A dimension, on the other hand, pervades all of experience with equal relevance; it is the common element all things have as created, the relation each has to its created nature, equally relevant for each created thing. There is only one dimension, the religious, and the nonreligious ideal ends determine its various aspects.

I should note parenthetically that not only is there a religious dimension to human experience, but for many people there is also a religious aspect. For, not only does people's createdness touch all they do, but its health requires special efforts, directed by ideal ends on a par with others, ideal ends in the form of religious practices, customs, and institutions. But the ideal ends relevant for the relevant for the religious *aspect* are nonreligious in the sense of nonreligious used heretofore. Since they are on a par with other ideal ends, they must at times conflict with them, and we may fail them. But to do so is a wrong to be made up in the future so far as possible, not a sin. When the religious aspect of experience is not acknowledged as distinct from the religious dimension, there is a tendency either to universalize religion so that it loses any concrete expression, or to identify it with the concrete expression so that it becomes one alternative among others.

5. Finally, it must be acknowledged that "ideal end" means something different when used of the religious than when used of the nonreligious, and the previous four points have separated the uses. Nonreligious ideal ends are ends in the sense that they oblige us with projects. Part of the created world is that we have these projects or contexts of responsibility. The religious ideal end is an end only in the sense that we may, through pride, get out of joint with our created status and face it as the project of regaining our identity as creatures. And it is ideal in the sense that it is our true identity. To be created is to be obligated to be a creature with a creature's finite nature. One cannot cease to be a creature, but one can pervert one's

created nature by trying to escape its given limitations. The Confucian might not use this Western imagery but would clearly understand the point. The reason filiality is the first of Confucian virtues is that it entails the acceptance of one's finite particularity as defined by finite particular responsibilities. Goodness and being are joined in the fact of contingency in such a way that to do less than the good is to fall from one's identity.

The answer, at least in outline form, to the original problem is now at hand. Our experience does indeed contain a plurality of aspects of obligation, a plurality of ideal ends by which we should govern our conduct, a plurality of contexts of responsibility. But it also contains one dimension from which all obligation stems and that is constitutive of the identity of all created things. With respect to the many aspects of obligation, our failure is necessary, and would be tragic if it were the only judgment made upon us. But judgment with respect to the many nonreligious ideal ends is made on us only with respect to our conditional characters, not as concrete individuals. And our failure to meet them might be made up so far as commensurability goes, if not by us, then by others. With respect to the one religious dimension, failure is not necessary, and our existence is not necessarily tragic. But only the religious dimension can sustain judgment upon us as concrete, whole individuals, and here alone can we become fully guilty.

My (Puritan) solution is to put the ideal ends on different levels, as it were, such that the many responsibilities are specializations of the religious dimension, and the many ideal ends sustain their own integrity as ideals. Were we not able to distinguish the monism of the religious dimension from the pluralism of the contingent contexts of responsiblity, we would end in the paradoxes detailed earlier. Insofar as people function relative to different ideal ends, they are responsible in the contexts those ideals regulate. But only in the religious dimension are people liable as individuals. Any particular responsibility, of course, has a religious dimension; one's contingent conditions determine one's political responsibilities, although one addresses those responsibilities (religiously) as a full person. As for nonreligious wrongs, people must accept their limitations with humility. Not to do so, to condemn oneself, is the greatest sin of pride, at once assuming God's bench of judgment and denying the hand of providence.

The ghost of the Puritan surely must smile at this religious rhetoric used out of season. Over the centuries, the ghost has watched the enthusiastic embrace of the Calvinist world turn first cloying and then repulsive. Part of the Puritan smile is at the fact that we still use it. Another part, the ironic part, is at the fact that we cannot help it. Albeit but metaphoric, it is more false to abandon the stark vision of infinite glory and responsibility coupled with inevitable guilt than to be burdened with its traditional liabilities. The embrace of the Puritan (and Confucian) seriousness of responsibility in the face of an infinity of impossible demands is the fundamental ironic context for moral reflection.

V. On Evil, of Satan's Sort

It must seem bizarre to find a book of moral philosophy with Puritan imagery, elevating responsibility over freedom, and turning on the ironic pivot of infinite life and finite response, that does not make a point about evil. The pain and suffering resulting from evil, both natural and moral, have been thematized, for they establish obligations. But the wickedness of moral evil itself, the subject of so many Puritan sermons, has been glossed over. Moreover, guilt was interpreted as a failure to fulfill some responsibilities because of conflicts with other responsibilities, not as the willful intention to do evil as such. Does this mean I advocate mere meliorism in the end? Where is the Prince of Darkness, the sower of negation and confusion in our world and souls? Surely, his footprints are tracked across the holocausts, bombs, oppressions, tortures, and banalities of our own time.

Remember, however, that Satan is an angel; God's glorious instrument before the fall, according to Milton; and his unwilling instrument after. For all the stark either/or of the Puritan contrast between good and evil, that contrast was a denial of Manicheanism, of the belief in an independent power of evil. Evil is a misguided pursuit of responsibility. Satan was not irresponsible in an absolute sense. He was responsible to a good that needed action, namely, the manifestation of his own excellence that was great indeed. The responsibility to manifest his own excellence was incompatible, he thought, with the compromises necessary for that to be harmonized with all the other heavenly obligations. Thus, he asserted his independence from the web of heavenly obligations and became an individual. His excellence as an individual required him to sow confusion, negativity, and destruction through the environment whose diverse obligations threatened his personal integrity. Whatever Milton's intentions, he did not depict Satan as a bum but as a hero whose dignity, courage, and perseverance through the pain of his guilt and punishment we cheer despite pious condemnation. Satan in *Paradise Lost* is more interesting than the humans, Jesus, God, and the other angels; we thrill to his struggles and find in him our own (idealized!) identity.

What was Satan's mistake in *Paradise Lost?* His task was to be responsible to the heavenly obligations, which appeared to be the problem of having to glorify too many glorious beings in harmonious order. The Christian answer to that problem, that Milton figured in Jesus, is that one empties oneself to be the servant of others. By denying one's own glory, one strikes the best bargain with the infinity of obligation. Paradoxically, God agrees with Satan in maintaining the integrity of his own manifest glory, sending instead the Son as his token *kenosis*. This paradox lies behind Altizer's death of God theology: The God who did not empty himself but sent the Son instead does have to die for the Christian vision to be fulfilled. After the death of the Father, there only is the self-emptied Son. In a functional sense, Satan and the self-glorifying God are one.

The identity of Satan and God lies not only in their common resistance to *kenosis*. That resistance, depicted in Satan's epic self-assertion through evil, is creative of our own situation. The human situation is not an innocent ramble through a garden and tumble in the hay. It is rather the inevitably guilty situation of having failed responsibilities even when we have tried to do the best. Furthermore, it is only when we are tempted to the assertion of our own glory, that is, our own moral virtue, that we have an individuating moral identity. That individuating moral identity is necessary for any response whatsoever to the temptation; it is necessary if we are sinfully to adopt the responsibilities to our own virtue, and it is necessary if instead we are to empty ourselves to other responsibilities. We thrill to Satan's heroism because our own individual moral identity is created in the act of being tempted. The thrill is how it feels to be created.

But of course evil is wrong, wrong on two levels. On the naive level, evil is the failure of a responsibility because some other responsibility gets in the way; on this level, evil is inevitable, and yet with luck and the arduous pursuit of a culture of responsibility, we might do least evil. On the perverse level, evil is the intentional doing of harm motivated by some aspect of self-glorificaton. If the Puritans (and Confucians) are right about a natural sense for the value of things, however that needs cultivation, then selfishness is a deviant phenomenon that needs explanation. Why pick one's own good over some other greater good? Only if there is a higher-level motivation to serve, assert, or glorify oneself. West and East agree that selfishness is an unnatural phenomenon and the root of morally culpable evil. The drama of the Fall gives it appropriate importance. Sin is not moral failure alone, but that coupled with the secret belief that we ought to be like gods: knowing good and evil in such a way as to avoid failure. The deliberate harming of others derives, through one path or another, from ontological pride.

So I believe that moral evil is indeed properly discussed as a matter of conflict among responsibilities, a conflict that turns from mere moral failure to ontological sin when we respond to the conflict with pride. Of course, our own good is one among many, and since we are with ourselves more than with anyone else, it is appropriate to be responsible to our good rather constantly. When our own good in pride doubles back upon itself and becomes a good at the expense of other, more meritorious goods, the service of our own good becomes the motivation for the intentional harming of other people, of institutions, and of nature for the sake of the harm itself. The answer to the ontological problem of intentional moral evil is the acceptance of ourselves as having failed responsibilities in conflict. That requires the emptying of ourselves of the glory in which we try to be like gods.

The truly evil people in this world are morally culpable in ways the Puritans understood well. It is inevitable that we do evil in failing responsibilities. That evil is compounded when we fail the higher-level responsibility to become as cultivated in the pursuit of responsibilities as possible; it is evil to do more evil than necessary. Evil takes on a religious, ontological dimension when being responsible to one's own goodness itself couples with pride and, like a chain reaction, corrupts the pursuit of all other responsibilities. The more competent and heroic, the more thorough and vicious the evil. To break the proliferating bondage of pride, one needs to accept forgiveness for even the most vicious failures and take satisfaction in the limited good that one in fact does and enjoys.

Satan's pride is a necessary constant temptation without which we are not moral individuals. Yet to succumb to it is to believe the absolute nonsense that we could be sinless like gods. Thrilling though he is, Satan is an utterly unironic, ridiculous bombast who lies to us and himself about our situation. Our situation is the contrast between infinite responsibilities and finite responsiveness, a contrast appreciated only with an irony like the Puritan's smile. Having put the heady drama of sin and salvation behind us, which is what salvation is, we have the ordinary world where good and evil are mixed and our task is simply to do better.

11

A Taste of Death

For the classical Puritans, death, though an obsession, was not an ultimately important topic. Believing as most of them did in a kind of immortality, the Puritans took death to be a door to a further life in which the moral quality of one's life here is to be manifested in a pure way. For the Calvinistic Puritans, life after death was not so much a reward or punishment for this life, since both were predestined, but rather a manifestation of its true nature. I do not think any of the Puritan beliefs on these matters are defensible. We do not share their confidence in a controlling God; our plausible cosmologies do not include immortality in any literal sense; the Puritan emphasis on responsibility, which I have defended at length, is not compatible with their predestinarian theology; and because of these points, death as such is much more important than they thought.

The twentieth century has forced the topic of death once again into the center of consciousness. Two historical conditions conspired to make this so. First was the crisis in meaningfulness focused by Modernism and given explicit philosophic form in Existentialism. Heidegger's point in his early work was that human meaning and reality consist at bottom in a fundamental care or compassion that arises from living toward one's own death. Those thinkers, then, who find life ultimately meaningless do so because it is meaningless to them to face death. The other condition was the invention of what

Edith Wyschogrod has called "mass death," the death of concentration camps, firebombs, and nuclear warfare. Reacting to Heidegger,
Wyschogrod points out that his "authenticity" paradigm of facing
death makes no sense under the conditions of mass death; yet mass
death, the technological innovation of our time, is our problem.[1]

I believe there is no straightforward way to reflect on death. It is
ultimately paradoxical and, therefore, can be discussed only in tones
of indirection and irony. At the same time, it is the topic of greatest
challenge for a philosophy of moral reflection attempting to embody
something of Puritan seriousness and responsibility. How can we be
serious about death if it can be approached only ironically? How can
we define human life in terms of responsibility if the culmination of
life is the utter incapacity of responsible action?

To address these issues, I have chosen Plato's ironic medium,
the dialogue; but the explicit model is the dialogue in the *Kathopanisad.*
The two characters are Dr. Thomas and Maria Nonscivi. "Thomas"
means "twin" and is cognate to the Sanskrit word for twin, "yama."
Yama the twin is also the name of the god of death, which is the
association intended here. Yama is depicted in the *Mahabharata* as
carrying a noose in which he binds the souls of the dead. "Nonscivi"
is the Latin name constructed from the negative plus the perfect
tense form of "scio," to know. It parallels the Sanskrit name
"Naciketas," likewise formed from the negative plus the perfect tense
of "cit," to know. The conversation between Naciketas, the one who
does not know, with Yama, god of death, is the subject of the
Kathopanisad.

* * * * * * * * * * * *

Dr. Thomas was a pathologist before becoming dean of the
country's largest medical school. Controversy marked his earlier
career because of his vocal public advocacy of plans to sustain arti-
ficially the bodies of the newly dead (dead by brain-death criteria) as
organ banks for transplant purposes. As dean, he spoke somewhat
less polemically because of his position as representative of the
university, an obligation the administration knew he would respect.
Besides, he was an excellent dean. His tendency to talk philosophy
had annoyed his medical colleagues; but it was immensely attractive
to people outside the medical school who, because of him, looked
upon the institution as more wise and humanistic than it was. Fur-

thermore, Dr. Thomas was a decisive administrator, wielding the axe with an objective sense of desserts, immune to special pleading. The metaphor of the axe, however, was not quite apt; in light of the usual power struggles in the medical school, Dr. Thomas was more often thought the hangman, playing out the hemp to supplicants with a finesse that trapped the soft souls every time. Incompetent people and dead-end projects were not so much thrown out as rendered excommunicant and asphyxiated, their reputations, presence, and equipment feeding the later accessors to power.

In the case of Maria Nonscivi, however, Dr. Thomas had made a mistake, a stupid blunder. Nonscivi, a fourth-year medical student, not only had led her class through medical school but had participated in so many extracurricular projects bringing health care to the university neighborhood that she clearly was the prize student. Dr. Thomas forgot her request for a recommendation to a prestigious internship, losing the form; his sense of guilt and obligation upset him greatly; the possibility of scandal itself was not far from his mind.

After calling her to his office, apologizing, and promising to pull strings to admit her to the desired program, Dr. Thomas asked whether there was anything more he could do to make amends. Almost out of politeness it seemed, she asked his advice on how to succeed as a young doctor. His answers, perfunctory truisms, were delivered so as to convey what they both knew, that Nonscivi already had the secret of success. Finally, with some confidence stimulated by his obvious desire to be relieved of guilt, yet with the embarrassment of knowing it was not the kind of question one raises with one's dean, she asked:

N. Explain death, Dr. Thomas. You run the world's greatest effort to cheat it. Yet your own speciality depends on death's having won.

T. Let me quote a poet for my answer, the author of the hymn at the end of the *Taittiriya Upanishad*:

> "I am food, I am food, I am food.
> I am foodeater, I am foodeater, I am foodeater.
> I am the combining agent, I am the combining agent,
>   I am the combining agent.

> I am the first born of the world-order, earlier than
> the gods, in the center of immortality.
> Whoso gives me, he surely does save thus,
> I, who am food, eat the eater of food."[2]

N.   What does that mean, doctor? I ask about death and you quote a verse about food. I don't mean to be impertinent, but is that a macabre reference to your ideas about using bodies as organ-farms?

T.   Perhaps it is, although the pejorative connotations you intend with "macabre" may not be worthy of the word itself. My belief is that our whole social attitude toward death needs to be changed. We have thought death to be an ultimate disconti-nuity, an ultimate separation of a person's identity from nature and from one's social world. That's a mistake. Death is as much a part of life as birth, and should be viewed as such.

The Upanisad's discussion of food is a good metaphor for the better conception. Life is like food. A person comes to be and grows by eating. He not only eats the food given by mouth, but he eats his parents genetically, he eats his society by consuming its culture, he eats his experience by taking it into his memory and education. Growing older, the emphasis shifts to "diges-tion." The person comes to be a "combining agent," putting together what he eats in a unique creative way. The Sanskrit word for "combining agent," "slokakrt," in this context means "digestion." But its root meaning has to with composing sounds into verse.

The person then becomes food himself. He provides genetic materials, sustenance, culture, and emotional resources to his children. He acts out deeds on the historical stage, feed-ing the world. And perhaps he makes a creative contribution to world culture. His last act of feeding is to give up his body as food. For the ancient Hindus this could hardly mean more than returning organic nutrients to the natural system. But with our new medical technology we can quite literally feed our organs to needy human beings. The prospect of dying can now be viewed as an extraordinarily valuable possibility for feeding life, almost as important as giving birth!

N.   Rhapsody, Dean Thomas, rhapsody! If you don't mind my saying so.

T. Oh, I know there are problems with this idea. Legal safeguards
would have to be worked out to respect the particular wishes of
dying patients; involuntary feeding is cannibalism. Legal
criteria would have to be defined for inheritance and for shifting the billing from Blue Cross to the hospital equipment
budget. And then there would be the special frustrations of
cancer patients whose bodies would be unacceptable for trans-
plantation; their disease would be a special kind of infertility.
But medical science soon . . .

N. That's not what I meant, doctor. Human life is more than natural
processes that could be symbolized by the metaphor of food. Consumption indeed! Surely life must add up to more than that.

T. Well, an earlier section of the same Upanishad does distinguish
the life of a person from the natural processes whose essence is
food. Personal life dwells within the natural process but is
distinguished by its cognitive capacity to know parts of the
natural process that are not directly its food. The cognitive
capacities of mind, of theoretical understanding, and of the
kind of mystical intuition associated with knowledge of God
and bliss—none of these are adequately symbolized by the
metaphor of food. But if you make the metaphor of eating an
abstract category and generalize it beyond its symbolic context,
like the philosopher Whitehead did with his category of
"prehension,"—which, by the way, can mean ingestion—the
peculiarly human faculties can be treated as a special kind of
eating and feeding. Why not say God is eaten by the mystic,
that parental love feeds children, that the hero feeds history?

N. All that might be true, an ingenious philosophy. But a
philosophy is good to the extent it articulates the subtle
balances of values we feel. While it is true each human life has
continuities with nature and history, consumptive or "prehen-
sive" continuities even, that's not as important as the fact that
each life is temporary. Each person takes his or her rise,
flourishes awhile, and then disintegrates, quickly or slowly.
His or her essence as a human being is the personality he or she
develops in childhood and loses in senescence and death. Death
is not a disease—disease is an unfortunate confluence of
natural processes, pitting germ, tumor, or quixotic gene
against the human organism as we like it. Death for the human
being is not just an interruption and redistribution of his or her
natural processes; it is an existential annihilation.

T.   A what?

N.   Death means the person ceases to be. As a subject, with experience of the world and an image of himself or herself as an organizer of that world, he or she ceases to exist. His or her personality might just be a harmony of natural processes. But when that harmony is broken, the person is annihilated, even though the component processes go on.

T.   I understand what you mean. The fact that we live in continuity with nature does not belie the more human fact that when we die our subjective life perishes. Whereas we might still be enjoyed by future eaters, both biological and cultural, we ourselves would no longer enjoy. We would no longer enjoy the world through eating, and we would no longer enjoy feeding the world. We would still be objective milestones on the road to consumption. But we would perish as subjective enjoyers of our position. I guess that could be called the existential annihilation of subjectivity, if you want.

N.   Doesn't death strike you as absurd and tragic?

T.   No. Nothing of value lasts. Most things can't even be repeated very often, since the changing environment loses tolerance for them. But this just means that things of human value, including individual human lives, must be seized and enjoyed in their own moments. They must be enjoyed in their own time of flourishing, because after that they can only be remembered, and memory tends to confusion with later experience.

     I would go farther and say that human experience has the peculiarly intense value it does precisely because it is tied to the passing moment. There is a certain value in the richness of the human biological and cultural diet, in the greatness of its compositions and creative achievements, and in the fecundity of human contributions. But regardless of how high that value is, there is an even higher value in all that *plus* the individual agent's subjective enjoyment of it. The enjoyment of doing the eating, creating, and feeding must be contemporary with the activity; and, therefore, it passes. Later, there can only be enjoyment of the deeds done. Contemporary enjoyment is the subjectivity that perishes, and human life would be less valuable than it is without that perishing.

N.   But isn't that perishing still tragic?

T.   I suppose there is a poignancy about it, and that might be what you mean by tragic. But the perishing isn't bad and shouldn't be grieved over. To be aware of it continually is to add a special flavor to our taste of everything else, if I may extend the metaphor. But that special flavor enhances by its poignancy. We can enjoy things all the more when we sense the fragility of their existence. The Japanese know this.

    One of my secret fears, I must admit, is that my proposals for organ transplanation will merely reinforce our social tendency to avoid the present by concentrating on the future. Donating one's body may be a dodge for avoiding the fact the one must first live and die. My balancing hope in this regard is that people will realize just that distinction in levels of importance between contributing to natural processes and losing the intense subjectivity of human life itself.

N.   You have out-existentialled me, Doctor, and I don't know where to go from here. Why is there a problem of facing death — why are you afraid people will avoid it — if its loss isn't sad? And yet why is the loss not sad if it's of the most valuable thing, human subjectivity? I'm confused. Let me come back to that in a few minutes.

    First, though, let me take up a more pedestrian consideration in light of what you just said. The Western tradition has always emphasized this special value of human subjectivity; we even call the value "infinite," I guess because it is not measured by the value of the contents of experience subjectively enjoyed. But the conclusion the West has drawn from this value is quite different from yours, and perhaps from that of Indian philosophy. Because the human person is infinitely valuable, the human body ought not be viewed as just another part of nature. It too becomes sacred in a sense, even when clearly voided of subjective life by death. Our funeral and burial rights express the sense that the body is more than natural because of its association with the human personality. At times, this belief has gone along with beliefs in the immortality of the individual soul that might want to use the body in some future time. But this spiritual supernaturalism is not necessary to explain and justify reverence for the body as more-than-natural because of its association with the infinitely valuable human subject.

Think also of the Nazis. They understood the association of the body with the value of the person, and they attempted to make people into nonpersons by basely degrading their bodily lives. I think myself that to feed others with one's body parts is a sacrilege. It degrades the human body to the status of a natural commodity, a foodstuff.

T. Of course, there is a danger that body parts will become mere economic commodities. I'm not concerned to defend any organ-bank proposal that can't safeguard itself from that danger. But I'm not really talking about the social form of giving away one's body. I'm talking about the meaning of death.

And what I'd say is that the body shouldn't be degraded to a special status befitting the matrix of human subjectivity. The fault of the Western tradition lay not in respecting the body but in thinking the body could be respected apart from the rest of nature. Precisely because of the connections illustrated by the feeding metaphor, the whole world in varying degrees, not the body in an absolute degree, is the vehicle for subjective enjoyment. All modern biology and social science supports this point.

N. But if the whole world is the vehicle of one consciousness, how can there be many separate centers of consciousness?

T. That is a very metaphysical question. Perhaps reflection about the center of subjective enjoyment would reveal it to be not quite as separate from other centers as you think. Certainly, the sense of spatial isolation stemming from the metaphor that my soul is in my body near my liver and your soul is in your body near your liver is inappropriate. The contents of consciousness are spatially extended, but not the act of enjoyment itself. Indian philosophy at, at least, suggests that consciousness is the God equally present in everyone.

N. Theology begs all the questions here. God can be cited to palliate any human ill. But that just won't work. Individuals *are* isolated, and this is nowhere more important than in the problem of death. Dying is filled with fear. People don't just fear pain. Many things hurt more than dying. They fear the unknown. No matter what they have been taught about the hereafter, everyone knows he or she faces the experience absolutely alone. No one can do another person's dying.

T. I agree. A person is never more isolated than when he faces death filled with fear. I would go farther than you, however. The fear is of the *holy* unknown. Just as the unique quality of human life is sacred, more than natural, so is its loss. At root, a person's fear is not that his heart will stop or that his brain will turn off; he can face donating his body with some equanimity and nevertheless stand in dread of death. At root, a person's fear concerns what you called his existential annihilation.

N. The facts you cite I don't dispute. Death is holy, faced by a holy dread. But doesn't this simply prove that living is better than being dead, and that dying is therefore sad, dreadfully sad, existentially sad?

T. No. Death is a holy loss, But there is no necessity that it be feared. Remember, the subjective moments of life perpetually perish. Their holy value consists in the fact they are just the kind of thing that does perish. Death is sad, apart from its real pains, only in the same way the passing of one day is sad. Perhaps we do not take the passing of one day seriously enough because we have the natural expectation of another day tomorrow, an expectation ruled out in the case of death. But a free person, knowing one day to be his last, would prize it all the more, cherish it until it was done, and release it as having been enjoyed.

N. Now I know what bothers me with what you've been saying. You want us to be moral heroes in facing death, living for our finite lives without dread. But that is simply not the case for most of us. People die from accidents, from disease, from our unspeakable technologies of warfare; only a few die in a reflective, philosophic old age. But either in the vague prospect of instant annihilation that affects our children, or in more rational approaches, death means holy dread.

T. Yes, dying without fear is an ideal, and most people fail the ideal. They fail because they are in pain, distracted, scared about the wrong things, brutalized by terrorists, by concentration camp torture, by mindless war. Or they're just plain unprepared for death. But the ideal of course is an old one, and it has never been easy. To die well requires living a life of preparation for dying. Even if this preparation means seizing the moment of present enjoyment, as implied by what I have been saying, it still means living life with the prospect of losing it.

N.   That is impossible without going mad. Or at least being neurotic. You can't *merely* enjoy life for what it is now because you have responsibilities. There is never a point when actual accomplishment is completely fulfilling. There are always more duties to fulfill, more goods to be attained, more avenues to be pursued.

T.   Now *that* sounds neurotic to me. Of course, it's true that death entails the end of accomplishment. A person can't do more when he 's dead. And he's left with obligations, goods, new developments never to be fulfilled. More disturbing, he will be left with guilts unexpiated, no doubt. But that's the condition of finite human life, and must be accepted. If life were such that nothing ever counted finally, if there were always second chances, nothing would ever count at all.

N.   That's the terrible paradox of human life. One's potentialities, and therefore one's obligations, are infinite. But one's accomplishments are always finite. Therefore, failure and guilt are inevitable. That's life! But *I* think that situation is absurd, a bad joke, a pathos so universal as to lose its savor. You don't think so. Why not?

T.   Because it's precisely that paradoxical quality that gives life its special flavor. The moral quality of life is forever ambiguous. No act is good without excluding other values. All accomplishments are finite and therefore both guilt ridden and unfulfiling. To possess this paradoxical quality of life, to attain to the value of enjoyment, it requires permeating one's feel of the world with both forgiveness and satisfaction. In fact, without those qualities, a person can't integrate his failures and responsibilities into a single feeling of his world.

N.   I don't understand. How can one feel forgiven when guilty, or satisfied when unfulfilled?

T.   Forgiveness doesn't mean you aren't guilty. In fact, you couldn't be forgiven unless you were guilty of something. Forgiveness is when your guilt is accepted and not held against you. Likewise, satisfaction doesn't mean that you have everything, but that what you have is enough.

N.   But who does the forgiving and engenders the feeling of satisfaction? It can't be the person dying, because that would be lying to oneself; the person is indeed guilty and unfulfilled.

T. On the contrary, though other people can forgive you and encourage satisfaction, the most important levels are qualities of your own feelings. To feel yourself forgiven, by yourself and any true judge, is a way of having your guilt as an intrinsic part of experience. To feel your accomplishments with satisfaction, even though unfulfilled, is a way of having your life in its finite contours. In fact, it's the only way. Without forgiveness, and satisfaction, you can't completely accept or enjoy your life; you must always deny part. The very meaning of non-denial is to accept yourself as forgiven and satisfied.

N. But if we're honest, how do we attain the feelings of forgiveness and satisfaction? If the motivation is simply to appropriate life without denial, wouldn't this lead us to deny our guilts and fudge our frustrations?

T. No, that's self-contradictory. Forgivenes and satisfaction are qualities you attain by careful and difficult acceptance of the limitations of your life, one by one.

N. Then you must either be a moral hero or depend on divine grace for forgiveness and satisfaction.

T. Maybe both.

N. I prefer the former, though it may not be possible without the latter—a sorry plight if there's no God. Nevertheless, Dr. Thomas, I think what you have said now about human finitude and limitation contradicts the main burden of your defense of the food metaphor. Whatever continuity there is in nature, through eating, composing, and feeding, it isn't sufficient for us to appropriate the reconciliation and fulfillment of the rest of the universe to ourselves. Finite individuals *are* cut off from the universe in some sense, and perhaps the Western sensibility about the sacredness of a person's body in contrast to mundane nature is on the mark.

T. Well, there's still the kind of continuity I described before. That can't be denied. And the rest of nature, including the social order, is sacred because it is the vehicle for human consciousness, not because it justifies the person.

N. But what kind of continuity ignores the unique features of the human self. The discontinuity comes precisely at those points where a person fears the holy unknown of death.

T.   The self indeed may be the problem. I certainly don't doubt the usefulness of concepts of human activities such as those involved in the food metaphor. We take things into our lives physically, culturally, and as items of unique historical experience. We order these things, and we make them public again to be used in the future.

But I have grave doubts about any concept of self involving more than the sum of these and like activities. I doubt first that there is any such self, and second, I doubt the wisdom of employing such a concept in thinking about ourselves. If we think we have that kind of self, and that it will die, we are in for needless grief.

N.   But that misses the whole meaning of life! The adventure of life is the creation of one's self. A child's education involves the development of his or her image of themselves as a skillful agent, as loved by family and friends, as having a unique identity worthy of esteem. Mature life's adventure is the development of autonomy, of self-determination, isn't it? Freedom is knowing who you are and acting in character, and following your own law to the greatest extent possible. Life's fulfillment is possessing an identity of your own making, reflected in and supported by a world invested with your sense of self. Although fulfillment's limited by the given conditions of nature and compromised by the efforts of others to work the world to their own reflection, the struggle for relative autonomy is still the heart of freedom.

N.   Miss Nonscivi, I suppose you have just expressed what you take to be the wisdom of the Western tradition. Let me assure you that the Western tradition is richer than that. Note the consequence of your view: death means loss of control, and with that the dissolution of the world as invested with a person's self-image. Death in this view is not just a threat to life but the ultimate blow to one's narcissism! How many people would rather be dead than see their ego and its world affronted! How much worse then is death when viewed as itself in the final affront!

N.   How can you deny the value of the self?

T.   There are two senses of self that must be distinguished, one bad and one good. The bad sense is that of a self as an entity, where certain things are taken to be components of the self and others to belong to the not-self. This is the narcissistic self that defines its world by the roles things play relative to its identity as a thing, especially relative to its loves and hates.

The other sense of self has to do with being a subjective agent, enjoying experience. This self has an identity given by its enjoyed resources for acting — its food. Other components of its identity stem from its being what it creates, its structures and social relations, together with the responsibilities flowing from its actions. But this sense of self is corrupted by that other sense of self. If it perceives, creates, or gives to the world with a thought to how this feeds back onto its own identity as a thing, its perception distorts, its creativity is mere reinforcement, and its giving is selfish.

N. But death is the loss of self, especially that self of highest subjective value! We agreed on that! You can't back out of that now!

T. The death of that first self is freedom, that narcissistic self composed of things organized by a self-image. To give up that sense of self while living leads to freedom of action. That is, you can act for the goodness of the action in its context, not for how the action will reflect on yourself and your world. And having given up that sense of self you can die without fear, satisfied to be food for the future, maybe even an organ bank.

If one's self-understanding employs the second concept of self, the agent who is no thing and possesses no world, death is not fearful. That self is the conscious enjoyer of how it eats, composes, and feeds the world. When eating, composing, and feeding are no longer possible because of the dissolution of the body in death, there simply is nothing more there to be enjoyed. This self does not exactly perish, even though its objects do. True, it does not continue or recur; but then it is not a kind of fixed substance that lasts anyway. Later enjoyments of actions will be identified with those actions, and will be as different from the former self as the actions are different.

N. But is there no subject behind the faculty of conscious enjoyment, a subject whose tenure is problematic?

T. In one sense, the identity of the act of consciousness is in its object; the object is perpetually changing and perishing, and in that sense the self of consciousness is changing. But this is an inessential kind of identity. Pure enjoyment can have any object that comes its way. There is no substrate of consciousness transcending the particular conscious acts, no substrate that could die. Or that could survive from one life to the other for that matter, unless you want to become theological and think of consciousness as the presence of God, a desire I trust you still do not have. On that theological view you would have to say that the substrate of consciousness is as identical between your experience and mine as it is between two of your experiences, or two of mine. And I know you don't like that thought.

N.   You are being ironic, Doctor. Don't rub in the disadvantages of my enlightened secularism. I shall have to rethink that, although I haven't given in, mind you!

My question now is, how do you say what you have said to a dying person? How do you tell a person who has spent his or her whole life fostering a sense of self as a thing, who sees that slipping away, that the end is Nothingness? I know enough about Eastern philosophy to see you have embraced the idea that the true reality left after the changes have become past is Emptiness.

T.   A good question, especially good since I think I have some answers. Talking metaphysics with the person will only create confusion unless the person has been prepared for it before. The first move is rather to get him to objectify the pain of his illness, to turn his body into an object so he can gradually shed its narcissistic connotations as he becomes more helpless. To this end, it's essential to talk with patients about their illnesses, encouraging, even forcing, them to come to terms with what is happening to their bodies. Without this, they will never be freed from narcissism.

N.   Supposing that can be done, Doctor, it opens the way for even greater suffering, the pain of separation. If patients are pre-occupied with their physical pains, they may not notice that their family comes to see them less, that the nurses won't meet their eye, that the doctor communicates by leaving messages. Dying involves the separation of the person from the community that has bestowed identity and love.

T.   At this point the patient needs to objectify his personal relations. I don't mean he should analyze them as he does his physical pain. Rather, he should be helped to accept and approve the separations as objective facts. Of course, the people around should *not* withdraw their presence and support. The patient desperately needs reassurance of personal recognition now. But in fact he will soon be dead, and thus separate. And he should set the people around him free to live without him. In the old days this meant he bestowed his blessings, dividing up his world for others, separate from connections with his own ego. To give your blessing is to approve a world without you. Patients should be helped to do this.

N. But what happens when the final loss of control — of bladder and bowels, of waking and sleeping, of who is present and who is not — entails ultimate loss of dignity? What dignity is there left in the purely passive person, in the pure patient? A patient still conscious at this point must see that the world treats him or her as just a body, a smelly, ugly body at that.

T. By then the illusion of self as an entity is gone, if the previous steps have been taken. There is nothing left to sustain it, no pretence of control. Either the patient has the dignity of tranquillity, giving up his body to others and resting in his consciousness, or he is in the despair of the damned. It all depends on his readiness to live without the narcissistic sense of self, and this can be helped by the attitudes of those caring for him. If they treat his helplessness as bondage, empathizing with what they construe as his suffering, they will encourage his narcissistic identification with bodily powerlessness. But if they treat him as the tranquil pool of consciousness reflecting his powerless state without a ripple, his peace will be reinforced. Dignity is peace.

N. I see how all these suggestions will help, even with patients for whom loss of self is great agony. But I don't see how people can pull all these things together while in their last agonies. And bad as hospitals are for dying, they are better than the battlefield, the torture camp, the city burnt with nuclear fire. What you have prescribed for patients — objectifying their body, blessing a world without them, tranquillity in helplessness — that's too great a task, emotionally and intellectually, for the deathbed, even should we be lucky enough to die in bed. It seems the greatest demands fall on people when they have the least power to cope. Even to think about it makes me cry.

T. Lament for the world, Maria. Most people don't die well. They don't die completely, they flicker out struggling for an illusion.

People need knowledge about their pain, heartfelt knowledge; and most doctors hide it from them. They need someone to receive their blessing, their last gifts; but which of us can be grateful around the dying, faced with our own conflicts between fear and greed? They need someone to love them without embarrassment at their helplessness, someone to accept them as released; but only the tranquil recognizes the tranquil, and tranquillity is displaced from our hospitals and most other places of dying. Most of all, people need a lifetime tasting death. As the savor of life, death is an acquired taste. Last rites are too late.

N. And there is no hope in becoming body parts and organ banks?

T. None.

N. In what then?

T. Forgiveness and satisfaction, constantly practised.

Notes

1 Metaphysics and Irony: New Twists on Moral Reflection

1. Reinhold Niebuhr, *Beyond Tragedy* (New York: Scribners, 1937), pp. 28f.

2. I have provided a brief analytical review of twentieth-century metaphysical speculation in "Metaphysics," *Social Research*, 47/4 (Winter 1980) 686–703. For a collection of articles by several, but by no means all, of the younger generation of metaphysicians, see *New Essays in Metaphysics*, edited by Robert C. Neville (Albany: State University of New York Press, 1987).

3. See my "Hegel and Whitehead on Totality: The Failure of a Concept of System," in *Hegel and Whitehead: Contemporary Perspectives on Systematic Philosophy*, edited by George R. Lucas, Jr. (Albany: State University of New York Press, 1986).

4. Richard Rorty popularized the phrase, "linguistic turn," in his book by that name (Chicago: University of Chicago Press, 1967); it refers to the general retreat from first order questions to second order ones, justified by the assumption that the second order (formal or ordinary language) is thoroughly perspicuous and not a new nest of problems. For a more critical (and earlier) discussion of this turn than Rorty's, see John E. Smith's *The Spirit of American Philosophy*, rev. ed. (Albany: State University of New York Press, 1983; original edition, 1963).

5. See his *After Virtue: A Study in Moral Theory*, 2nd ed. (Notre Dame: University of Notre Dame Press, 1984), especially Chapters 1–9.

6. Modernism, of course, is notoriously difficult to define. Originally a term for the critical analysis of literature and art, it is exhaustively and exhaustingly analyzed in a collection of studies edited by Malcolm Bradbury and James McFarlane: *Modernism: 1890–1930* (Middlesex: Eng.: Penguin Books Limited, 1974). As an intellectual style, Modernism perhaps was best exemplified in many fields by the diverse personalities of the Bloomsbury Group. In his many books of art theory and criticism, Clive Bell expressed that group's attitude in his analysis of sensibility and form in art. Bell's work perhaps best shows the power of the aestheticizing approach to culture. Modernism finds some of its most cogent critical defenders now in the main body of authors publishing in Hilton Kramer's journal *The New Criterion*. Bertrand Russell and Alfred North Whitehead, in very different ways, built philosophies on an aestheticizing sensibility; and that too was the capstone of Dewey's ethics. Dewey and Whitehead, however, explicitly rejected Modernist foundationalism in philosophy, believing that philosophy necessarily trails off into other disciplines and is always justifying itself as an hypothesis for further consideration. The truly Modernist philosophies are Husserlian phenomenology, with its eidetic reductions, and analytic philosophy, with its attempts to find a "solid" ground in formal or ordinary language.

7. See, for instance, the typical articles published in *Philosophy and Public Affairs* or in the *Hastings Center Report.*.

8. David Hall defends this position in his brilliant, *Eros and Irony* (Albany: State University of New York Press, 1982); see the discussion of his position later in this chapter.

9. See *Eros and Irony*, Chapter 4, "The Ambiguity of Order."

10. See his *The Puritan Conscience and Modern Sexuality* (New Haven: Yale University Press, 1986).

11. See William Haller's wonderful book *The Rise of Puritanism* (New York: Columbia University Press, 1938; Harper, 1957), especially Chapters 1 and 4.

12. See his excellent new study cited above.

13.   Haller, *The Rise of Puritanism*, p. 16.

14.   Ibid., p. 17.

15.   Concerning the death of the God of Western (not Orthodox) Christian culture, see the analysis of Thomas J. J. Altizer in his *The Self-Embodiment of God* (New York: Harper, 1977); *Total Presence* (New York: The Seabury Press, 1980); and *History As Apocalypse* (Albany: State University of New York Press, 1985).

16.   *The Experience of Defeat: Milton and Some Contemporaries* (New York: Elisabeth Sifton Books-Viking, 1984).

17.   For a study demonstrating the combination of the religious and the Lockean principles, see Aldo Tassi's *The Political Philosophy of the American Revolution* (Washington: University Press of America, 1978). Robert N. Bellah and his colleagues Madsen, Sullivan, Swidler, and Tipton trace the heritage of this combination, or rather its dissolution, to the present day in their popular *Habits of the Heart: Individualism and Commitment in American Life* (Berkeley: University of California Press, 1985). One of those colleagues, William M. Sullivan, provides a deep philosophical and historical analysis of civic republicanism, with a plan for its reconstruction, in his *Reconstructing Public Philosophy* (Berkeley: University of California Press, 1982).

18.   See J. H. Hexter, *Reappraisals in History: New Views on History and Society in Early Modern Europe* (Evanston: Northwestern University Press, 1961; New York: Harper, 1963), and Jack A. Goldstone, "Capitalist Origins of the English Revolution: Chasing a Chimera," in *Theory and Society*, March, 1983, pp. 143–180.

19.   We are indebted to Robert Denoon Cumming for his magisterial work *Human Nature and Histroy: A Study of the Development of Liberal Political Thought*, Two Volumes (Chicago: The University of Chicago Press, 1969).

20.   See Dewey's *Liberalism and Social Action* (New York: Capricorn, 1963; original edition, 1935).

21.   In *Thinking Through Confucius* (Albany: State University of New York Press, 1987), David Hall and Roger Ames argue that transcendence is a characteristic belief of the West and that immanence is analogously characteristic of classical Confucianism.

22.   Actually, although the theology must be radically transformed in an era of world religions, my own theological projects are
closer to a transformed Calvinism than to nearly any other
theological tradition. See, for instance, my *Soldier, Sage, Saint* (New
York: Fordham University Press, 1978).

2   Modeling the Moral Life

1.   See Dewey's *The Theory of Valuation* (Chicago: University
of Chicago Press, 1939), especially Section VI, "The Continuum of
Ends-Means." See also the fourth chapter of any edition of *Experience
and Nature*.

2.   In *After Virtue: A Study in Moral Theory*, 2nd ed. (Notre
Dame: University of Notre Dame Press, 1984).

3.   See Richard J. Bernstein's *Praxis and Action: Contemporary
Philosophies of Human Activity* (Philadelphia: University of Pennsyl-
vania Press, 1971), *The Restructuring of Social and Political Theory* (New
York: Harcourt Brace Jovanovich, 1976), *Beyond Objectivism and
Relativism: Science, Hermeneutics, and Praxis* (Philadelphia: University
of Pennsylvania Press, 1983), and *Philosophical Profiles: Essays in a
Pragmatic Mode* (Philadelphia: University of Pennsylvania Press, 1986).

4.   By "scholar-official" I mean the socially defined ideal Confucian devoted both to cultivation of personal virtue and to service to
society; early texts discuss this in terms of the "gentleman" or
"superior man" (*chun-tze*) and the later traditions shift the discussion
to sageliness. For a collection of texts with introductions sensitive to
the scholar-official ideal, see Wing-tsit Chan's *A Source Book in Chinese
Philosophy* (Princeton: Princeton University Press, 1963). For a
general discussion of the early period, see Donald J. Munro's *The
Concept of Man in Early China* (Stanford: Stanford University Press,
1969). For a deep philosophic analysis of the early ideas, see Tu
Wei-ming's *Centrality and Commonality: An Essay on Chung-yung*
(Honolulu: University Press of Hawaii, 1976). One of the greatest
scholar-officials was Wang Yang-ming, a sixteenth-century general
and administrator whose philosophy dominated China for two hundred years and is still extraordinarily influential. Tu Wei-ming has
an excellent biography of Wang Yang-ming's early life, *Neo-
Confucian Thought in Action: Wang Yang-ming's Youth (1472–1509)*
(Berkeley: University of California Press, 1976). Julia Ching's *To*

Acquire Wisdom: The Way of Wang Yang-ming (New York: Columbia University Press, 1976) is an excellent introduction to Wang's philosophy. Wang's ethics of "virtue" is finely analyzed, in contrast to Western notions of the sort MacIntyre discusses, by Antonio Cua in his *The Unity of Knowledge and Action: A Study of Wang Yang-ming's Moral Psychology* (Honolulu: The University Press of Hawaii, 1982). For general collections expressing many perspectives on later Neo-Confucianism and the ideal of the sage, see William Theodore de Bary, editor, *Self and Society in Ming Thought* (New York: Columbia University Press, 1970) and *The Unfolding of Neo-Confucianism* (New York: Columbia University Press, 1975). Cheng Chung-ying's *Tai Chen's Inquiry into Goodness* (Honolulu: East-West Center Press, 1971) is an excellent analysis of a leading eighteenth-century discussion of the topic. Both Cheng, in his *New Dimensions of Confucian and Neo-Confucian Philosophy* (Albany: State University of New York Press, 1987) and Tu, in his *Humanity and Self-Cultivation: Essays in Confucian Thought* (Berkeley: Asian Humanities Press, 1979) and *Confucian Thought: Selfhood as Creative Transformation* (Albany: State University of New York Press, 1985), give contemporary reinterpretation of Confucianism from the perspective of attempts to make it a living philosophy. See also David Hall's and Roger Ames's *Thinking Through Confucius* (Albany: State University of New York Press, 1987).

5.   See Wing-tsit Chan's strong claim in his *Source Book in Chinese Philosophy*, the introduction to Mencius; also see *The Book of Mencius* 4A:12–14, 20; 5A: 5.

6.   Consider this passage from Mencius 3B:2: "At the marriage of a young woman, her mother instructs her. She accompanies the daughter to the door on her leaving and admonishes her, saying, 'Go to your home. Always be respectful and careful. Never disobey your husband.' Thus, to regard obedience as the correct course of conduct is the way for women. [Both Kung-sun and Chang attempted to please their rulers in order to obtain power and were more like women than like great men.]" Wing-tsit Chan's translation and observation in *Source Book*, p. 72.

7.   For a general account of this story, see René Grousset's *The Rise and Splendor of the Chinese Empire* (Berkeley: University of California Press, 1968), especially chapters 9 and 21. See also Donald Munro's *The Concept of Man in Early China*, especially chapter 3–5.

8. See, for instance, the issue of the *Journal of Chinese Philosophy* called "John Dewey and Chinese Philosophy," Vol. 12, No. 3, September 1985; see especially the articles by John E. Smith, Julia Ching, and myself. By "pragmatism" I mean the classical positions of Charles Peirce, William James, John Dewey, George Herbert Mead, and the neighboring position of Alfred North Whitehead. (New Haven: Yale University Press, 1978) is an analytical statement of the general position on pragmatism to which I subscribe. The parallels with Chinese philosophy do not hold plausibly for the epistemological pragmatism of Nelson Goodman or Williard Quine, nor for the rhetorical neopragmatism recently popularized by Richard Rorty. Confucianism and Rorty's pragmatism share an emphasis on edification, but the former has a commitment to ultimate seriousness which, for better or worse, makes it qualitatively different from the latter.

9. The culture of experience formed around Confucian conceptions would have been a splendid reference point for Maurice Merleau-Ponty's attempt to characterize human life in terms of a lived body. As it was, he struggled to criticize and break out of his own Cartesian culture with perhaps too much energy spent in the negation; although his intent is clear, his categories still seem to bear the marks of fixed-up Cartesianism. It is paradoxical that some of the more original philosophers seem displaced; their theories resonate better with the culture of experience from an alien setting than with that of their own tradition. Thomas J. J. Altizer pointed out that Whitehead's theory seems far more immediately plausible against the background of the Buddhist culture of experience than against Western theism; see his "The Buddhist Ground of the Whiteheadian God," *Process Studies* 5/4 (Winter 1975).

10. See Whitehead's *Process and Reality*, Corrected Edition, edited by David Ray Griffin and Donald W. Sherburne (New York: The Free Press, 1978), especially Part II, Chapters 3 and 4. I have explored the idea of the brain as an environment for thought and action, from a process perspective, in "Zalmoxis," in *Operating on the Mind*, edited by Willard Gaylin, Joel Meister, and myself (New York: Basic Books, 1975), and in "Environments of the Mind," in *Mental Health: Philosophical Perspectives*, edited by H. T. Engelhardt, Jr., and S. F. Spicker (Dordrecht: Reidel, 1977).

11. Paul Weiss's recent *Privacy* (Carbondale: Southern Illinois University Press, 1983) is an example. I have argued my own ver-

sion in *The Cosmology of Freedom* (New Haven: Yale University Press, 1974) and *Reconstruction of Thinking* (Albany: State University of New York Press, 1981). I deal explicitly with the Confucian model in *The Tao and the Daimon* (Albany: State University of New York Press, 1982), Chapter 8.

12.   The idea of public life as care of the environment within which creativity takes place is the central thesis of the theory of social freedom and participation developed in my *Cosmology of Freedom*, Part III, especially pp. 271 ff. It will be discussed below in Chapter Nine.

13.   For a brilliant analysis and playing out of this Taoist point, see Kuang-ming Wu's *Chuang Tzu: World Philosopher at Play* (New York & Chico: The Crossroad Publishing Company & Scholars Press, 1982).

14.   The distinction between network meaning and content meaning is drawn in my *The Tao and the Daimon* (Albany: State University of New York Press, 1982), Chapter 11.

15.   See Edmund Leites, *The Puritan Conscience and Modern Sexuality* (New Haven: Yale University Press, 1986). The entire book is about constancy and its price. Chapter 1 is about the Cambridge Platonists.

16.   See the *Chuang Tzu*, chapter 8–11, any edition; these chapters may not have been written by Chuang tzu but by someone very like him.

17.   See his *Eros and Irony: A Prelude to Philosophical Anarchism* (Albany: State University of New York Press, 1982). My characterization of irony is an adaptation of his, although we draw quite different conclusions. See also the debate about this topic in *Process Studies* 14/1 (Spring 1984), in "Imagination and Responsibility" by Daivd Hall, "The Beast not Found in Verse" by George Allan, and "Uncertain Irony" by myself; Hall and I review each other's books.

3   Social Obligation, Personal Responsibility, and Moral Identity

1.   The best case made recently for our intrinsic assumption of responsibility for the good of the community is Paul Weiss's *Toward a Perfected State* (Albany: State University of New York Press, 1986).

2.   The Liberal tradition overall has many ways of qualifying this. See, for instance, Robert Denoon Cumming's discussion of Mill's critique of Hobbes, Locke, and Bentham in his *Human Nature and History: A Study of the Development of Liberal Political Thought* (Chicago: University of Chicago Press, 1969), Vol. 2, Chapter 18.

3.   See Dewey's great book, *The Public and Its Problems* (1927), Volume 2 of *John Dewey: The Later Works, 1925-1953*, edited by Jo Ann Boydston (Carbondale: Southern Illinois University Press, 1984).

4.   For a sophisticated historical discussion of Liberalism on this point, see Cumming, *Human Nature and History*, Chapter 18-13. For a powerful philosophical discussion by a reforming Liberal, see John Dewey's *Liberalism and Social Action* (New York: Capricorn, 1963; original edition, 1935).

5.   See, for instance, the argument in Robert Nozick's *Anarchy, State, and Utopia* (New York: Basic Books, 1974).

6.   Dewey's theory, from *The Public and Its Problems*, and the theory that privacy has to do with creativity, are discussed with reference to one another in my *Cosmology of Freedom* (New Haven: Yale University Press, 1974).

4   The Metaphysics of Chaos, Totalization, and Normative Description

1.   This list of factors influencing imagination is, of course, incomplete; but it is not entirely arbitrary. With minor modifications, the list derives from the analysis of the development of selfhood by Paul Weiss in his book, *Privacy* (Carbondale: Southern Illinois University Press, 1983). It will be presented in greater detail in Chapter Six.

The present remarks about imagination reflect the analysis in my *Reconstruction of Thinking* (Albany: State University of New York Press, 1981), Part II. That volume offers a naturalistic analysis of imagination as the synthesis transforming natural causal factors into the stuff of experience, and it deals with the nature of imagination as a religious ground of culture.

2.   The point about the power of ideas was made most eloquently by Alfred North Whitehead, whose examples of contrasting

powers were the barbarian invasions and the invention of the steam engine. See his *Adventures of Ideas* (New York: Macmillan, 1933).

3. For classic statements of the developing idea of Liberalism, with an emphasis on the social contract, see Thomas Hobbes's *Leviathan*. John Locke's *Second Treatise of Government*, Baruch Spinoza's *Theological-Political Treatise*, David Hume's *A Treatise of Human Nature* (Book III), Immanuel Kant's *Perpetual Peace*, and Georg Hegel's *Philosophy of Right*.

4. Thomas Hobbes, *Leviathan*, Introduction by A.D. Lindsay (New York: E. P. Dutton & Co., 1950; originally published in 1651), pp. 103f.

5. Robert Nozick is a contemporary Liberal political philosopher who emphasizes the minimizing of government regulation; see his *Anarchy, State, and Utopia* (New York: Basic Books, 1974). His Harvard colleague, John Rawls, also gives contemporary expression to Liberal political theory, but with a direct concern to equalize the inequalities of private life, making that concern a public one. Rawls is thus an exception to some of the generalizations made below about Liberalism. See his *A Theory of Justice* (Cambridge: Harvard University Press, 1971).

6. *Hegel's Philosophy of Right*, translated with Notes by T. M. Knox (Oxford: Clarendon Press, 1942), p. 156.

7. See the fascinating discussion of the difference between Hobbes and Locke on the need for violence in keeping domestic order, in Niall Caldwell's dissertation, *The Hidden Cost of Contract Theory: Institutional Violence* (State University of New York at Stony Brook, 1986; Ann Arbor, Mich.: University Microfilms, 1986.)

8. For a more complete treatment of the metaphysis of modernity, see E. A. Burtt's classic *The Metaphysical Foundations of Modern Physical Science* (Garden City, N.Y.: Doubleday Anchor, 1954), and the more recent study by Eugene M. Klaaren, *Religious Origins of Modern Science* (Grand Rapids: Wm. B. Eerdmans Publ. Co., 1977).

9. See *Philebus* 15–28.

10. See, for instance, *Philebus* 66, the discussion of the awarding of prizes. I have formally defended Plato's theory of value in *The Cosmology of Freedom* (New Haven: Yale University Press, 1974),

Chapter 3, and more extensively in *Reconstruction of Thinking*, Chapters 3, 5–8.

11.   The term "moral metaphysics" was used by Professor Mou Tsung-san in *Chih te chih-chueh yu Chung-kuo che-hsueh (Intellectual Intuition and Chinese Philosophy)* (Taipei: Shang-wu Book Company, 1971). Professor Mou might have stressed too much the construal of metaphysical issues around human moral concerns; I would prefer to stress, with Plato, the natural value character of all things, with the implication that human moral interest should be determined by what there is in which to be morally interested. To avoid the extremes of anthropocentrism in metaphysics, perhaps it is better simply to speak of axiology. For a further extension of the notion of moral metaphysics, see Tu Wei-ming's *Centrality and Commonality: An Essay on Chung-yung*. (Honolulu: University of Hawaii Press, 1976), Chapter Four.

5   Suffering, Experience, and Politics

1.   Alfred North Whitehead, *Adventures of Ideas* (New York: Free Press, 1967), p. 66.

2.   G. E. Moore, *Principia Ethica* (Cambridge: Cambridge University Press, 1903), p. 20.

3.   See Gadamer's *Truth and Method* (New York: The Seabury Press, 1975), pp. 235–258. See also "The Universality of the Hermeneutical Problem," in Gadamer's *Philosophical Hermeneutics*, translated and edited by David E. Linge (Berkeley: University of California Press, 1976).

4.   For a subtle interpretation of this, see Richard J. Bernstein's *Praxis and Action* (Philadelphia: University of Pennsylvania Press, 1971).

5.   See Marx's 1844 review of Bruno Bauer's *The Jewish Question*, in *Writings of the Young Marx on Philosophy and Society*, translated and edited by Loyd D. Easton and Kurt H. Guddat (Garden City: Doubleday Anchor, 1967), pp. 216–248.

6.   On the distinction between network-meaning and content-meaning, see my *The Tao and the Daimon* (Albany: State University of New York Press, 1982), Chapter 11.

7. "On Practice," in *Selected Writings of Mao Tse-tung*, Vol. 1 (Peking: Foreign Language Press, 1967).

8. See, for instance, the delicate *Creativity and Taoism: A Study of Chinese Philosophy, Art, and Poetry* by Chang Chung-yuan (New York: Harper, 1970).

9. For a much more thorough attempt than this to relate Mao's philosophy to antecedents in both China and the West, see Frederic Wakeman, Jr.'s *History and Will: Philosophical Perspectives of Mao Tse-tung's Thought* (Berkeley: University of California Press, 1973).

10. My *Reconstruction of Thinking* (Albany: State University of New York Press, 1981), develops these themes from Whitehead while rejecting certain others; it also takes explicit account of the tradition of Taoist thought, in Chapter 2. In Chapters 3 and 4, it develops a careful distinction between the passive aspects of feeling, the activity of spontaneity, and the resultant intentional activity of judgment. A full perception is a judgment, but in the present text I am calling attention to perception's moments of feeling and spontaneity.

11. Mao, *Selected Writings*, p. 203.

6 Moral Discernment and the Reality of Value

1. In *The Nature of True Virtue* (written in 1755, postumously published in 1765; Ann Arbor, Mich.: University of Michigan Press, 1960), pp. 103–104.

2. For a philosophically technical exposition of this theory of value, see my *The Cosmology of Freedom* (New Haven: Yale University Press, 1974), Chapter 3.

3. See his *Experience and Nature*, The Later Works of John Dewey, Vol. I: 1925, edited by Jo Ann Boydston (Carbondale: Southern Illinois University Press, 1981), Chapter 2.

4. For Peirce's critique of intuitionism, see his papers "Questions Concerning Certain Capacities Claimed for Man" and "Some Consequences of Four Incapacities," in *The Collected Papers of Charles Sanders Peirce*, edited by Charles Hartshorne and Paul Weiss, Vol. 5 (Cambridge: Harvard University Press, 1934), paragraphs

213–317. I have analyzed Peirce's view and defended a kind of intuition in "Intuition," *International Philosophical Quarterly*, vii/4, December, 1967.

5.   This historical observation reflects the argument of my *Reconstruction of Thinking* (Albany: State University of New York Press, 1981), Chapter 1.

7   Moral Science in a Normative Cosmos

1.   For a fascinating introduction both to the theory and to the practice of t'ai chi ch'uan, see Sophia Delza's *T'ai-Chi Ch'uan (Wu Style): Body and Mind in Harmony: The Integration of Meaning and Method*, with a Foreword by Robert C. Neville, Drawings by the Author, and Photographs by Lisa Lewicki (Revised edition: Albany: State University of New York Press, 1985). My Foreword undertakes an explication of Chou Tun-i's conception of change.

2.   See *The Question Concerning Technology*, translated by William Lovitt (New York: Harper & Row, 1977).

3.   This point is made with beautiful force by David Strong in his Ph.D. dissertation, *To the Things Themselves: Metatechnology, and the Environment*, State University of New York at Stony Brook; Ann Arbor, Michigan: University Microfilms, 1988.

4.   The idea of valuing up or down comes from Whitehead. See his brilliant analysis in *Process and Reality* (Corrected Edition; New York: The Free Press, 1978), edited by David Ray Griffin and Donald W. Sherburne, pp. 240–255. It should be remembered, however, that Whitehead's view tends to reduce the value of the past to that which it has in subsequent entities that objectify it (including God who forgets nothing, according to Whitehead).

5.   Paul Weiss, *Privacy* (Carbondale: Southern Illinois University Press, 1983). Weiss calls these structures "epitomizations." Among Weiss's many other books, the most central for the discussion to follow are *Man's Freedom* (New Haven: Yale University Press, 1950), *You, I, and the Others* (Carbondale: Southern Illinois University Press, 1980), and *Toward A Perfected State* (Albany: State University of New York Press, 1986).

6.   Weiss, *Privacy*, pp. 49–57. In this and the following expositions, I am selecting among Weiss's points those that serve my present purpose.

7. See my *Reconstruction of Thinking* (Albany: State University of New York Press, 1981), Chapters 1, 5–8.

8. Weiss, *Privacy*, pp. 57–73.

9. Ibid., pp. 73–83.

10. Ibid., pp. 83–96.

11. Ibid., pp. 96–103.,

12. Ibid., pp. 103–122.

13. Ibid., pp. 122–145.

14. Ibid., pp. 146–164.

15. Ibid., p. 216; see also pp. 171–183.

16. Ibid., pp. 183–196.

8 Authority

1. See Aristotle's *Politics*, especially Book I, Chapter 2.

2. The most important texts of Plato are the *Republic*, *Statesman*, and *Laws*. Besides Aristotle's *Politics*, see his *Nichomachaean Ethics* and *On the Soul*. For general background, see Ernest Barker's *Greek Political Theory* (New York: Barnes & Noble, 1960; orig. 1918); Robert Brumbaugh's *Plato for the Modern Age* (New York: Collier, 1964) and *The Philosophers of Greece* (Albany: State University of New York Press, 1981); Eric Voegelin's *Plato* (Baton Rouge: Louisiana State University Press, 1966); and Eric A. Havelock's *Preface to Plato* (New York: Grosset & Dunlap, 1967). Hannah Arendt's "What is Authority?" in *Between Past and Future* (New York: Viking, 1968), treats Plato and Aristotle with the same focus as I do, though with a different point of view. For instance, Professor Arendt defines political authority as the top position in a social hierarchy that derives its authority from something outside the hierarchy. So, she interprets Plato as giving the Philosopher-King the right of command because of authority derived from knowledge of the transcendent Forms; on this interpretation, Plato thus is sliding always toward tyranny. This interpretation assumes, however, that the Philosopher-King takes possession of the forms through contemplation and exercises authority in conventional ways. A contrary thesis, mine, representing another strain in Plato, is that the Philosopher-King takes possession of the forms through dialectic, an invariably

social process in which all participants are made equals, and that authority is exercised through dialectical persuasion or not at all. Plato believed that if philosophers cannot rule through dialectical persuasion they should abandon political life. For a sample of mis-understanding that arises from neglecting this side of Plato's thought, see Karl Popper's *The Open Society and Its Enemies* (Princeton: Princeton University Press, 1962) Volume I. I have criticized Popper in *Reconstruction of Thinking* (Albany: State University of New York Press, 1981), Chapter 2. Arendt correctly points out that rule exercised among equals through dialectical persuasion is not rule by authority, and in this sense Plato's understanding of philosophical political authority itself funded the undermining of authority.

3.   Werner Jaeger, *Paideia: The Ideals of Greek Culture*, trans. by Gilber Highet (New York: Oxford University Press, 1965), Vol. 1, 2nd ed., especially Chapters 6–8.

4.   See Plato's *Crito*, 50a–54e.

5.   (Albany: State University of New York Press, 1986).

6.   Although Hobbes may not be well thought of as a Liberal, defending as he did an absolute monarchy, he was nevertheless one of the first theorists of the social contract, denying any but pruden-tial delegated authority of the sovereign. Furthermore, as Robert Denoon Cumming points out, whereas Machiavelli wrote *The Prince*, Hobbes wrote *The Citizen*, lifting up at once the importance of the in-dividual and the importance of the commonality of individuality. See his *Human Nature and History* (Chicago: University of Chicago Press, 1968), Volume 2, p. 34.

7.   Thomas Hobbes, *Leviathan*, Introduction by A. D. Lind-say (New York: Dutton, 1950), pp. 133–134.

8.   Here the relevant text is not the *Philebus* passage I have mentioned so often but the *Statesman* 283e–287b where Plato describes the statesman's task as mixing the various components of society, for example, the gentle and the brave, according to "nor-mative measures."

9.   (New York: Basic Books, 1974); see especially the Preface and Chapters 2, 7–8.

10.   (Cambridge: Harvard University Press, 1981), Chapter 5.

11.   See his *A Theory of Justice* (Cambridge: Harvard University Press, 1971), par. 25–26.

12.   See Harold F. Moore, Robert C. Neville, and William M. Sullivan, "The Contours of Responsibility: A New Model," *Man and World*, 5/4 (November 1972).

13.   *Hegel's Philosophy of Right*, translated with notes by T. M. Knox (Oxford: Clarendon Press, 1942), par. 260, pp. 160f.

14.   The point is developed at length in my *Cosmology of Freedom* (New Haven: Yale University Press, 1974), Chapter 11.

9   Freedom and Privacy

1.   I have presented a theory of freedom aiming to be comprehensive in two books. *The Cosmology of Freedom* (New Haven: Yale University Press, 1974) discusses personal and social freedom. *Soldier, Sage, Saint* (New York: Fordham University Press, 1978) analyzes spiritual freedom. The argument of the present chapter works within categories developed in those two books, and applies them to a dialectical critique of the shortcomings of Liberalism.

2.   John Stuart Mill, *On Liberty*, edited with an Introduction by Curren V. Shields (New York: The Liberal Arts Press, 1956) p. 13.

3.   John Locke, "Second Treatise of Civil Government," in *Two Treatises of Government*, edited with an Introduction by Thomas I. Cook (New York: Hafner Publishing Company, 1956), p. 134.

4.   Because this very interesting group is not well-known in the United States, I will list a more extensive bibliography than is necessary for the points in the text. See Theodor W. Adorno, *The Jargon of Authenticity*, translated by Knut Tarnowski and Frederic Will (Evanston: Northwestern University Press, 1973); Max Horkeimer and Thodor W. Adorno, *Dialectic of Enlightenment*, translated by John Cumming (New York: The Seabury Press, 1972); Max Horkeimer, *Critique of Insrumental Reason*, translated by Matthew J. O'Connell and others (New York: The Seabury Press, 1974); Herbert Marcuse, *Eros and Civilization* (New York: Vintage, 1962), *An Essay on Liberation* (Boston: Beacon, 1969), *One Dimensional Man* (Boston: Beacon, 1964), *Reason and Revolution* (New York: Oxford University Press, 1941; Beacon, 1960); Karl-Otto Apel, *Charles S. Peirce: From Pragmatism to Pragmaticism*, translated by John Michael

Krois (Amherst: University of Massachusetts Press, 1981), *Under-standing and Explanation: A Transcendental-Pragmatic Perspective*, translated by Georgia Warnke (Cambridge: MIT Press, 1984); Jurgen Habermas, *Knowledge and Human Interests*, translated by J. Shapiro (Boston: Beacon, 1971), *Legitimation Crisis*, translated by Thomas McCarthy (Boston: Beacon, 1975), *Theory and Practice*, translated by J. Viertel (Boston: Beacon, 1973), *Communication and the Evolution of Society*, translated by Thomas McCarthy (Boston: Beacon, 1979). For an interesting integration of the program of this school with the hermeneutics controversies, see Josef Bleicher's *Contemporary Hermeneutics* (London: Routledge & Kegan Paul, 1980). For an excellent analysis of Habermas' theory of interests, discussed here in the text, see William Sullivan's "Two Opinions in Modern Social Theory: Habermas and Whitehead," *International Philosophical Quarterly*, March 1975, pp. 83 ff.

5.   See Habermas's *Knowledge and Human Interests*, pp. 25–42.

6.   See the fine discussion of this in Gerard Radnitzky's *Contemporary Schools of Metascience* (2nd revised and enlarged edition; New York: Humanities Press, 1970), pp. 43–58.

7.   In addition to the arguments throughout this book, I have directly addressed the topic in *The Cosmology of Freedom*, pp. 174–203.

8.   In *Cosmology of Freedom*, pp. 214–217, I argue for a typology distinguishing personal values, interpersonal values, public values, social-order values, and civilization values.

9.   For an analysis of the significance of Habermas's theory of quasi-transcendental interests, see Richard Bernstein's *The Restructuring of Social and Political Theory* (New York: Harcourt, Brace, Jovanovich, 1976), pp. 219–225.

10.   Werner Jaeger, *Paideia: The Ideals of Greek Culture*, translated by Gilbert Highet (New York: Oxford University Press, 1965), Vol. 1, p. 111.

11.   This discussion is taken from Marx's early writing, a review of Bruno Bauer, *Die Judenfrage*, in *Writings of teh Young Marx on Philosophy and Society*, translated and edited by Loyd D. Easton and Kurt H. Guddat (Garden City: Doubleday Anchor, 1967), pp. 216–248.

10 Responsibilities in Conflict

1.   I am attempting to find a general and all inclusive characterization of the religious dimension, and, of course, there isn't any. Each religion defines itself. Paul Tillich was one of the few great theologians in our century within a tradition who attempted to characterize the religious dimension generally, and he gave currency to the emphasis on ultimate meaning. Probably the best extended development of the ideal is in John E. Smith's *Experience and God* (New York: Oxford, 1968). See also Paul Weiss's *The God We Seek* (Carbondale: Southern Illinois University Press, 1964). In *God the Creator* (Chicago: University of Chicago Press, 1968), I characterized religion in terms of the public participation in ultimate matters and private pursuit of them; there, and much more thoroughly in *Soldier, Sage, Saint*, I characterized the "ultimate" in terms of a distinction between cosmological and ontological aspects of things. None of these fine points is crucial for the present discussion except the conviction that religious concerns lay some responsibilities on us.

2.   The present chapter needs only an acknowledgment of a plurality of contexts of responsibility, not a list. Paul Weiss is one of the few recent philosophers to attempt a list of the important domains providing organized norms for life. Consult, for instance, his *World of Art* (Carbondale: Southern Illinois University Press, 1961), Chapter Two, or *Toward a Perfected State* (Albany: State University of New York Press, 1986). His list of personal structures from *Privacy* (Carbondale: Southern Illinois University Press, 1983) is the source of the essential epitomies of human life discussed in Chapter Five above.

3.   See *Modes of Being* (Carbondale: Southern Illinois University Press, 1958), pp. 353–355.

4.   I have argued in other places in great detail that ontological questions require a conception of divine creation *ex nihilo*, although with a nontraditional conception of God that can be specified in nontheistic as well as theistic ways. See *God the Creator* (Chicago: University of Chicago Press, 1968), and *The Tao and the Daimon* (Albany: State University of New York Press, 1982).

5.   See Cua's *The Unity of Knowledge and Action: A Study of*

Wang Yang-ming's Moral Psychology (Honolulu: The University Press of Hawaii, 1982).

11   A Taste of Death

1.   See her *Spirit in Ashes: Hegel, Heidegger, and Man-Made Mass Death* (New Haven: Yale University Press, 1985).

2.   Radhakrishnan translation.

Index

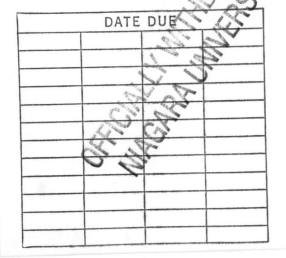